UNDERSTANDING
MEDIA
ETHICS

SAGE was founded in 1965 by Sara Miller McCune to support the dissemination of usable knowledge by publishing innovative and high-quality research and teaching content. Today, we publish more than 750 journals, including those of more than 300 learned societies, more than 800 new books per year, and a growing range of library products including archives, data, case studies, reports, conference highlights, and video. SAGE remains majority-owned by our founder, and after Sara's lifetime will become owned by a charitable trust that secures our continued independence.

Los Angeles | London | Washington DC | New Delhi | Singapore

UNDERSTANDING
MEDIA
ETHICS

David Sanford Horner

Los Angeles | London | New Delhi
Singapore | Washington DC

CONTENTS

LIST OF TABLES

PREFACE

HOW TO USE THIS BOOK

This book is for students of the media. Its aim is to promote an understanding of media ethics. In other words, the kinds of moral issues and dilemmas that daily confront media practitioners and policy makers. I take 'Media Ethics' to be a species of applied ethics akin to medical ethics, business ethics and computer ethics. Each chapter addresses a single theme in the field of Media Ethics, such as violence or pornography. The chapters are therefore relatively independent one from another and do not necessarily need to be read in the sequence in which they are presented. However, the reader might benefit from reading Chapter 1 on moral judgement as a way into how we ought to approach moral issues and dilemmas that the other chapters explore. Similarly, the concluding chapter presents some more general reflections on the nature and origins of wrong-doing.

Within the chapters there are a number of features intended to aid the student in getting the most out of the material and in thinking through and making moral judgements on specific topics. Boxes entitled 'A Judgement Call' present the student with a moral issue which may be actual or hypothetical but is in need of some resolution. These judgement calls are intended to help students to sharpen their analytical abilities and appreciate the complexities of moral decision making. Material helpful in resolving the dilemmas presented will be found in the adjacent text. Example boxes include specific examples to illustrate general principles, arguments and themes, and Definition boxes define important concepts. Some of these key concepts are repeated throughout the book as an aid to making the chapters relatively autonomous. Key arguments are summarized in the Summary of Arguments boxes.

Each chapter is accompanied by an article from a journal which is available from Sage. A short introduction, 'How to Use This Article', draws attention to the connection between the chapter and the featured article. These articles are intended to take the reader more deeply into the primary literature of Media Ethics. This takes the form of a focus on empirical research relevant to the chapter, or a deeper theoretical interrogation of the material, or a combination of both. In addition to the featured article, there is also guidance on further reading relative to the chapter. Hopefully, these features will contribute to the our general aim of understanding Media Ethics and its implications for media practice.

ACKNOWLEDGEMENTS

I would like to thank the University of Brighton for the support from its sabbatical scheme which helped to get this project off the ground. I would also like to thank the very helpful criticisms of the reviewers of the various drafts of this book. Their insightful contributions have helped to make this a much better performance than it would otherwise have been. The same may also be said about the guidance and support contributed by Mila Steele, my Commissioning Editor at Sage. In addition, I would like to thank particularly Dr Chris Boyne for his collaboration over the many years, during which we co-taught Communication Ethics and subsequently Media Ethics to media students at the University of Brighton. And last, but certainly not least, I want to thank the many cohorts of students whom I have had the pleasure of teaching over the years and from whom I have learned so much. The frailties and the faults of this work are, of course, all my own.

PART I
FOUNDATIONS

INTRODUCTION

WHY MEDIA ETHICS?

A 27-year-old prince is partying in an exclusive suite of a Las Vegas hotel while on leave from his military duties. He and several of his female companions are naked, apparently following a game of 'strip billiards'. One of his fellow revellers uses a mobile phone to photograph these antics. The rather poor and indistinct photographs are then subsequently sold for $10,000 to a celebrity website. The prince is clearly shown to be wearing nothing but a wrist watch and a distinctive necklace. The photographs are rapidly and globally available for anyone to view. In contrast, the press and broadcast media in the prince's own country, after representations from the Palace, do not publish the photographs. It is claimed that the prince is merely 'letting off steam'. However, eventually a tabloid newspaper with a distinctive record for populist and prurient journalism breaks ranks and publishes the photographs in 'the public interest'.

Now, in themselves, these events may appear in many ways to be trivial and of little significance in a world beset by natural and manmade disasters. However, even in their apparent banality they expose questions that go to the heart of the culture and ethical practices of the individual members of the public, media practitioners and professional media organizations. For example, is the initial and subsequent publication of the photographs a gross intrusion into the prince's privacy, driven by little more than the desire for profit? After all, the events took place at a private function in a private space. Was the subsequent re-publication of the photographs in a national newspaper merely compounding the initial intrusion? Or was the publication of the photographs against the wishes of the Palace a defence of press freedom and in the interests of the public? It would be a dangerous precedent for news media to suppress stories merely to placate the rich and the powerful. Is there a genuine ethical dilemma here? Or was the newspaper in breach of the self-regulatory code of practice governing what the paper ought or ought not to print? Can there really be a distinction between the public and the private for royal persons? And what of the companion of the prince who took the photograph? Was this not an act of the betrayal of trust enabled by new mobile technologies? Interestingly, the initial 'intrusion' was not by a journalist. Is this 'citizen journalism'? What about the actions of the prince himself. Might we not feel there is something genuinely reprehensible in his behaviour? Isn't the expectation supposed to be that privilege brings with it important social and moral responsibilities? Like a Russian doll, this relatively simple case reveals layers of moral complexity. At each stage, essentially moral judgements were being made about what it was permissible to do.

Viewed from the perspective of media professionals, this small story demonstrates a variety of moral issues. Media industries become ever more socially, culturally and economically pervasive and powerful. A private hotel room becomes a global phenomenon. Public perception of the media resolves itself into a sense of a decline in standards, involving bias, inaccuracy, unfair treatment, invasion of privacy, trivialization, manipulation and exploitation. It is in this context that this book seeks to understand the ethical dimension of media practice and analyse the moral obligations of media practitioners and media institutions. The object of the exercise is to provide conceptual and analytical tools to enable the reader to come to grips with important ethical problems in the field. It seems beyond doubt that media practitioners need to develop acute and reflective moral awareness. It is only on that basis that media professionals might make sounder and more secure moral choices.

If further evidence is needed for the importance of our subject, we need look no further than the UK's Leveson Inquiry into the culture, practice and ethics of the press in the United Kingdom. In July 2011, Lord Leveson was appointed by the British Prime Minister, David Cameron, as a consequence of the revelations about illegal phone hacking by journalists at the *News of the World*, to conduct a wide-ranging inquiry into the press. What is at stake in this inquiry goes beyond the malpractices of a few journalists at one particular newspaper. The phone hacking scandal has become a lens through which to view the morality of the relationships between the media, the police and the political elite. There is no reason to suppose that print journalism in the UK is fundamentally different from journalism in other liberal democratic countries. What the inquiry has revealed are significant moral failures to maintain appropriate relationships between the media and those it should scrutinize in the public interest. In other words, it raises fundamental questions about the implicit (moral) contract between the media and major institutions in a democratic society. Lord Justice Leveson opened the hearings on 14 November 2011 by saying: 'The press provides an essential check on all aspects of public life. That is why any failure within the media affects all of us. At the heart of this Inquiry, therefore, may be one simple question: who guards the guardians?' (Leveson Inquiry, 2011)

The scope of the inquiry is indicated by the range of witnesses called, including newspaper reporters, management, proprietors, police officers and politicians, public figures (including those involved with press regulation itself) as well as well-known celebrities. The witnesses gave testimony under oath and there was a strong adversarial element in the confrontation between the lawyers and the witnesses. The stated intention of the inquiry that followed from this wide-ranging investigation was to 'make recommendations on the future of press regulation and governance consistent with maintaining freedom of the press and ensuring the highest ethical and professional standards' (Leveson Inquiry, 2011). The Leveson Inquiry raises many of the key issues of moral judgement and practice in the media that we will be covering in this book, not least the nature of the professional responsibilities of media professionals.

DEFINING MEDIA ETHICS

Ethics, as a discipline, as an area of study, is generally conceived to be the philosophical study of morality (Wiggins, 2006, p. 9). It is the rational discussion of the process of making moral judgements. Media Ethics is more specifically the philosophical study of morality in the context of media institutions and professional practice, including the ethics of media content. Our concern, as suggested above, is with the moral choices made in this context, the values that influence them, notions of moral good and of what constitutes right- and wrong-doing. It follows from this that Media Ethics is a species of applied ethics akin to medical ethics, business ethics, and computer ethics, applied ethics being 'the application of ethical theories to practical situations where there are moral choices, which have implications for professionals, and which may often be challenged in the courts' (Thompson, 2000, p. 179).

Typically, the kinds of questions which Media Ethics tends to address include the following: Is it right or wrong to broadcast material that may offend some sections of the television audience? Is it right or wrong to make confidential documents freely available? Is it right or wrong to subordinate considerations of privacy to the public interest or the interests of the public? Is it right to lie to get a good story? Are there certain types of media content that should be highly regulated or censored? Is the value of media production to be judged by the pleasure it stimulates in an audience? Are sensationalism and trivialization necessarily of moral concern? Do the visual media have particular responsibilities for their impacts on audiences? Do they desensitize people to the moral implications of what they represent? Do the media overall have significant moral effects? To what extent must the media maintain balance and objectivity?

As has already been suggested, answering such questions will be bound up with our conceptions of the purpose or purposes of the media. They are also bound up with our conceptions of what, from a moral point of view, is 'good 'or 'bad'; what constitutes 'right' or 'wrong action'. Answering such questions also involves us in having some notion of what may be good from a moral point of view generally and also what might constitute goodness in particular times and places. What do we mean by moral issues in general? Should making people happy be the goal for the media? Or should the media be a neutral conduit for information or entertainment? In other words, it may not be the job of the media to have any moral goals over and above the observance of the commonplaces of everyday morality. What constitutes bad media practice? The objective of this book is to provide some understanding and guidance as to how we begin to answer these types of question and how we might shape our practice in the light of ethical considerations.

Our definition of Media Ethics suggests that moral judgement, choice and action are things that might reasonably be argued about and about which we can possess knowledge rather than simply feelings, beliefs or opinions. In other words, we can understand and resolve at least some of our moral problems and dilemmas. This is in itself by no means an uncontroversial claim. As we will see in Chapter 1, there is plenty of debate about what it means to claim that an action is right or wrong, or that something is good or bad, and whether these are cognitively or non-cognitively based. At the more extreme, nihilistic and post-modern end of the spectrum, it is argued that there are no moral truths (in any objective, copper-bottomed sense) and that distinctions such as right and wrong or good or bad ultimately also have no solid foundation (Baggini and Fosl, 2007, p. 225). It will also be one of the objectives of this book to show that this is false.

MORALITY AND LEGALITY

It is important to recognize a distinction between what might be ethical and what might be legal. The field of media law intersects with, but is distinct from, Media Ethics. Dilemmas frequently arise where there may be a conflict between morality and legality. We can meaningfully distinguish the question 'Is it immoral?' from the question 'Is it illegal?' Filming someone in the street without their consent may not be illegal but we certainly might have moral misgivings, depending on the circumstances. We can, and do, distinguish immoral behaviour from illegal behaviour. However, there is an important theological and philosophical tradition of thinking about morality as being derived from 'natural' law. The idea that the universe itself is shot through with a moral law, like a structure put there by the gods or God so that an analogy can be legitimately drawn between 'moral law' and 'legal rules'. For example, appeals to the idea of 'natural rights' often rely on such a conception.

The problem of morality is precisely thought to be the problem of formulating moral rules in much the same way that we enact laws. Legal systems essentially do two things. Firstly, they stipulate behaviour. Secondly, they aim to make people behave better; they exert pressure to curb objectionable ways of behaving. It seems attractive to see morality operating on a similar model. Both legal systems and morality seem to have similar concerns in attempting to prevent objectionable behaviour. However, the moral philosopher Geoffrey Warnock (1971) points out that the rules of morality and legal rules differ in a number of significant respects.

Firstly, moral rules are not formally made by anybody or any authoritative institution. There is no inherent moral structure to the universe. Moral beliefs and moral systems tend to evolve over time relatively spontaneously to meet the exigencies of the situations in which human beings find themselves. We can perhaps see something of this process in action as we come to terms with the implications of emergent digital media that may create new dilemmas where our existing moral concepts and rules may be difficult to apply (see Chapter 12).

Secondly, moral systems don't usually entail formal institutions of detection, trial and punishment. The Press Complaints Commission (PCC) in the UK gave judgement on complaints made about the press by the public. However, adherence to its code of practice was voluntary.

Thirdly, legal rules define an action as wrong (illegal) on the basis that it was, in Warnock's phrase, 'antecedently objectionable'. In other words, some behaviour or action is thought to be objectionable before it was subsequently made illegal. If moral rules existed on the same model as legal systems, then certain kinds of behaviour wouldn't be immoral before a moral rule was created. But, for example, that would imply that the publication of paedophilic images of child torture wasn't morally wrong until there was a rule that said it was. There's something puzzling, if not obviously wrong, about such a conclusion.

Fourthly, in the case of legal rules there is a clear distinction to be made between the 'effect' of the rules and the 'basis' of the rules. The 'effect' is to make certain kinds of behaviour illegal (or to constitute certain rights). The foundation of law is in non-legal or pre-legal views. Consider, for example, the case of hacking. The ability to hack arose as networked computing developed. There were no laws making it a criminal offence so the behaviour of hackers was not 'illegal'. However, hacking was seen by most people as wrong, even though it was not illegal. Similarly, the moral view is that advertising should be truthful and honest or that certain kinds of material might 'deprave and corrupt'.

Fifthly, the effect/basis model doesn't seem to work for morality. In the case of morality, the forming of a rule seems to add nothing to the view that certain kinds of actions are morally wrong, for example, lying. A rule that says you shouldn't tell lies seems to add nothing to the view that lying is wrong.

It makes perfect sense to criticize certain laws as immoral (although a *prima facie* duty in any civilized society must be to obey the law). In Nazi Germany, for example, German radio stations were forbidden to broadcast Jazz music. Jazz was seen by the Nazis as degenerate because it was largely the product of racially inferior black musicians. Clearly, any such law or regulation prohibiting Jazz on such grounds is immoral in a very fundamental sense. We can argue that such a prohibition is fundamentally wrong because it violates an antecedent moral idea – that of justice. It must be unjust on at least two counts. In the first place, it seems that banning a whole genre of music is draconian and unfair. But secondly, and more importantly, the grounds on which the ban rests are immoral in the sense that it treats a certain set of human beings in an inhuman way. In this book we are primarily concerned with Media Ethics rather than Media Law, but this is not to fail to recognize that the two are intimately linked. Morality is connected to, but logically prior to, legality.

Moral values are embodied in the answers to the questions 'What ends are good?' and 'What actions are right or wrong?' The answers to those questions are usually formulated by reference to general principles, principles such as 'we ought always to aim for the greatest happiness of the greatest number', or 'we ought to aim to minimize the total suffering of all sentient beings', or we ought only to dedicate ourselves to the service of God, or 'that it is right and proper for everyone to look after themselves' (Mackie, 1990, p. 9). In later chapters we will investigate how such general principles function in relationship to our everyday experience of moral decision making. Clearly, if we have an established notion of what is morally good, this will determine what we ought to do to achieve that good. In other words, our sense of what is morally good determines what the right thing to do must be.

FACTS AND VALUES

In this section we draw two further important distinctions for ethical analysis: the distinction between statements of fact (descriptions of what *is* the case) and statements of value (what *ought* to be the case), and a related distinction between descriptive ethics and normative ethics.

Description and Evaluation

A central claim of much Anglo-American moral philosophy in the twentieth century is that there is a fundamental, logical gap between statements about 'what *is* the case' and statements of 'what *ought* to be the case'. According to this doctrine, it is not possible to derive conclusions about what *ought* to happen in a moral sense simply from statements about what the natural or social world is, as a matter of fact, like. The consequence of this view is the ruling out of 'naturalistic' accounts of morality, for example, the idea that we can identify goodness with some natural property, such as that value is associated with being more evolved or being stronger ('might is right') or being more beautiful.

The argument has its roots in the work of the great Scottish Enlightenment philosopher and historian David Hume (1711–1776), and is sometimes referred to as 'Hume's Law'. Hume pointed out that any argument which resulted in a conclusion which contained an *ought* statement must also contain a premise with an *ought* in order to be a valid argument. Given that statements about how the world is are factual, then we cannot read off, or derive, values from such descriptive accounts. What Hume's Law rules out of court is 'strictly any attempt to deduce conclusions about what ideally ought to be the case from any premise or premises stating only what is supposed, actually and already is the case' (Flew, 1985, p. 136). Morality must have its roots in something other than, say, the laws of evolution or even the existence of God. The illicit derivation of moral conclusions from purely factual premises is also known as 'the naturalistic fallacy': the fallacy of identifying goodness with some or other natural feature or property of the world is a term first coined by the philosopher G.E. Moore (Warnock, 1960, pp. 1–28). For example, from the fact that many people, as they do, desire to be happy, it cannot be deduced that happiness in itself is desirable.

Descriptive Ethics and Normative Ethics

Descriptive ethics, as the name suggests, is about the description of moral norms, values and choices which may be held in a particular culture or society – simply as a matter of fact. It was the case that in the 1930s the USA had a code which regulated the motion picture industry on moral grounds, the Hayes Code. It was under this code, for example, that the cartoon *Betty Boop* was censored for its salacious content. However, the fact that such a code existed says nothing about its rightness or wrongness. Descriptive ethics, to the extent that it may give an account of such a code and an explanation for its existence, is not concerned with the cogency or otherwise of the justification. Descriptive ethics is an aspect of sociology, psychology, anthropology or history (Nowell-Smith, 1965, p. 12). The objective of descriptive ethics is to gather the facts about what people consider to be good or bad, right or wrong, in a particular social group. It is not about whether the norms held by a culture or society or media professional are right or whether the goals they are pursuing are morally good in themselves. It seems to me that one of the many pitfalls of media analysis is to fail to make an appropriate distinction between the description of media practices and their moral evaluation (normative Media Ethics).

Normative ethics, on the contrary, is about the grounds on which we justify our moral values, judgements and actions. The fact, as we will discuss in the next chapter, that a majority of people in a particular social group adopt a particular moral behaviour doesn't make that behaviour right. There is an important and allied distinction, as indicated above, between what as a matter of fact may be *desired* by any person or group and what is *desirable*. Sociological, psychological and legal studies may be informative about what people's preferences and desires (factually) are, but do not, and cannot, by themselves, determine what those preferences *ought* to be. This distinction implies that we may sensibly talk about the rightness or wrongness of particular sets of values. People's preferences and moral judgements may be open to being shown to be just plain wrong! These ideas will be developed further in Chapter 2.

A descriptive approach to the distribution of paedophilic imagery would be concerned with the facts about the extent of the distribution, the nature of the imagery and the demographics of its producers and consumers and so on. A normative inquiry is about whether the production and consumption are morally permissible. It is concerned with the bases or principles on which we would want to say that even possessing such imagery is morally reprehensible.

OVERVIEW OF THE BOOK

The book is constructed broadly around two general types of moral theory: consequentialist and deontological. *Consequentialism* is a generic word to embrace all those theories which assert that we should make our moral judgements and decide on a course of action on the basis of the results it will produce. The right action is then, on balance, the one which will produce the best outcome set against the

outcomes of the other options which are available. The most well-known consequentialist theory is that of utilitarianism, which advocates that the right action or
policy is the one which will, on balance, produce more pleasure than pain. In contrast, *deontology* refers to those ethical theories which place duty as the fulcrum of
morality. This view assumes that some acts are just obligatory whatever the consequences may be. When confronted with the need to make an ethical judgement
we must ask ourselves what our duty is. Dilemmas arise here when we might have
a conflict of duties. The contrast between this deontological approach and that of
consequentialism, as we will note, forms two poles for the structure of the book.
We will view particular media issues through the lens of particular moral theories.

Chapter 1 provides a general foundation for what follows by examining the
nature of moral judgement itself. It aims to overcome sceptical arguments that
suggest moral judgements, in the final analysis, will always be subjective, relative
and merely a matter of feeling. If that were the case, the current enterprise would
be of little purpose. But, on the contrary, we can, and often do, argue about moral
problems in a rational way. So it does make sense to talk about the objectivity of
moral judgements. In Chapter 2 we discuss a popular, consequentialist method
of reaching moral judgements based on the notion that we ought always to maximize pleasure and minimize pain. The meaning of this general principle for Media
Ethics is illustrated with an analysis of a much discussed controversy sparked by
Russell Brand and Jonathan Ross. This consequentialist theme is continued in
Chapter 3 by taking a more refined utilitarian view and applying it to the debate
about media markets and public service broadcasting. We consider, from a moral
point of view, whether there is a legitimate distinction to be made between higher
and lower pleasures. If there is, then it may be morally right to override the operation of media markets in favour of some types of media content. In this chapter we
look in particular at the clash between Rupert Murdoch and the BBC.

Chapters 4, 5 and 6 grapple with the key issue of freedom of speech and the
media. In particular, we consider the grounds on which media freedoms may
be restricted in terms of causing harm or offence. Chapter 4 outlines a general
defence of media freedoms based on the work of the nineteenth-century philosopher John Stuart Mill. His arguments continue to this day to represent the liberal
democratic paradigm for the liberty of thought and discussion. Mill states a general principle – the liberty principle – which maintains that freedom of speech
may only be restricted on grounds of harm. Chapters 5 and 6 explore the limits
of this liberal paradigm through a discussion of violence and pornography. They
examine the grounds on which it may be legitimate to censor media content. The
book generally assumes that the ethical judgements we discuss are made within
a broadly liberal democratic framework. The problem with totalitarian regimes is
that the kinds of deliberations we are discussing are simply foreclosed by political
or religious fiat.

In Chapter 7 we change gear from the consequentialist approaches of the previous chapters to consider the idea of morality as based on duty. We discuss the duty
to tell the truth as being fundamental to media practice. Kant's moral philosophy is

presented as a paradigm example of a deontological moral theory. Kant's approach is used to show why it is that truth-telling in both ordinary life and in media contexts is so fundamental. Kant's theory provides a comprehensive theory of moral decision making which is then further explored in Chapters 8, 9 and 10. In these chapters moral issues around the nature of visual representation, stereotyping and privacy, respectively, are explored. Chapter 11 discusses the morality of whistle-blowing in the context, particularly, of the work of Julian Assange (WikiLeaks) and Edward Snowden. Chapter 12 examines the moral impact of emergent digital media. Central questions here concern the extent to which emergent media create novel and puzzling ethical situations which our existing moral concepts and rules do not address. Do we need a new digital ethics? Finally, in Chapter 13 I return to some more general considerations about the nature of moral wrong-doing. When is it reasonable to blame people for their actions? Are morally wrong acts simply committed out of ignorance? What I hope to demonstrate is that to act morally is to act rationally; to act immorally is always to act irrationally; and that morality is not a sideshow to the real business of the world.

1
MORAL JUDGEMENTS

Ethical practice in the media requires moral judgements. I will refer to these as 'judgement calls'. Thinking and reasoning about ethical questions is a sterile pursuit if it does not lead to decisions and actions. And making such judgements is a key aspect of being a media professional (or indeed any other kind of professional). In this chapter we will look at making moral judgements and try to establish key elements in judging and choosing how to act morally. We will do this by considering some beliefs about moral judgements to the effect that they are either obvious or impossible! We will focus on moral scepticism: the belief that it is not possible to make valid, objective, moral judgements. This is closely related to another view that morality is simply a personal and private matter.

We will analyse four important claims about making moral judgements which are frequently invoked to support the sceptics' arguments. These are: that people disagree about solutions to moral problems; that we are in no position to judge others; that ethics ultimately is a private matter; and that morality is simply a matter for individual societies or cultures to determine. If the claims of scepticism (see Box 1.1) are really sound, we will be hard-pressed to show the fundamental importance of morality to media practices. However, we will show that a thorough-going scepticism is unfounded and that we can in fact make valid and well-grounded moral judgements. The fact that people frequently disagree about moral issues provides no grounds for believing that we can never agree about moral issues or what might constitute sound, moral policies to underpin media practices. Similarly, we can show that there are standards and grounds on which sound moral judgements can be reached. The claim that 'ethics is simply a private matter' is logically incoherent and the allied claims of cultural relativism in moral matters are similarly flawed. Making moral judgements is more than having certain feelings of approval or disapproval or of expressing those feelings. In the light of the discussion, we identify certain key elements in making moral judgements: for example, establishing the facts of the case; identifying appropriate moral principles; making reasonable, valid arguments; and, finally, exercising moral imagination in understanding the range of interests involved in moral situations.

The controversy sparked by the publication of drawings or cartoons of the Prophet Mohammad in the Danish press provides a good example of a situation where a moral judgement had to be made (see Box 1.2). The judgement call is whether or not it is morally right to go ahead and publish the cartoons. This is a genuine dilemma in the sense that whether you publish or don't publish there are potential negative moral consequences. On one side of the argument is freedom of speech. Media freedom is a key value in liberal democratic societies. Such freedom is an important condition in maintaining individual autonomy, in the development of civic rights and in the promotion of the public interest. On the other side of the argument is the very high probability many Muslims will be offended at the blasphemy of the depiction of the Prophet and, at the same time, will be outraged by the implied association of Islam with terrorism. In the event, the publication of the drawings did in fact lead to a major campaign by Muslim groups against the newspaper, with demonstrations and threats of violence against the journalists involved. The case raised wider issues of the role of Muslims in Danish society (Lægaard, 2007). But the nub of this argument, from our point of view, is whether or not 'giving offence' to religious sensibilities provides sufficient grounds for suppressing or restraining freedom of speech. We will return to this clash between free speech and offence in Chapter 6.

1.1 DEFINITION
Moral scepticism

Moral scepticism is the belief that it is not possible to make objectively valid moral judgements. The practical upshot of such a belief must be that we must reject moral constraints for ourselves, but it also means that we are not in a position to criticize others for behaving badly because we have no grounds for such judgements.

1.2 A JUDGEMENT CALL
The Cartoon Controversy

Imagine yourself in the position of the editor of the Danish newspaper *Jyllands-Posten*. You have before you the twelve drawings of the Prophet Mohammad. The satirical cartoons arise from the fact that a Danish author claimed not to be able to find an illustrator for a

(Continued)

(Continued)

children's book about Mohammad. One of the drawings depicts Mohammad in the desert; two combine Islamic symbols with Mohammad; one drawing depicts Mohammad as a boy writing on a blackboard 'the editors of *Jyllands-Poston* are a bunch of reactionary provocateurs'. Other drawings clearly make the association between Islam, Muslims and the Prophet and terrorism. One cartoon depicts Mohammad with a turban shaped like a bomb that is about to go off with a verse from the Qur'an inscribed upon it. In another drawing the Prophet is shown to a line of suicide bombers: 'Stop. Stop. We ran out of virgins.' Two of the cartoons link the Prophet to the oppression of women. Finally, two of the drawings refer to fears of the cartoonists that the pictures themselves will trigger a campaign of revenge against themselves.

Would it be right to publish or would it be better not to publish?

OBSTACLES TO MORAL JUDGEMENTS

To make progress in understanding Media Ethics and the process of making judgements it is important to clear away a number of hindrances to the very idea of moral truth or independent standards of judgement. The obstacles are of a number of different kinds. Firstly, let's consider the claim that the moral judgements are intuitively obvious and arise spontaneously from our particular upbringing, cultural background or religious persuasion. They are just a matter of common sense. This may be an obstacle in that it proclaims that no reasoning is required to come to moral judgements. Secondly, there is a fashionable but corrosive moral scepticism which purports to show that we can't make moral judgements at all. Of course, if we were to say that we *shouldn't* make moral judgements, that in itself would be a judgement of a kind! Thirdly, there is a view that moral judgement is inherently 'subjective', such that when I condemn some action, say the journalistic intrusion into the private life of a person, I am only describing a personal view, attitude or feeling much in the same way that I might prefer coffee to tea. Clearing away such hindrances will help to throw into stronger relief how we can deal with practical moral judgements in media contexts.

Moral Judgements are Intuitive and Obvious

First, let's examine the popular response that it is just plain obvious what those judgements should be. No tutoring is required here! We just intuitively know what the right thing to do is whether we are a media professional or an ordinary person in the street. Intuitively, we are all aware, or at least pre-consciously aware, of our moral obligations, what right and wrong actions are and what moral goodness and moral evil are. This may be all right as far as it goes. It is clearly the case that at some basic level we can command and make use of the rich moral vocabulary built into our language, such that when confronted by some moral decision we don't have to go about re-inventing the moral wheel.

1.3 A JUDGEMENT CALL
Press freedom and the Leveson dilemma

Lord Leveson's Inquiry was charged with considering whether or not current arrangements for the self-regulation of the press in the UK were adequate. This was against the background of evidence of widespread phone hacking and intrusion into the privacy of celebrities, public figures and victims of crime.

a) The first horn of the dilemma is the assumption that the press ought to be free of state intervention and regulation in order to be able 'to speak truth to power'. A free press is important in the defence of individual liberty and civic rights. The duty of the press must be to inform the public of what is in the public interest, particularly in the scrutiny of government policy and decision making. But unfettered media create the very conditions in which journalistic practice tends to develop in unethical ways.

b) The second horn of the dilemma is that a stringent framework of state control and regulation may prevent the development of systematic unethical culture and practice. But such a regime would put power in the hands of government and politicians to muzzle the press when their interests are threatened. Political control may prevent the media from performing their role as critics of powerful institutions and the state.

Can we escape this dilemma? Are their institutional ways of balancing the public interests and the interests of the press?

The problem with this straightforward approach becomes apparent the moment people begin to articulate conflicting moral views, for example, disagreement about whether or not a particular broadcast should have been made or a particular photograph published. Such disagreements frequently revolve around matters of principle rather than matters of fact. For example, central to the Leveson Inquiry is a fundamental disagreement as to the principles that should guide regulation of the press (see Box 1.3). On one side, strong arguments have been presented that anything other than self-regulation would compromise press freedom. In contrast, many of those who feel they have been traduced and intruded upon by the press argue that, as a matter of principle, regulation should be independent, tougher and more punitive. The resolution of these conflicting positions must be a matter of reasoning about fundamental principles and far from intuitively obvious (Cohen-Almagor, 2014).

Moral Scepticism

It is such disagreement and apparent insolubility, or the lack of agreement on moral questions, that are partly responsible for another significant obstacle: moral scepticism. The moral philosopher, Mary Midgley, has written extensively on the origins and diagnosis of this condition in *Can't We Make Moral Judgements?* (1991). She differentiates between an 'enquiring scepticism', by which we pose genuine questions in pursuit of answers, and 'dogmatic scepticism'. This latter kind of scepticism rejects the view that answers are possible and that we are equipped to make soundly based judgements:

> ... moral questions are (as is often said) just a matter of everybody's own subjective opinion, of their taste. In the terms of this hypothesis, people can no more 'impose judgements' on one another here than they can impose their own taste in clothes or in food. This seems to mean that moral judgements are not really in any ordinary sense judgements at all. 'Making judgements' in this sphere is not so much wrong as impossible. The veto on doing it is something like the veto on witchcraft: it forbids us to pretend to do something which in fact cannot be done. (Midgley, 1991, p. 2)

If this were truly how things stand, then the whole enterprise of Media Ethics would be a vain one. One of the reasons that Mary Midgley suggests that people adopt this view is the bogus notion that it is in the interests of the wider freedom of the individual that we should refrain from judging others even to the extent seeing criminal action not as a case for punishment but, at most, as a case for treatment. According to this view, we have no rational grounds for considering actions as either criminal or morally evil because there are no actions which are bad in themselves and no citizens are bad in themselves. The most that judgement can do is to reflect our personal preferences. There is, in this sense, no such thing as 'moral truth'. This sceptical attitude is frequently informed by a kind of world-weary cynicism: 'when we look at the big words – justice, equality, freedom, rights – we see only bids for power and clashes of power, or we see only hypocrisy, or see only our own opinions, unworthy to be foisted onto others' (Blackburn, 2001, p. 9).

Four Beliefs Underlying Scepticism

Underlying scepticism are four related beliefs which I will summarize here. In the next section we will go on to refute these beliefs. In this way, we can begin to see the possibility and key elements of moral judgement. The first belief is that because people often disagree on solutions to moral issues, ultimately, there can be no resolutions. Disagreement is taken by sceptics to be an indication that, in the final analysis, disagreements are insoluble and thus the enterprise is futile. Anyone who has listened to the arguments presented on the UK's radio show *The Moral Maze* will find ample evidence to support this view. The protagonists apparently never find a way out of the maze; they remain entrenched in their positions; no one ever appears to concede that they are wrong; no agreement is ever reached. There is a vertiginous, endless cycle of debate. However, from the fact that we sometimes disagree it doesn't logically follow that we can never agree or that consensus cannot be reached on the resolution to a moral problem.

The second belief takes the form of self-doubt about making judgements at all: 'Well, after all, who am I to judge others?' Here, judging others is characterized as being 'judgemental' or 'moralistic' (see Midgley, 1991, pp. 1–9). Thirdly, there is a belief that morality is 'simply' a private matter. Our personal moral attitudes can have no purchase on the public world. Finally, scepticism about ethical reasoning is often founded on the belief that morality, if not entirely a personal matter, is very much a local matter. In other words, the moral norms which shape our moral judgements are simply outcomes of the decisions of individual cultures. This position is often characterized as cultural or moral relativism.

Having briefly identified these symptoms of moral scepticism we may now proceed to examine the possible cures for the malady. If the claims of scepticism are really sound, we will be hard-pressed to show the fundamental importance of morality to media practices.

1.4 SUMMARY OF ARGUMENTS
Meeting the claims of scepticism

Ethical diversity: 'People disagree on solutions to moral issues.'

- But there are many non-moral areas of human activity where experts disagree.
- But there is a high level of consensus about moral values both within and between cultures.
- But disagreements may often be resolved by reference to publicly available facts; not all disagreements are about principles.

Moralism: 'Who am I to judge others?'

- But there is a difference between making a moral judgement based on evidence and moralizing.
- But to judge is to evaluate or discriminate by agreed standards, not simply to condemn.
- But in the course of social life we frequently must make informed judgements.

Individual relativism: 'Morality is simply a private matter.'

- But like the idea of a 'private language', the idea of a private morality is conceptually incoherent.
- But there is an important distinction to be made between moral choices and personal preferences.
- But morality is a public institution represented in our commonly shared moral vocabulary.

Cultural relativism: 'Morality is simply a matter for individual cultures to decide.'

- But this assumes that a system is moral simply because a majority in a culture decides it is moral.
- But this ignores the distinction between descriptive ('is') statements and normative claims ('ought').
- But this assumes that people can never reach agreement on some moral principles.

Adapted from Tavani (2011, p. 53)

RESPONDING TO MORAL SCEPTICISM

This section reviews the responses we can make to the moral sceptic. We can show that moral judgements can, and must, be made on rational grounds rather than on personal intuition or preference.

Shared Values and Facts

Firstly, how do we address the problem that people do indeed, as a matter of fact, disagree on solutions to moral issues? Beyond the media context, we need only consider questions such as euthanasia or abortion to encounter profound and deep clashes of moral views. Within a media context, equally, there are profound disagreements arising from diverging moral values, as we saw in the case of the Cartoon Controversy (see Box 1.2). For example, there are strong disagreements on media censorship between those who espouse libertarian and those who espouse conservative values. However, the simple fact of such disagreements, profound though they may be, doesn't by itself provide grounds for thinking that no resolution or compromises are possible or that reasoned arguments are of no account. If that were really the case, then inquiries, such as that by Lord Justice Leveson, would be futile. Equally, experts in many areas of theoretical and practical endeavour may disagree on key problems in their fields. And this not confined to the humanities, social sciences or the professions. Think, for example, of the disagreements between cosmologists and theoretical physicists about the origins of the universe. The occurrence of such disagreements does not lead to the wholesale rejection of cosmology as a discipline that is not worth pursuing. On the contrary, the more difficult the problem the more worthwhile is the endeavour. And so it is with moral dilemmas.

Secondly, by concentrating on disagreement the sceptics also fail to acknowledge that there are many moral values and issues on which people do agree. Such agreements are often different cultural expressions of the same values. We might say that the clash of customs and, by extension, what is now referred to as 'the clash of civilizations', are a much over-egged pudding. The ancient Greek historian Herodotus provides us with a helpful illustration from his *Histories* (Book 111, chapter 38; see Box 1.5). Mary Midgley points out that there is a profound sense in which this story does not date. Our contemporary news media are constantly representing the collision of customs and habits. However, for our purposes, the story has a deeper lesson because beneath the strongly held funeral customs lays a shared value. What the Greeks and the Callatiae both demonstrate is a deep, shared value of respect for their dead parents.

1.5 EXAMPLE
A shared value

The following historical example illustrates the fact that beneath very different social practices there may yet be a common value. The story, as told by the ancient Greek historian Herodotus, concerns various practices by different communities with regard to the treatment of the dead bodies of parents. Darius, the King of Persia, asked the Greeks who were attending his court what amount of money would be required to induce them to eat the dead bodies of their fathers. They responded, because this would have transgressed a major taboo, that they would not do it for any money in the world. Later, and in the presence of the Greeks, Darius posed a related question to Indians of the tribe of Callatiae. An interpreter was present so that everyone understood perfectly the question and the answer. Darius asked the Callatiae what amount of money would be required to induce them to burn the bodies of their dead parents. They reacted in horror and asked the King not mention such a dreadful thing. Callatiae clearly had a taboo that forbade them to burn the dead bodies of their parents. Thus the customs of the Greeks forbade them to eat dead bodies whereas for the Callatiae this was precisely what custom required. Herodotus draws the conclusion that custom is 'king of all'.

However, we can also see that although these two groups had very different customs, they nevertheless shared a profound respect in their treatment of the dead.

Thirdly, one of the important lessons for the resolution of moral issues is the importance of distinguishing between disagreements about fundamental principles and disagreements about facts. Disagreement may often be resolved simply by paying attention to the facts. We may agree that, in principle, from a moral point of view, that harmful social actions are wrong and that society has a right to intervene to prevent harm. But do people tend to emulate what they see on screen? If that is true, we have a factual case for regulating or censoring material which may lead people to commit socially harmful acts. Of course, moral arguments about public policy are more complex than this might suggest. For example, the evidence may be more difficult to assess – violent films, for example, might not influence most people but may influence the behaviour of a small, vulnerable, but significant element of the population. Michael Moore's controversial film *Bowling for Columbine* (2002) illustrates the point. However, it does highlight the possibility of making progress by examining the facts, undertaking research and finding areas of agreement in principle. The upshot, then, is that we must not fail to differentiate between disagreements about principles and disagreements about facts.

Finally, in analysing any moral question we need to unearth the sources of conflict. As we have seen, disagreements may arise over facts, but disagreements may also arise over the fact that we may not agree about interests affected by some moral rule. A remedy here, as the moral philosopher R.M. Hare suggests, lies not in the search for facts but in the use of the imagination: 'For if my action is going to affect the interests of a number of people, and I ask myself what course of action I can prescribe universally for people in just this situation, then what I shall have to do, in order to answer this question, is to put myself imaginatively in the place of the other parties' (Hare, 1963, p. 123). Conflict may arise or fail to be resolved because we lack the imaginative faculty not to imagine ourselves in the situation of the other but to imagine ourselves *as the other*. In the case of the Cartoon Controversy, as an editor, I may have to imagine what it would be like to be a member of a Muslim community exposed to blasphemous imagery.

Judgement Implies Standards

Let's now turn to our second obstacle in the way of ethical reasoning: 'Who am I to judge others?' This seems partly to arise from a liberal, in the broad sense of the word, reluctance to risk diversity of views by openly condemning. But it also may arise from the failure to make another important distinction. There is a world of difference between the act of judging (which surely implies making a judgement in relationship to some established criteria or standards) and being a judgemental person. 'Being judgemental' has a much narrower meaning, 'poking your nose into other people's affairs or forming crude opinions about things that you don't understand, and expressing them offensively' (Midgley, 1991, pp. 1–2).

There is a fundamental difference between a narrow interpretation of judging, simply 'finding fault' and condemning, and judging as 'evaluation'. There must inevitably be circumstances in which media professionals are called upon to make moral decisions based on judging what the right thing to do is in particular situations. Similarly, we must be concerned, where necessary, to evaluate the moral behaviour of journalists, TV producers, performers, script writers, network managers, and so on. Judgements of various kinds are unavoidable.

This distinction is also related to a further one; the distinction between 'moralizing' and making a moral judgement. Moralizing is judging dogmatically whereas making moral judgement ought to be a rational process in which the judgements we make and the actions we take are rooted in sound (evidential) reasons. In contrast to the dogmatic sceptic who professes that we can have no knowledge sufficient to make moral judgements, the moralist is dogmatic in another way in claiming to have all the answers in advance! Moralism is the attempt to instruct the audience in a particular, favoured set of moral rules and beliefs. Forms of moralism are rife in the editorial columns of daily newspapers, but we can, and do, distinguish editorializing from reporting, with the aspiration to be factual and accurate. Genuine ethical enquiry does not suppose that it has all the answers or, indeed, some infallible decision procedure for solving moral problems and dilemmas.

Morality is a Public Matter

The third obstacle to ethical reasoning is the claim that morality is simply a private matter. Enough has been said already to indicate what might be wrong with this claim. However, we must acknowledge that, of course, there is a sense in which the moral beliefs that I hold are personal in the banal sense that they are the beliefs that *I* hold. However, the moral language that we use and its meanings are essentially part of language as a public system or institution, as the linguistic philosopher J.L. Austin points out: 'our common stock of words embodies all the distinctions men [*sic*] have found worth drawing, and the connexions they have found worth marking, in the lifetimes of many generations' (Austin, 1970, pp. 181–182).

There can be no private morality that is not derived from a public system. For moral vocabulary to have meaning it must (logically) be a public vocabulary. The reasons for this are to be found in the famous argument advanced by

Ludwig Wittgenstein (1889–1951) against the logical possibility of a private language at all. To simplify a complex argument: the gist of the matter is that the use of a language involves some idea of correct or incorrect usage. This in turn depends on the possibility of being able to check that you are using a word correctly. However, the very privateness of a private language means that there can be no such checking, thus rendering the very idea of a private language impossible: 'Without some independent criterion, a third party so to speak, there is only my impression that I am following my private definition correctly' (Sheehan, 2001, p. 49).

There is a clear difference between making a moral judgement and acting upon it and simply having a personal preference for some choice of action. The identification of moral choice with personal preference has been described as an 'Individually Subjectivist Theory' (Raphael, 1989, p. 24). To say that 'producing and distributing pornographic images is wrong' is not like saying 'the pornographic images are colourful', although the statements are grammatically similar. 'Wrong' does not describe a property of the images in the way that 'colourful' does. According to our 'Individually Subjectivist Theory', wrong simply means I feel disapproval for such images. This, of course, leaves the gate wide open for you to disagree, based on your personal reactions and feelings about the images.

1.6 DEFINITIONS
Contrasting moral subjectivism and objectivism

Subjectivism

This is roughly the view that moral value is not grounded in some independent (external) reality but in our beliefs or our emotional responses or our attitudes. In other words, various kinds of judgements refer only to 'subjects' (people). For example, 'Ice-cream is delicious' is a subjective claim. Its truth or falsity depends on what we may feel or think about it. Such claims may be said to be neither true nor false. Similarly, moral claims are neither true nor false. On this account, the value of telling the truth depends on our belief, our feeling about it or our attitude of approval or disapproval. Subjectivism is usually contrasted with objectivism.

Objectivism

This is the view that moral values, such as goodness, inhere in, or are intrinsic to, actions or persons. Such objective values are sometimes compared to properties of objects in that they exist independent of our apprehension of them. Objective moral judgements may therefore be true or false and are independent of what anyone happens to think or feel about them. For example, 'Ice-cream is white' is either true or false and can be shown to be so by observation. Similarly, telling the truth is always an objectively good action.

The theory claims essentially to tell us that the meaning of any sentence of the form 'x action is right' and 'y action is wrong' or 'w is good person' and 'z is a bad person' can be translated into statements of approval or disapproval. However, this subjectivist approach (see Box 1.6) soon runs into logical difficulties when we consider a difference of opinion over moral judgement. Suppose we are considering the control and regulation of pornography. David says 'The production and distribution of pornography are always wrong' whereas Bill's opinion is that 'The production and distribution of pornography are sometimes right' (for example, it may be all right for consumption by consenting adults in private). Clearly there is a contradiction between the two statements. According the subjectivist theory, these translate as David says 'I always disapprove of the production and distribution of pornography' and Bill says 'I sometimes approve of the production and distribution of pornography'. The effect of this translation is to remove the contradiction between the two statements. They in effect reduce the statements to autobiographical description (facts about what they approve or disapprove of). This is similar to statements of preference as when David says 'I always like to eat burgers for lunch' and Bill says 'I never eat burgers for lunch or at any other time!' But surely, in differences of belief over moral questions of this kind, the protagonists are engaging in something other than merely stating their preference?

In a debate about pornography they might go on to adduce reasons for and against their respective positions. David may be claiming that pornography is harmful, tending 'to deprave or corrupt', for example, whereas Bill might want to contest the 'harmful' claim. But whatever the nature of the reasons they are doing something more than simply describing their preferences. If subjectivism was a true account and morality was simply a private matter then David and Bill would not be contradicting each other – which they plainly are! (Raphael, 1989, p. 24)

The subjectivist theorist may be more tenacious and claim that David and Bill are simply deluded and are simply arguing about their feelings. However, the subjectivist theory claims to tell us what it really means to say 'x action is right' and 'y action is wrong' or 'w is good person' and 'z is a bad person'. But what a sentence means is a function of the circumstances of its use and its logical character. It simply is the case that we do use statements such as 'x is a wrong action' and 'y is a good action' as contradictories. It just won't do to say people are deluded: 'The proper use of a sentence is its actual, normal use and the meaning of a sentence is to be gathered from its use. 'X is right' cannot mean the same as 'I approve of X'. The Individually Subjectivist Theory is false. We have spent some time unpacking the subjectivist approach because, as we will see, the mode of argument it develops is an influential one and, in a modified form, plays an important role in the common claim that 'morality is simply a matter for individual cultures to decide' a popular view which is characterized as 'cultural relativism'.

1.7 DEFINITIONS
Varieties of subjectivism

Individual subjectivism

This is the theory that moral judgements and choices are simply a function of private preferences. Morality is, and can only be, simply a private matter. In other words, I may choose to make my moral decisions only by reference to my own moral standards, which may be radically different from yours. Values are then relative to any particular person's subjective beliefs, feelings or attitudes. In this case there can be no independently established standards of behaviour.

Social subjectivism

This is the theory that moral judgements and choice are a function of the specific moral codes and values prevailing in a particular society or community at a particular time. Morality is the consensual outcome of whatever the majority decide. As a consequence, the standards of morality which I must uphold are therefore those of the community to which I belong. Values are therefore *relative* to those which are determined by the consensus in the community. In this case there can be no possibility of independent moral criticism of the prevailing moral consensus.

Relativism is Incoherent

It is frequently asserted that moral codes and values represent the decisions of particular societies relative to particular times and places (see Box 1.7). The implication is that a system is moral because a majority of people hold the moral beliefs that they do, as a matter of fact, hold. This is a form of relativism – cultural relativism – but is also very similar to the subjectivist arguments above. Such a view is often associated with the idea of toleration (Blackburn, 2001, p. 19). If it is the case that moral values may be relative to different societies in different times and places, then this undercuts any claims to the universal or transcultural values of morality. In England in the eighteenth century, most people would have considered the publication of blasphemous writings morally wrong and worthy of punishment. In a predominantly God-fearing society, blaspheming would be a moral wrong and mark out a bad person. This situation is not unknown in some contemporary, theocratic societies. In liberal, democratic societies, the majority of people would no longer consider blasphemy a moral evil. An extrapolation of this view would be to suggest therefore that the 'moral majority' should hold sway.

The relativist view shares much in common with the Individual Subjectivist and is vulnerable to similar kinds of arguments. The theory described above and can usefully be described as a 'Socially Subjectivist Theory' (Raphael, 1991, p. 25). It rests on a similar view of what it means to say some action is right or wrong or some person is good or bad. On this theory, 'x is right', for example, means 'the majority of people in my society approve of x'. However, clearly, I might hold a moral view that is in the minority but still argue that my moral belief is founded on reasonable grounds. For example, 'it is morally right that pornography should be available to those adults who choose to want to use it, even though the majority of people in society disapprove of it'. But the Socially Subjectivist Theory implies that this moral belief – 'that it is right that pornography should be available to those adults who choose to want it' – should be translated as 'most people in my society approve of pornography for those who want it'. This is now clearly in contradiction with the original moral claim and is absurd. But the original statement is well formed and makes perfectly good sense.

Raphael concludes that: 'Ethical predicates, then, do not describe the feelings of the speaker or the society at large. It seems clear that the meaning and the logical function of such expressions are not captured by saying that they describe feelings' (Raphael, 1989, p. 25). There is a world of difference between describing the kinds of moral values and rules that a particular culture may have, as a matter of fact, and the justification of those values and rules. This refers back to our distinction in the Introduction between descriptive and normative ethics. Simply to say that these are the moral rules that some particular culture has developed cannot mean that these are the rules and values that it *ought* to adopt.

Emotivism or Hurrah/Boo Ethics

The cultural relativist position is also associated with the belief that people can never reach agreement on moral principles. This view is often sustained by another view of moral language, which is again related to feelings. In this case it is claimed that moral beliefs and moral claims do not describe feelings but rather express them. The Expressive Theory attempts to avoid the difficulties of our previous Subjectivist Theories by arguing that value judgements in general, and moral judgements in particular, evince or express our feelings. This view is also referred to as Emotivism or the Hurrah/Boo Theory (Ayer, 1967, pp. 102–120).

This theory is associated with a philosophical movement of the early to mid-twentieth century known as Logical Positivism. The Logical Positivists made much of the logical gap between statements of fact and statements of value. Moral beliefs about the world are very different from factual beliefs. Moral claims are more like expressions of pain, delight, anger, etc. They express or evince my feelings. They have no purchase on empirical facts (the truths of the sciences); in effect, they express an attitude or feeling about the world. So if I claim that 'producing pornography is morally justifiable', then I am not stating that I have a feeling of approval but I am just expressing that feeling. In the same way, if I was to hit my head on a low beam I might cry out in pain. However, if someone was to challenge me and say 'producing pornography is morally unjustifiable', again they would be giving expression to a contrary feeling (not simply describing their emotions). Hence the Expressive Theory has this Boo versus Hurrah characteristic.

1.8 DEFINITION
Emotivism or Boo/Hurrah Ethics

Emotivism

Broadly, this is a view of ethics that maintains that ethical judgements are expressions of a speaker's emotional states rather than claims that such judgements are either true or false. This view makes a distinction between describing our feelings about things in the world and expressions of those feelings. Moral judgements are not descriptions or statements of our feelings about the world, but direct expressions of those feelings. In making moral judgements, in arriving at a moral decision when confronted by a moral dilemma, we are giving expression to an emotional response in favour, our approbation (hurrah), or against, our disapprobation (boo).

Boo/Hurrah

In other words, I cheer for my moral belief and you for yours. If we are simply expressing our feelings, then there apparently can be no question of discussing or agreeing on principles. On this basis, those celebrities who appeared at the Leveson Inquiry and argued that intrusion into their privacy was morally wrong were merely expressing a feeling they had. And similarly those journalists who argued that it was not immoral to report on the private doings of public persons were also expressing their feelings. On this account, there are no grounds for arguments about public interest or the interest of the public. However, when we do discuss these matters there clearly is a contradiction here and a contradiction which can be argued through by reasoned argument and by reference to facts and principles.

But the Expressive Theory has similar logical difficulties to the ones we have already discussed. When people adopt different moral positions they are doing more than cheering or booing. The language which they use cannot simply be translated as feelings. They are in effect expressing opinions and if I want to convert you to or persuade you of my moral belief, I would begin to state the reasons why I hold the particular views which I do in fact hold. Thus a simple equation between value judgements and feelings cannot be right. There are standards and criteria for applying value terms which I would reasonably refer to. If we think about choosing a camera for some particular photojournalistic job – one particular camera will satisfy some relevant standards or criteria appropriate for the job in a way another camera may not. I have grounds then to support my view that this is the camera for the job. Listing the qualities of a good camera is not like cheering! Similarly, when we come to discuss the moral qualities of a person we will invoke certain standards of behaviour to which this person matches up, or list the degree and extent of the person's virtues or vices. The Expressive Theorist may try to claim that those standards themselves are but expressions of feelings. But the analogy with a spontaneous emission of pain is not tenable. Reasons are not like involuntary cries of pain.

Table 1.1 Elements of moral judgement

Element	Description
Facts	In order to arrive at a reasonable judgement we need to know as far as we can the 'facts of the case'.
Relevant ethical principles	To determine how we ought to act, or what policy should be adopted, we need to consider what relevant universal rules or principles bear on the situation and what are their relative weights; for example, does justice or fairness have priority over others such as benevolence?
Argument	In coming to a judgement we need, if called upon, to show we have reasonable grounds for believing what we do believe to be the right judgement.
Moral imagination	We need to consider the relevant interests of all those involved or affected; this may not just be a question of imagining myself in someone else's place, but imaging what it is like to be them.

Adapted from Hare (1963, pp. 86–111)

CHAPTER REVIEW

By removing these various subjectivist types of theories I hope to show that making moral judgements and choosing a course of action or developing a policy are not an arbitrary matter. Moral judgements involve the deployments of facts, developing a logical argument, identifying appropriate moral principles and the exercise of moral imagination. Although people may, and frequently do, argue about the solutions to ethical problems, it is because of these aspects that it is possible to do so in a reasoned way and with some expectation of reaching reasonable solutions.

However, there is a difference between the soundness of an argument and persuading someone to accept it. I might present Rupert Murdoch with a brilliantly argued case as to why he should dismember his media empire for the greater good of the media industry and society in general, and my premise may be impeccable and the logic of the argument valid, and yet he would, I suspect, remain unmoved. A good argument may not necessarily be persuasive, especially where specific interests are involved. But we have also shown that morality must mean making reference to some standard of behaviour which is over and above any such particular individual or collective interest. In the coming chapters we will examine a range of moral ideas and principles that have been proposed as the foundations of such moral standards and their implications for media practices.

FURTHER READING

Cohen-Almagor, R. (2014) 'After Leveson: recommendations for instituting the Public and Press Council', *The International Journal of Press/Politics*, 19(2): 202–225. Useful for a good review of the work of the Leveson Inquiry and the underlying moral principles that ought to inform a new Public and Press Council.

Frost, C. (2000) *Media Ethics and Self-regulation*. Harlow. Pearson Education. See particularly Chapter 3, 'Media morality' (pp. 23–47), which provides a general overview of press ethics.

Gordon, A.D., Kittross, J.M. and Reuss, C. (eds) (1996) *Controversies in Media Ethics*. White Plains, NY: Longman. See particularly Overview, 'Foundations for Media Ethics', by John C. Merrill (pp. 1–26), which provides a useful introduction to a range of ethical theories.

Lægaard, S. (2007) 'The Cartoon Controversy: offence, identity, oppression?', *Political Studies*, 55: 481–498. An excellent account of the Danish Cartoon Controversy, primarily from a Danish perspective, it covers both legal and ethical dimensions. The author also broadens the discussion into questions of its relevance to identity and oppression in relationship to the Muslim community in Denmark.

Plaisance, P.L. (2009) *Media Ethics: Key Principles for Responsible Practice*. London: Sage. See particularly Chapter 1, 'Ethics theory: an overview' (pp. 1–20), for a review of basic ethical theory.

Sanders, K. (2006) *Ethics and Journalism*. London: Sage. See particularly Chapter 1, 'Ethics and journalism' (pp. 14–26), for a sceptical discussion of the relationship between ethics and journalism.

HOW TO USE THIS ARTICLE

Go to https://study.sagepub.com/horner to access the following journal article:

Luckhurst, T. and Phippen, L. (2014) 'Good behaviour can be taught', *British Journalism Review*, 25: 56–61.

The argument of Chapter 1 has emphasized the need for and nature of moral judgement in media practice. This article by Tim Luckhurst and Lesley Phippen of the Centre for Journalism at the University of Kent may be used to underscore the importance of moral judgement in journalistic practice. They extend the discussion of the chapter by engaging with a long-standing debate about whether we can best promote morally driven professional behaviour through the (mechanical) rules or through education in fundamental principles. They argue that current ethical problems in the press, demonstrated by Leveson, will not be addressed by a rule-based approach. They believe that would-be media practitioners must have ethical values embedded in their learning. They identify four core principles: accuracy, sincerity, hospitality and the responsibility to bear witness. In addition, this must be linked to what journalism is for in liberal democracies. They argue that good journalism is not a product of rule following, but of fundamental ethical commitments. Students should study and emulate the work of the great reporters and journalists of the past. They conclude that 'the difference between ethics and rule-based regulation is that the latter promises much but delivers little, whereas ethical education promises only to encourage thought and frequently spawns outstanding journalism'. We might add that these strictures, which are directed at journalism, may equally well apply to media practitioners more generally.

PART II
DESIRABLE ENDS

2
PLEASURE

In Chapter 1 we argued that it seems reasonable to suggest that moral judgements in Media Ethics are not arbitrary, relative or a matter of subjective preference. In other words, when faced with moral problems and dilemmas we must be able to make well founded and reasonable moral judgements. In this chapter we will examine a particular type of approach to how we might determine what a morally right action is and what the goal of our actions ought to be. This approach is broadly known as consequentialist. It proposes that the rightness or wrongness of an action is determined by the consequences that flow from that action and the tendency of that action to lead to inherently good or bad states of affairs. This, of course, leaves open the question as to what a good or bad state of affairs might be. To this there may be a variety of answers. One very influential answer, which we will focus on in this chapter, is that happiness is the one intrinsically good thing which we should aim to achieve. Now this could mean the happiness of the individual (hedonism) or it could mean the collective happiness or welfare. The latter view is usually referred to as utilitarianism. Thus, for media professionals trying to resolve a moral dilemma, it implies that, of the options available to us, we must choose the one which will lead to the greater happiness overall. When confronted by the need to make a moral choice, say when pressed as a journalist to disclose sources, I must weigh the consequences of disclosure against non-disclosure to work out, all things considered, which will produce the 'best' consequences.

In the chapter we will relate this consequentialist approach to one of the standard defences, for example, of media intrusion into the private lives of public figures. This defence is usually that the intrusion is justified in 'the public interest'. We can see that this defence has much in common with the consequentialist approach in that it elevates the public interest to the status of the public good. In effect, the public interest carries more moral weight than an individual's privacy, and maximizing the public good constitutes 'the best state of affairs'. We will then examine a specific controversy about media behaviour and morality in the light of this kind of moral theory. The case is that of a controversial radio broadcast in 2008 on the BBC involving Jonathan Ross and Russell Brand. The offensive content of the show raised the question of whether or not it was morally right to broadcast, especially given that this was a public service broadcasting organization, and what are the appropriate moral standards to apply in such cases.

The chapter goes on to broaden out this discussion by focusing on a particular and influential theory in the consequentialist tradition about how we ought to determine standards of behaviour. Jeremy Bentham (1749–1832) was a legal reformer and moral philosopher who believed he could establish an objective moral standard and method for moral judgement in the interest of social reform. For Bentham, the cornerstone of moral judgement is 'utility' (interpreted as pleasure) or 'the Greatest Happiness Principle'. It is plausible to argue that one of the key purposes of the media is to provide pleasure for audiences. In other words, if we are considering media content, then such content is moral and deserves to be broadcast if it maximizes the pleasure of the audience. From pleasure as a normative principle, Bentham argues, can be derived not only individual moral judgements, but also the policies which institutions and governments ought to follow to realize this principle. This approach to ethics is intuitively attractive as it appeals to a general aspiration to be happy. The chapter concludes with some criticisms of this approach.

2.1 DEFINITION
Hedonism

'Hedonism takes as its fundamental idea that the ultimate human good is happiness. The only state of being that is of value, in and of itself, is happiness or pleasure. The only state of being which is bad is unhappiness (or pain).'

'Usually the pleasure in question has been thought to be the subject's own pleasure, and so the view has been a form of egoism; but there is no reason in theory why it should not be the pleasure of humans, or even sentient beings generally.' Honderich (1995, p. 337)

RIGHT ACTION AND THE PUBLIC INTEREST
Normative Ethics and Consequentialism

Normative Ethics refers to those kinds of moral theories which recommend moral norms or rules that people ought to follow. The contrast is with Descriptive Ethics, which is an area of study which describes the particular moral values that people hold as a matter of fact. One influential response to the question 'What is the right action to take?', as we saw above, is that the right thing to do must depend, or be decided, on the basis of the outcomes of actions we take, by the consequences the actions bring about. In other words, moral judgement is based on an evaluation or weighing of the range of possible options that might be selected and then on the selection of the one that leads to the best consequences, all things considered. This is the gist of the range of moral theories that are conventionally described as 'consequentialist'. Notice that in this context what people intended is subsidiary to how things actually turn out: 'The right thing to do is whatever will produce the best state of affairs, all things considered' (Sandel, 2009, p. 33). The 'all things considered' clause is important given the frequency with which the actual, as opposed to the intended, outcomes of our actions are unpredictable.

However, this just pushes the argument back a further stage since we need to be able to characterize what 'best state of affairs' actually means in specific situations. If I am to make a judgement on consequences, I need to know what are 'good' consequences from a moral point of view. Consequentialist styles of thinking about moral questions are profoundly influential, especially in the formation of public policy. Much of contemporary policy making in the media and in other sectors, including government, is influenced by this notion that the rightness of actions and policies must depend on what happens, on outcomes, on succeeding states of affairs. In Media Ethics this idea is captured in the concept of the 'the public interest'.

The moral defence of acting in 'the public interest', even when laws have been clearly broken, is the crux of much debate about privacy and press intrusion (Archard, 1998; Sanders, 2006, pp. 77–92; Solove, 2008). Acting in the public interest is proposed as a way of providing moral legitimacy to intrusion in that it promotes, if not maximizes, the common good, for example, through the exposure of corruption or criminal activity. But the idea of 'the public interest' proves to be a slippery one. Morrison and Svennevig (2007), in researching the defence of public interest and intrusion into privacy, were unable to find any recognizable definition of public interest. What they found was that the application of the concept was very much context-dependent, so there might not be 'the public interest' but there may be 'a public interest' in specific circumstances. For example, this may apply to particular fields, such as public health, safety, military security and the like. In addition, the public interest is constructed from the values of a particular society representing the specific values that people hold and wish to have maintained. This may mean, they argue, that in particular cases intrusion into privacy may be defended not only on grounds of preventing possible harm to the community (the public interest) but also on grounds of the moral implications of particular acts or for reasons of social solidarity (Morrison and Svennevig, 2007, p. 45).

Consequentialism and the Public Interest

It has already been suggested that to determine what is right in some particular circumstance, say whether or not it would be right to hack into private telephone conversations, must (logically) have a concept of some ultimate, primary or intrinsic value, whether this is indeed happiness or social solidarity. It is this value which will in turn determine or allow us to decide what constitutes 'the best state of affairs'. In the case of phone hacking, when called upon to justify the hacking, which is illegal, this is done in such terms as 'in the public interest' or 'for the public good'. The breach of privacy and subsequent publication of the information gathered is justified because in some way this has promoted or added to the general welfare. Criminality or the blatant hypocrisy of some politicians may have been exposed. We are again arguing that 'the best state of affairs' is defined in terms of the public good or the public interest. The use of illicit methods, employed frequently as we now know from the Leveson Inquiry, may be justified in the public interest because, in the words of the Press Complaints Commission's *Editors' Code of Practice*, they lead to 'detecting or exposing crime or a serious misdemeanour, protecting public health and safety, or preventing the public from being misled by some statement or action of an individual or organization' (Press Complaints Commission, 2012).

It has been widely accepted that the public interest is not equivalent to whatever happens 'to interest the public' (Sanders, 2006, p. 48). The phrase connotes something that is impersonal, an abstract idea, which is not simply the aggregate sum of the public's interests. This emphasizes the need to distinguish the two by some other principle. As we have seen, the meaning of 'the public interest' is by no means always clear. The utilitarian approach typically may be used in the sense of 'the end justifying the means'. So, in the case described in Box 2.3, clearly the method used by the journalist to obtain the story is unethical by normal standards but, if it can be established that the ultimate end was in the public interest, then it may be morally justified. If we accept that the exposure of corrupt sporting practices is in the public interest, then the journalist was right. But a counter-argument might be that a greater public interest may be served if the country wins a gold medal, creating widespread rejoicing and happiness.

A key question is always 'Who defines the public good or the public interest and by what means and in what fields?' Frequently, governments will try to arrogate to themselves the power to define what is or is not in the public interest, especially on grounds of national security. As we will see later, the philosopher Jeremy Bentham (1749–1832) comes up with what he takes to be an objective method of determining 'the greatest good of the greatest number' and hence an objective normative principle for defining the public interest or the public good. This was particularly attractive in the period in which he was writing, which was one of great social injustice, corruption and arbitrary legal processes.

2.2 DEFINITION
Consequentialism and utilitarianism

Consequentialism

'Any outlook that holds that the rightness or wrongness of an action always depends on the consequences of the action, on its tendency to lead to intrinsically good or bad states of affairs.'

Utilitarianism

'...a species of consequentialism in that it takes happiness as the one intrinsically good thing at which actions and social arrangements are supposed to be aimed.'

'[Utilitarianism in a narrower sense] holds that there is just one moral principle, to seek the happiness of the greatest number; that "happiness" here means pleasure and the absence of pain; and that the one moral principle – since it is the one moral principle – is to be applied to each individual situation.'

Williams (2008, p. 82)

2.3 A JUDGEMENT CALL
Can I lie if (I think) it's in the public interest?

Suppose an investigative journalist has reasons to suspect that some international sportswomen may be susceptible to taking bribes to influence the outcome of netball matches. However, it is thought that this is so far not the case. There is an international gambling syndicate interested in making millions of dollars from fixing matches. The women are likely to play in their country's netball team in the next Olympic Games and have a high probability of winning a gold medal. The team enjoys widespread public support. The journalist poses as the representative of a rival syndicate and arranges to meet with the women. She goes to the meeting in the guise of a representative of a Russian oligarch. At the meeting, she is armed with a digital camera and sound recording equipment. She makes an offer to the women of a large sum of money to fix their next match. They seem to be persuaded because the money would support their Olympic training regime and agree to fix the result of their next (minor) match in return for the bribe. The whole transaction is caught on camera. Public exposure of the meeting and the bribe would certainly lead to disqualification from the Olympics, possible legal action and the disappointment of their many thousands of fans.

Suppose you are an editor. You must decide whether or not to run the story. The journalist has already made her judgement by deciding to get the story in the way that she has – by deception. Was the journalist right? Do you back the journalist's judgement and broadcast the story? Is the revelation of the corrupt practices in the public interest? If you believe it is, how do you know? What other steps might you take?

THE RUSSELL BRAND AND JONATHAN ROSS CONTROVERSY
'The Prank'

On the afternoon of Wednesday 15 October 2008, the BBC presenter Jonathan Ross left an obscene message on the answering machine of the actor Andrew

Sachs as part of a pre-recorded session for Russell Brand's BBC Radio 2 show. Sachs most famously had been the Spanish waiter, Manuel, foil for demented seaside hotel owner, Basil Fawlty, played by John Cleese, in the comedy series *Fawlty Towers* (1975–1979). In the telephone call reference was made to comedian and presenter, Russell Brand, having had sex with Sachs' granddaughter. Cooked up by Ross and Brand, the telephone call was intended as a comedic 'prank'.

The BBC producer of Brand's show, Nic Philips (subsequently referred to by the press as a 'junior' producer), having heard the pre-recording emailed David Barber, BBC's Head of Compliance, to discuss the 'pre-recording' and, in particular, the use of an obscene word in the call. The problem seemed to be the use of an obscenity rather than the substance of the call itself. Philips was seeking clearance to broadcast the show. In an email of Thursday 16 October at 3 pm, Nic Philips again emailed David Barber defining the issue: 'The problem comes when Jonathan says that Russell "******" Sachs' granddaughter. … I would say take it out but if it forms the crux of the call and is VERY funny… Russell and Jonathan both very keen for it to go out' (quoted in Martin, 2008, p. 4).

Barber then listened to the relevant sections twice. He then sent an email, on the same day, consulting the Radio 2 Controller, Lesley Douglas: 'Jonathan uses the f-word 52 mins [*sic*] into the first hour in a sequence about Russell "*******" Andrew Sachs' granddaughter. They are speaking into Sachs' answering machine at the time, and it's very funny – there then follow more calls to the answer phone in the 2nd hour, again v [*sic*] funny.' Note the stress on the comedic value of the 'prank' in these exchanges.

Barber was clear that the material should be kept in the show. He makes three key points. Firstly, that it should be broadcast but with the inclusion of a '"strong language" warning at the top of the hour'. This, he felt, would be better than simply bleeping out the offending word. Secondly, the nature of the material was compatible with the show. His view was that given the timing of the broadcast (early morning) and the audience expectations for Brand's show, the material was 'editorially justified'. Thirdly, he was also under the impression that Sachs had consented to the broadcast. Lesley Douglas responded the following day, at 12.22, with a simple 'yes' authorizing the broadcast of the suspect material – allegedly from her Blackberry. At 12.24 on David Barber emailed Nic Philips, the producer, informing him of the Controller's approval: 'I've just got sign off from [the Controller] so keep.'

In addition to seeking internal sanction for the broadcast Nic Philips had also contacted Andrew Sachs to get his consent for the broadcast. However, Philips and Sachs have very different accounts of the conversation about the messages. Philips thought that he had obtained Sachs' permission. Subsequently, Sachs claimed that he had asked that the producer 'tone down' the material. However, at no point does it seem that Philips conveyed Sachs' request to either Barber or Lesley Douglas.

2.4 A JUDGEMENT CALL
To broadcast or not to broadcast?

The show was transmitted on Saturday 18 October. The production team did not finish editing the show until shortly before it was to be broadcast. In the final editing some offensive material was edited out by Nic Philips. However, he did not fill out and submit the BBC's required compliance form until the next week (Martin, 2008, p. 4). BBC producers are required to complete a compliance form to point out any potentially offensive material. This would include, as in the Sachs' case, sexual content and strong language. The form must include a justification for the inclusion of such material. The aim is to ensure the compliance of pre-recorded material with the BBC's own editorial guidelines and Ofcom's broadcasting code. In other words, compliance is concerned with both internal and external standards. The focus of the compliance is on the protection of the public from offensive material. When asked why he did not submit the compliance form earlier, Nic Philips said that this was because he knew that there was no one to read it at Radio 2 – presumably because it was the weekend (Martin, 2008, p. 4)!

Given the background outlined in the text, the question is 'Was the judgement to broadcast the show right or wrong?' Even if the programme had failed to meet the required standards of compliance before it was broadcast, could this be justified if ultimately more people were happy with the broadcast than were offended by it? Does the end justify the means in this case?

2.5 DEFINITION
Moral panic

'A term introduced in the sociology of media and youth cultures ... but now in general use to describe the way a particular incident or apparent trend becomes a national issue of concern to a MASS of the population. What is particular about this public response is its "moral" dimension, where this term alludes to the way the behaviour of certain groups is understood as deviant or a threat to an accepted morality and way of life, or where highly profiled events and tendencies are seen as the symptoms of a social malaise.'

Brooker (1999, pp. 164–165)

Competing Standards

The transmission of the programme created a storm, with all the characteristics of a 'moral panic' (see Box 2.5). Ross and Brand's actions were greeted by a large degree of public opprobrium, although they were not without their supporters among a younger audience. In addition to the accusation of offensiveness, it was also claimed that the broadcast breached the privacy of Andrew Sachs and of his granddaughter. The BBC came in for heavy criticism for allowing the transmission and was condemned for the fact that no senior executive had listened to the pre-recording. But the question of the moral rightness or wrongness of the broadcast became entwined with a broader public and political debate about the BBC's funding mechanism – the licence fee. The government had been considering proposals to break the BBC's monopoly of the licence fee and, for example, possibly sharing it with a rival, Channel 4. In effect, the Ross and Brand affair fuelled the lobby for further deregulation and curtailment of public service broadcasting on the grounds that the BBC was failing to maintain appropriate standards. In response, the BBC Trust commissioned a report into the Brand Show but this was as much an attempt to stave off the wider threats to the BBC's monopoly of the licence fee.

If we put aside the questions about the failure of the internal procedures at the BBC, what seems to be more significant are the core questions of 'How standards of broadcasting should be determined?', 'What are the appropriate, applicable moral principles?', and importantly, 'Who should determine them?' This is a case where it could be argued that there was a real moral dilemma created by two competing core principles. Generally, the facts of the case were not in question, apart from whether or not Andrew Sachs had or had not consented to participation in the programme. On one side of the argument were those who claimed the broadcast was in bad taste and demonstrated a failure to maintain certain standards. The values which were invoked on this side of the argument were intrinsic values such as those of privacy and consent. The idea here is that, as a person, I have certain intrinsic rights that ought not to be overridden. Given these rights, the presenters and programme makers had an obligation to respect them. On the other side of the argument were those who felt that another celebrity was fair game for an amusing prank. In other words, the show was to be justified by its consequences: the end justified the means (see Box 2.4). Did it sufficiently amuse the audience? If the purpose of such programmes is to entertain and its intended audience are indeed entertained, then it was legitimate. (Remember that one of the key points David Barber made for broadcasting the show was that, in his view, the timing of the broadcast – in the early morning – and the audience's expectations for Brand's show meant that the material was 'editorially justified'.) This is fundamentally a consequentialist argument. If the majority of the listening audience enjoyed the show, then this justified the performance. This view is consistent with a broadly utilitarian approach which places maximizing pleasure as the guiding moral principle. Jeremy Bentham notoriously refers to the idea of natural rights as 'nonsense on stilts'. In the following section, we examine Bentham's system in more detail for, as the Harvard philosopher Michael Sandel suggests, 'The philosophy he launched has had an influential career. In fact, it exerts a powerful hold on the thinking of policy-makers, economists, business executives, ordinary citizens to this day' (Sandel, 2009, p. 34).

BENTHAM AND THE DEMOCRACY OF PLEASURES
Pleasure as 'the Good'

On Bentham's account, pleasure should be the cornerstone of our moral system. His system is a form of hedonism (see Box 2.1). If we want to know what the right thing to do is, then we have to consider the consequences of our actions. If we agree with the idea that actions should be judged according to their consequences, then we must, from a moral point of view, ask what are the consequences we aim to achieve? For Bentham, the answer to this question was clear: we should act so as to maximize pleasure and minimize pain. The rightness or wrongness of an action or a policy (because he was primarily concerned with social reform and public policy) should be determined by weighing up the costs and benefits. His most important work is *An Introduction to the Principles of Morals and Legislation*, first published in the revolutionary year of 1789 (Bentham, 1969). His work is sharply at odds with the predominant religious ideology and morality of the day, where God was the ultimate source of morality. He begins in the very first paragraph of Chapter I, 'Of the principle of utility', with this clear and radical statement of his central idea:

> Nature has placed mankind under the governance of two sovereign mas-
> ters, *pain* and *pleasure*. It is for them alone to point out what we ought to
> do, as well as to determine what we shall do. On the one hand the standard
> of right and wrong, on the other the chain of cause and effects, are fastened
> to their throne. They govern us in all we do, in all we say, in all we think:
> every effort we can make to throw off our subjection, will serve but to
> demonstrate and confirm it. (Bentham, 1969, p. 313)

The Principle of Utility

We are, according to Bentham, as a matter of fact, governed by pleasure and pain and we ought to make these two 'masters' the basis of our morality and law. Bentham goes on in the same paragraph to state:

> The principle of utility recognizes this subjection, and assumes it for the
> foundation of that system, the object of which is to rear the fabric of felicity
> by the hands of reason and law. Systems which attempt to question it, deal
> in sounds instead of sense, in caprice instead of reason, in darkness instead
> of light. (Bentham, 1969, p. 313)

Note that Bentham seems to move from factual statements about human psychology to an evaluative statement about what we ought to do as a consequence. This is a fundamental problem for utilitarianism; it appears to confuse what people *do*, as a matter of fact, desire with what *ought* to be desired. In effect, this is a fallacious argument which attempts to derive an evaluative conclusion from purely factual premises (Flew, 1985, pp. 134–138).

There are no half measures for Bentham. Once he had achieved this insight there was to be no retreat, no going back. This was not to be construed as individualistic hedonism, that is, that only our own selfish pleasure mattered (see Box 2.2). The consequences of actions were to be judged on the basis of their tendency to increase pleasure or pain for all whose interests were in question. This is 'the Greatest Happiness Principle' and it was to be applied universally. Bentham claims that 'the Greatest Happiness Principle' is the foundation of all morals and legislation; the highest principle of morality. He was not interested simply in constructing an abstract system, but in its practical application for social reform in the pursuit of greater happiness. By utility, he meant whatever was conducive to the production of pleasure or happiness and whatever led to the prevention or mitigation of pain or suffering. He believed that there could be no grounds for rejecting the principle of utility. He argued that those who defended notions of natural or intrinsic rights could only do so by arguing that in the long run they maximized happiness. To promote policies on grounds other than those of utility was simply irrational. All genuine moral problems could ultimately be translated into how to apply the principle of utility. On this basis, utility ought to determine both the actions of individual media practitioners and organizational and government policies.

2.6 DEFINITION
The principle of utility

Bentham's principle of utility is that an action or policy should be judged on the basis of the results it achieved. Those results should be assessed by the extent to which pleasure or happiness was promoted and/or pain was minimized. As a moral theory this is referred to as utilitarianism. Pleasure or 'the greatest happiness of the greatest number' is the ultimate good, subordinating all other moral principles, which then appear only as means to this end.

Applying the Utility Principle

In Chapter III of *The Principals of Morals and Legislation* Bentham outlines the mechanisms by which our individual hedonic impulses, our individual pursuit of pleasure, would be modified or reconciled to the pleasures and pains of others:

> There are four distinguishable sources from which pleasure and pain are in use to flow: considered separately, they may be termed the *physical*, the *political*, the *moral* and the *religious*: and inasmuch as pleasures and pains belonging to each of them are capable of giving a binding force to any law or rule of conduct, they may all of them be termed *sanctions*. (Bentham, 1969, p. 325)

Bentham argues that the effect of these sanctions in combination is to persuade people to pursue their own pleasures in such a manner that will be conducive to the production of pleasure and the avoidance of pain for others. The *physical* sanction is simply our experience of pain or pleasure as a natural consequence of our actions. The *political* sanction is the influence of laws and policy on our pleasures and pains. The *moral* sanction represents the influence of other people's attitudes towards us and the pressure of popular opinion in general. And finally, the *religious* sanction is the influence of our apprehension of divine rewards and punishments. In consequence, the job of the moralist and the policy maker or legislator is to so configure these various sanctions so as to maximize happiness overall (Norman, 1991, p. 125).

In this moral framework, I only value your happiness in an *instrumental* way. I'm only interested in your happiness to the extent that it promotes or hinders mine. I have no duty as such to promote your happiness; your happiness has no intrinsic worth. I, for example, make films or television programmes in pursuit of my own satisfaction not out of any sense of benevolence towards the audience. I feed the audience's pleasure because in the end that will promote my pleasure such as in developing a successful media career. In this context, sanctions match our individual desire for happiness to the general happiness. Codes of practice and legislation may curb my activities to bring them into line with what the general welfare or public interest requires.

For Bentham everyone's pleasure counted equally. This is, in effect, a democracy of pleasure in two senses. Firstly, in calculating the overall balance sheet of pleasure in any situation no one person's satisfaction counted more than another's. Secondly, all pleasures were to be counted as equal – that is, pleasure was purely a quantitative matter not a qualitative one. The symphonies of Gustav Mahler are to be valued on the same scale as the works of *Take That*: that is, the extent to which the consequences of their performance created pleasure and/or pain. Experiences only differ on the basis of the quantities of pleasure. Bentham not only provides a clear account of what ought to count as 'good', but he also provides a method for deciding in any circumstance what was the right course of action to take: 'the Felicific Calculus'. On this basis, a key indicator of what counts as 'good' in a moral sense might be audience ratings or circulation figures.

The Felicific Calculus: Who Should Decide?

A key question in regulating the media is 'Who is competent to make the judgements about the regulation of media content?' Bentham's answer to this question would be a purely administrative one. No special insight is necessary to make such judgements. Policy is to be determined by the application of 'the Felicific Calculus'. When confronted by any moral problem, the solution was to be found in calculating the relative balance of pleasure to pain to arrive at the moral course of action. This is why notions such as lying and truth-telling, in this version of utilitarianism, are context-dependent. On some occasions, more happiness may result rather than pain by lying. If you ask me 'Does this hairstyle suit me?', even though I think it doesn't, I might lie and say 'Of course, darling'. If my lie is exposed, I might argue that to have said otherwise would cause you pain while lying gave you pleasure.

But equally, and more seriously, we can see that here is a possible, rational justification for journalistic deception and malpractice in the interest of the public good (defined as 'the greatest happiness of the greatest number'). The *News of the World*, for example, was renowned for its use of deception to expose alleged corruption by celebrities, sportsmen, minor royalty and politicians. Balancing out the relative harm of the deception against the gain in public knowledge of corruption, using Bentham's method, can we not rationally and morally provide a justification for more or less routine acts of mendacity and deception (Sanders, 2006, pp. 40–52)?

Bentham used the term 'felicific calculus' for the method by which to arrive at the hedonistic value of an action. This value is the sum total of pleasure the action brings about. The elements to be taken into account in calculating individual and collective happiness are enumerated in Table 2.1. For the individual, Bentham argued that 'the value of a pleasure or pain considered by *it* will be greater or less' depending on the six elements listed in Table 2.1. However, he argues that 'fecundity' and 'purity' are properties of the act or event by which the pleasure or pain has been produced, rather than the value of the pleasure itself.

Table 2.1   Elements determining the value of a pleasure or pain

Element	Description
Its intensity	An intense pleasure is to be valued more than, say, a less intense pleasure that may last longer.
Its duration	A pleasure is to be valued more the longer it lasts.
Its certainty or uncertainty	A pleasure is of less value if its occurrence is less likely than some other pleasure.
Its propinquity or remoteness	Pleasures emanating at a distance are to be counted as lower value than those arising close to.
Its fecundity	'...the chance it has of being followed by sensations of the same kind: that is, pleasures, if it be a pleasure: pains, if it be a pain.'
Its purity	'...the chance it has of not being followed by sensations of an opposite kind: that is, pains, if it be pleasure; pleasures, if it be pain.'

Source: Bentham (1969, p. 327)

If we are determining the correctness of a judgement for more than one person, then the total value of the pleasure or pain will be determined by these same elements with the addition of a seventh element or circumstance: 'Its extent; that is, the number of persons to whom it extends; or (in other words) who are affected by it' (Bentham, 1969, p. 328).

Having enumerated these elements, Bentham makes short work of showing how we might then 'take an exact account … of the general tendency of any act, by which the interests of a community are affected' (Bentham, 1969, p. 328). This is to be achieved by working out the values of the pleasures and pains according to the six elements. This is to be calculated for each individual by balancing the values of pleasure against pain. The individual pleasures and pains would then be multiplied by the numbers of persons affected and the overall tendency to 'good' or 'evil' could be calculated.

In the case of Ross and Brand, the determination of whether they behaved badly or not would be entirely a function of the relative balance of pain or pleasure which resulted from their behaviour. We would have to work out all the values of pain and pleasure for members of the audience. We would also have to include the effects on Andrew Sachs and his granddaughter. This is the only standard, according to Bentham, which reasonably allows us to make a moral judgement. If we could establish that more people derived pleasure from Ross and Brand's performance, then we would have to acknowledge that they were right in doing what they did. The fact that Andrew Sachs suffered particularly from their 'prank' would simply be one element in the calculation. The 'victims' in this case, would not have special status. Other kinds of values, such as those of respect for privacy, are simply overridden by the appeal to the principle of utility.

LIMITATIONS OF BENTHAM'S SYSTEM

Bentham's system is attractive because of its apparent simplicity and its apparent suitability as means of policy making. To determine media regulatory policy, for example, a policy maker first identifies all the possible alternative policies, then calculates all the various costs and benefits for each alternative, and then calculates the option that delivers the best overall outcomes according to the principle of utility.

Problems of Method

This apparent simplicity hides a wealth of complexities. For example, Lord Justice Leveson, in concluding his inquiry on press regulation, let's imagine, might undertake a calculation on these lines based on a variety of options. Firstly, he could consider the costs and benefits of leaving the system of press self-regulation as it is. Secondly, he could consider the costs and benefits of a regulatory system which is independent of both the industry and government and has more powerful sanctions. Thirdly, he could consider regulation by a government authority, again with increased sanctions. Fourthly, he could consider a form of regulation which focuses more particularly on the processes of news gathering and publication while having a light-touch policy for matters of substance and content. With Bentham's method, in each case he would have to predict the consequences of each option for the overall good 'in the long run'. Again, it is difficult to see how this metaphorical weighing could be done with the kind of precision that Bentham implies (and he himself never achieved).

The method does seem to require ever larger amounts of data for relatively simple problems if we were seriously to try to apply the calculus. Is it practical? How do we get the data for the felicific calculus? Fundamentally, we do not have a standard for measuring pleasure. We can only use surrogate measures, responses to surveys, audience research, audience figures, circulation figures, and so on. But we don't have an homogeneous measure for pleasure. A further set of difficulties concern the basic principle. Is pleasure really what most people desire given that what people desire in terms of pleasure may be very different? The very idea of pleasure is vague. The impression of precision in the method is illusory. The 'weighing' of pleasures against pains is in the end metaphorical.

Unfairness

One important implication of this approach might be that we would be prepared to sacrifice innocent parties (e.g. Andrew Sachs in our example above) for the pleasure of the majority. We might well decide, for example, that if the public interest is indeed defined by pleasure, then it might be reasonable to have an open season on intrusion into the private lives of celebrities. In Bentham's system there can be no necessary right to privacy; the audience and circulation figures, as indicators of happiness, could rule media outputs. On the other hand, this should strike us as unjust. This is the problem. Bentham requires us to jettison much of our established moral vocabulary, by which we do feel able to talk meaningfully about respect, human dignity, sacrifice, and so forth. It does seem entirely reasonable (although in some circumstances debatable) to reject torture on principle as intrinsically bad (see Sandel, 2009, pp. 38–41). As noted above, Bentham asks us to subsume all existing moral concepts under one principle – that of utility. This, however, seems to be an impoverishment of our moral life. Rooted, as it is, in the view that actions should be judged by their consequences, the theory neglects altogether the importance of intentions irrespective of outcomes.

Back to Ross and Brand

So can we apply Bentham's analysis to the Ross and Brand case? We can at least see how the matter might be decided according to Bentham's principles. We would need in some way to determine 'the hedonic value' of the programme. Did it, on balance, produce more pain than pleasure for the audience? Certainly, the assumption of some of those who defended the show did so in precisely those terms. It was right to broadcast the programme because it did amuse and entertain the majority of those for whom it was intended. But here's one of the problems with Bentham's approach; it's just not obvious how the calculus is to be implemented. It may be that some sophisticated social science-based audience research may be helpful. But for Bentham, it is not the particularity of pains and pleasures we might suffer that is significant, but their duration and intensity. Now I think we can easily see that there are problems with this approach. We can measure time but in what units do we measure happiness? Is happiness indeed the kind of thing that can be measured? What instruments do we have for measuring the intensity of pleasure? Is it really sufficient to have a social survey of the audience which just asks them? Bentham appeals to his hedonic calculus as an objective measure, but just asking people would be far from objective.

In addition, there must be difficulties about calculating the probabilities about how certainly pleasure or pain may follow an action. If we are to use Bentham's method in an anticipatory way, and he surely intends this, then we need to be able to predict the outcomes in terms of pain and pleasure of all possible actions in a particular situation. Take the Ross and Brand case: if we were to use Bentham's method to decide in advance whether or not to broadcast, then we would at least have to know the relative balances of pleasure over pain for both broadcasting and non-broadcasting. Bentham himself acknowledges the difficulties of having to constantly apply the method:

> It is not to be expected that this process should be strictly pursued previously to every moral judgement, or to every legislative or judicial operation. It may, however, be always kept in view; and as near as the process actually pursued on these occasions approaches to it, so near will such process approach to the character of an exact one. (Bentham, 1969, p. 328)

In other words, it will be all right to do quite a bit of guessing as long as we keep the principle in view!

But is Bentham Right about Pleasure?

The scenario in Box 2.7, 'the Pleasure Machine', raises the fundamental issue as to whether Bentham's fundamental assumptions are right about pleasure as the supreme good. On offer, we have a choice of a simulated life of unalloyed pleasure in which all our ambitions and desires may be virtually fulfilled. We might be likely to choose this option if we felt that our well-being was solely constituted by pleasure. In contrast, we can choose to live a real life characterised by all the usual human stresses and strains, triumphs and disasters. Why might we refuse this offer of endless intense pleasure? Well, we can argue that well-being is not solely constituted by pleasure. For example, what about the sense of achievement after triumphing against the odds, or making a sacrifice which brings suffering in the interests of others, such as donating an organ in order to save a child's life? We value relationships with our family and friends even though, on some occasions, these may cause us pain and dissatisfaction. To live a life in a simulated environment, fed with pleasure, would, on this view, be a wasted life. (This, after all, is the situation depicted in the film *The Matrix* [1999] which the heroes are striving desperately to overcome.) So we would have reasons for refusing the pleasure machine on the basis that there are other things besides pleasure that we find intrinsically valuable.

2.7 A JUDGEMENT CALL
Whether or not to enter 'the Pleasure Machine'

Suppose, like the characters in the film *The Matrix* (1999), it was possible for you to live in a simulated environment in which you could enjoy any experience you desired. Neuropsychologists have designed a machine which can stimulate your brain so that you imagine you are actually experiencing what is, in effect, only a simulated experience. However, in reality you are floating in a life support tank connected to a supercomputer which is generating your experiences of the world. Before being plugged into this system you can specify all the most pleasurable experiences which you could ever imagine having. The catch here is that this is an all or nothing situation. You can't choose just to plug in for a short period. You have to commit to 'living' in this way for the rest of your natural life. The machine will ensure that you live the rest of your life in a state of intense pleasure. In addition, the simulation is so good that once plugged in you will not be aware of being in the tank or the fact that your experiences are artificially created. This is, in essence, a profoundly moral choice because it goes to the core of how we ought to live our lives and what we ought most to value.

Would you elect to live this life of simulated pleasure at the expense of effectively leaving a world of mixed pleasures and pains, successes and disappointments, triumphs and frustrations?

Adapted from Law (2007, p. 111)

CHAPTER REVIEW

In this chapter we began by considering the idea that we ought to make our moral choices based on whether or not those choices led, all things considered, to the best outcomes. This represents a generic type of moral theory which we referred to as consequentialist. We went on to consider a particular species of consequentialism, referred to as utilitarianism. Characteristically, utilitarianism holds that the best consequences can be defined in terms of pleasure or happiness. In other words, we ought to make moral judgements on the basis that the particular action chosen will be the one that will maximize pleasure for the individual or the community. In the latter form, this is encapsulated in the slogan 'the greatest happiness of the greatest number'. We then related this approach to moral decision making to the idea of the public interest. We discussed how a utilitarian approach is translatable into the concept of the public interest. In particular, we discussed how intrusions into the privacy of public figures may be justified by reference to the public interest – in other words, how the end (the public interest) might be justified by the means (intrusion).

We then considered in more detail Bentham's moral theory as a grand theory which he proposed would underpin all legislation and policy. Bentham's principle of utility seems an attractive way of reducing the complexities of moral judgement to measurable proportions. It seems consistent with a common-sense understanding that we generally aim for a more pleasurable life and shy away from pain both individually and collectively. It also seems attractive because the idea of utility is as equally applicable to the individual as it is to the community. It is not hard to see that many policy decisions are, in fact, based loosely on Bentham's principles: policy makers seek to balance the interests of stakeholders and 'calculate' the relative costs and benefits. At the time Bentham was writing, this was a bold and radical approach, opening the way to social reform against the dead hand of religion and political reaction.

Bentham's methods of determining what the moral thing to do is are also disarmingly powerful. It requires no special insights or feats of moral character. It is a purely arithmetical process. From a policy point of view, it can be seen as a neutral administrative procedure. If sanctions in the form of regulation are needed, the job of the administrator is simply to identify those policies which will tend to maximize the public good in terms of the maximization of pleasure and the mitigation of pain. This is, according to Bentham, a purely object process. However, as we will see in later chapters, in considering particular debates, this cannot be the whole story.

Bentham's principle also seems to be a good fit with essentially liberal market economies. The guiding principle is that everyone's preferences have equal value in the market. This also translates into a view of culture which refuses to privilege any particular type of cultural product and content. In the next chapter, we will see how this plays out in terms of the dispute between the advocates of public sector broadcasting and those of the market. One of the assumptions of public sector broadcasting is that there are certain kinds of media services and content that need to be protected and promoted, whether they are commercially viable or not. From Bentham's point of view, no such privileging is justifiable. But we have also seen that Bentham's hedonism is also vulnerable to criticism. Pleasure, as the primary consideration in determining our actions, can't be the end of the story. There just may be grounds for arguing that although pleasure is important, it is not the only thing that is important. We will explore this idea in the coming chapters.

FURTHER READING

Bentham, J. (1969) *An Introduction to the Principles of Morals and Legislation*, in D.D. Raphael (ed.), *British Moralists: 1650–1800. Volume II: Hume–Bentham*. Oxford: Clarendon Press. pp. 313–346 (1st edn, 1789). In this essay, Bentham outlines the basis of his theory and its method of application in terms of the 'hedonic calculus'. It is essential reading for coming to grips with the depth of Bentham's work.

Sandel, M.J. (2009) *Justice: What's the Right Thing to Do?* London: Allen Lane. See particularly Chapter 2, 'The greatest happiness principle/utilitarianism' (pp. 31–57), for a discussion and critique of Bentham and Mill on pleasure and happiness.

Sanders, K. (2006) *Ethics and Journalism*. London: Sage. See particularly Chapter 11, 'The bottom line' (pp. 128–138), for a discussion of media markets, dumbing down and journalistic integrity.

 ## HOW TO USE THIS ARTICLE

Go to https://study.sagepub.com/horner to access the following free journal article:

Morrison, David E. and Svennevig, Michael (2007) 'The defence of public interest and the intrusion of privacy', *Journalism*, 8: 44–65.

Use this article to take a more critical look at the concept of the public interest and its deployment in defence of intrusions into people's private lives. This is an empirical UK study based on a series of 13 in-depth interviews with key figures in radio, television, print and internet journalism, media regulation, pressure groups, trade bodies and media law. These interviews were followed up with eight focus groups and a nationally representative survey. The results of this empirical work produced insights into a more complex understanding of the factors involved in judging the rights of individuals to be protected from intrusion and the relative rights of the media to intrude. In particular, the authors highlight the unsatisfactory nature of the concept of 'the public interest'. In response, they offer an alternative concept – that of 'social importance'. The advantage of their proposed concept is, they argue, that it is 'readily operationizable and scalable in terms of intensity and in its potential applications'. For example, 'social importance' is more capable of addressing a question such as 'What is the social importance of a picture of a female news reader sunbathing on a holiday beach?'

3
MARKETS

In the previous chapter we saw how the idea of pleasure provided a fundamental principle in making moral judgements. In this chapter we discuss how the idea of pleasure as the ultimate good plays out in debates about the delivery of media content. One camp believes that 'free markets' are the best means of delivering the kinds of media content that audiences want. The interests of society are best served by allowing markets to govern the development of media institutions and the distribution of media products and services. In opposition to this idea is the belief that markets are imperfect and tend to lead to distorted and restricted outcomes in terms of diversity and plurality of content. And that there are some forms of media content that ought to be provided, on moral grounds, but cannot be left to the market. The best interests of society as a whole are served by at least some public provision of media products and services, that is, public service broadcasting to preserve cultural standards and to promote artistic and technical innovation.

In the next section we will look at some general arguments about the moral efficacy of markets, in particular the relationship between free markets in broadcasting and the idea of aesthetic and moral standards. We look at a significant debate which focuses on these issues of markets and ethics. This was a clash between the media moguls Rupert and James Murdoch and the BBC. The Murdochs have publicly argued that the BBC, through its public subsidy – the licence fee – and the scale of its operations, distorts the development of market-based media institutions and content. Our aim will be to draw out the ethical principles at stake in this debate. The Murdochs' position has much in common with Bentham's idea of the public good being, in effect, the aggregate of public pleasures. It is only when manifest harm stemming from media activities can be demonstrated that regulation of the market may be necessary.

In the following section we will discuss a modified form of utilitarianism, introducing a distinction between 'higher' and 'lower' pleasures which takes the argument in the opposite direction. John Stuart Mill (1806–1873) argues that there are some types of pleasure which are intrinsically better than others, and such pleasures are essential for a happy and fulfilled life. This distinction between higher and lower pleasures implies several things. Firstly, why it may be socially important to regulate for, and maintain, public service provision of a diverse range of media content and forestall an undue concentration of media ownership. And, secondly, it suggests the criteria on which such judgements about content ought to be made and by whom.

PLEASURE AS A GUIDE TO JUDGEMENTS ABOUT MEDIA CONTENT

The Equality of Pleasures

Let's consider some of the implications of Bentham's utilitarianism for standards in broadcasting. If we apply Bentham's method, we assess all media content by the same standard – that of whether it tends to promote happiness or reduce pain. The standard here is purely quantitative. More people may watch and enjoy *Sex and the City* as against, say, the BBC dramatization of D.H. Lawrence's *Women in Love*. The aggregate of preferences ought to shape future programme schedules. The relative balance between entertainment and news programming must reflect their tendency to add to the general happiness. Bentham recognizes no distinctions between types of pleasure. He accepts people's preferences at their face value. He recognizes no distinction, as John Stuart Mill came to do, between 'higher' and 'lower' pleasures. As the contemporary moral philosopher Michael Sandel (2009, p. 52) puts it: 'Some people like Mozart, others Madonna. Some ballet, others like bowling. Some read Plato, other *Penthouse*. Who is to say, Bentham might ask, which pleasures are higher, or worthier, or nobler than others?'

A Role for Public Service Broadcasting

This view seems to provide a pretty good fit with views about how markets operate in modern liberal democracies. The case for markets in a utilitarian framework is that generally the free operation of markets will tend to promote the general welfare, again defined in terms of the 'greatest happiness principle'. The simplistic view is that in exchanges between individuals making a bargain, both parties gain equally. If the exchange makes each better off in some way, then there is an overall increase in utility in society as long as no one is harmed in the process. Of course sceptics question this simple story. For example, the majority of exchanges take place between large corporations and individuals. There is frequently a huge power differential between our status as media consumers and the power of the media corporations. The power of corporations, it may be argued, means that our choices may in some sense not be entirely as free as they might appear (Vardy and Grosch, 1999, p. 262).

However, the fact of the concentration of media power may not affect the guiding principle that everyone's preferences have equal value in the marketplace. This translates, as we will see below, into a view of culture which refuses to privilege any particular type of cultural product, content or genre. On the basis of this logic, it would generally be wrong to intervene in the operation of the market. The only justification for the application of sanctions or regulation would be those also outlined by Bentham in his *Principles of Morals and Legislation* (Bentham, 1969). Law makers may only apply laws and sanctions according to the utility principle. But one of the assumptions of public sector broadcasting is that there are certain kinds of media services and content that need to be protected and promoted, whether they are commercially viable or not. From Bentham's point of view, I would argue that no such privileging is justifiable except on purely utilitarian grounds.

3.1 DEFINITION
Utilitarianism

'The creed which accepts as the foundation of morals, Utility, or the Greatest Happiness Principle, holds that actions are right in proportion as they tend to promote happiness, wrong as they tend to produce the reverse of happiness. By happiness is intended pleasure, and the absence of pain; by unhappiness, pain and the privation of pleasure. To give a clear view of the moral standard set up by the theory, much more requires to be said; in particular, what things it includes in the idea of pain and pleasure; and to what extent this is left an open question. But these supplementary explanations do not affect the theory of life on which this theory of morality is grounded – namely, that pleasure, and freedom from pain, are the only things desirable as ends; and that all desirable things (which are as numerous in the utilitarian as in any other scheme) are desirable either for the pleasure inherent in themselves, or as means to the promotion of pleasure and the prevention of pain.'

John Stuart Mill, 'Utilitarianism' (1964b, p. 6)

THE MURDOCHS' ATTACK
Rupert Murdoch's Attack on Public Service Broadcasting

The MacTaggart lectures, delivered annually in Edinburgh, Scotland, are an occasion when the great and the good reflect upon the state of the media industry. In a landmark lecture in 1989, Rupert Murdoch, the Chief Executive of News Corporation, delivered an attack on the poor state of British television, dominated as it was by the public service broadcasting of the BBC. He charged that the BBC's dramas were 'run by the costume department' (quoted in Sabbagh, 2009, p. 13). The prevalence of costume dramas was symptomatic. The genre reflected the values of a narrow elite of society in which 'strangulated English accents dominate dramas which are played out in rigid class-structured settings'. The apparent obsession of film and television with adaptations of the works of Jane Austen seems to emphasize his point. For Murdoch, the source of 'the problem' was precisely that public service broadcasting was not subject to the disciplines of the market: 'The fact that those who control British TV have always worked in a non-market environment, protected by public subsidy and state privilege, is a major reason why they are unsympathetic to markets and competition' (quoted in Sabbagh, 2009, p. 13).

Murdoch argued that the power of the public sector in broadcasting stifled innovation and was a barrier to increasing diversity of both means and content of broadcasting. He predicted the rise of multi-channel television at a time when Sky television was losing £2 million a week. His vision was that of market-driven media industries exploiting the benefits of new technologies in which television sets would be 'linked by fibre-optic cable to a global cornucopia of programming and nearly infinite libraries of data, education and entertainment'. This, remember, was in the pre-internet days of 1989. Murdoch argued that under the impact of market forces and such technological developments the debate was about multi-channel choice versus what was then, in the UK, the public service duopoly. He was in no doubt as to what would triumph.

James Murdoch's Attack on Public Sector Elitism

The resilience of these questions of principle and power is reflected in the fact that twenty years later, in 2009, in the same series of MacTaggart lectures, James Murdoch, Rupert Murdoch's son, returned to the same theme. The debate had not gone away. The younger Murdoch renewed the attack on public service broadcasting in general and the BBC in particular. His argument was again that the dominance of state-sponsored broadcasting ultimately led to a denial of choice. He had in his sights not only the BBC, but also the national broadcasting regulator, OfCom. Murdoch's charge was that, in conjunction, these two institutions had a stultifying effect on the development of broadcasting, producing a highly regulated sector. Firstly, this was wrong because it annihilated the customer in the sense that they were reduced to a position of passivity in need of protection. In contrast, the freedom of the customer to choose, to express their preferences in a free market, is at the heart of things for the commercial sector. Secondly, Murdoch argued that the way the BBC was expanding, fuelled by the power of public subsidy – the licence fee – was a threat to democracy, especially through its dominance of online news provision. Thirdly, the Corporation was not subject to the disciplines of the market, particularly in the salaries it paid to attract major celebrities (such as Jonathan Ross). The licence fee again allowed the BBC the freedom to remunerate its 'stars' unconstrained by any normal commercial logic.

James Murdoch returned to his father's theme of the essential elitism embedded in public service broadcasting. He drew a religious analogy in describing the central tenets of public service broadcasting, likening them to 'Creationism'; in other words, the belief that 'a managed process with an omniscient authority is the only way to achieve successful outcomes' (quoted in Sabbagh, 2009, p. 13). 'Creationism' was the doctrine that markets were inadequate and not to be trusted and should be sub-jected to state direction. This, he claimed, was a view that was reminiscent of the interventionist view of failing British industry in the 1970s, that is, it was the job of the state to make good industrial failure through its own direction.

These criticisms were also levelled at the regulatory authority, OfCom. The authority seemed only too ready to intervene with adjudications on what broad-casters were allowed to say or not say. Such interventions, he claimed, ought to be limited to 'intervention only on the evidence of actual serious harm to the interests of consumers' (quoted Sabbagh, 2009, p. 13). Murdoch also challenged the 'impartiality rule', OfCom's requirement that broadcasters produce impartial news. Murdoch argued that this was a largely impossible demand to meet: 'the mere selection of stories and their place in the running order is itself a process full of unacknowledged partiality'.

The BBC Strikes Back

Sir Michael Lyon, the then chairman of the BBC Trust, responded to James Murdoch's attack by claiming that there was no necessary antagonism between the public and private sector. The licence fee principle meant that the BBC must serve 'all' the audi-ence. However, this does not necessarily have to happen to the detriment of other service providers. At the same time, he argued: 'We have to be careful not to reduce the whole of broadcasting to some simple economic transactions. The BBC's public purposes stress the importance of well tested principles of educating and informing, and an impartial contribution to debate' (quoted in Sabbagh, 2009, p. 13).

A more strident response to Murdoch's criticisms was made a year later, in August 2010, again through the opportunity presented by the annual MacTaggart lectures. Mark Thompson, the Director General of the BBC, sharply criticized News Corp for its overly dominant position in the broadcasting landscape in the UK. Firstly, Thompson cited survey figures which showed the popularity of BBC programming, indicating the continuing overwhelming support for public service broadcasting: 'The purists have spent a generation making the free market case for abolishing the licence fee, the British public agree with them less now than they did when they started' (quoted in Robinson, 2010, p. 15). These are clearly moral purposes and can be construed in a utilitarian sense of serving the greater public interest.

Secondly, Thompson attacked News Corp for its failure to invest in original programming. In response to James Murdoch's claim that the BBC should be much smaller, Thompson argues that far from the BBC being too big, the real threat comes precisely from Sky being the biggest force in television with sub-scription revenues of £4.8 billion. But its failure to invest in new programmes threatens the whole sector: ' ... it's time that Sky pulled its weight by invest-ing much, much more in British talent and British content' (quoted in Robinson, 2010, p. 15). Murdoch's claim is that the public service provision is being met by Sky News and Sky Arts, which are both loss-making and serve niche markets. However, Thompson's argument is that Sky's marketing budget is greater than the total amount of money in ITV1's programme budget.

Thirdly, Thompson raised the spectre of cross-media ownership. At the time of the lecture News Corp was attempting to take control of Sky by extending its share from 39% to over 50%. Thompson argued that this would give News Corporation 'a concentration of cross-media ownership that would not be allowed in the United States or Australia' (quoted in Robinson, 2010, p. 15). News Corp would then be dominant in television broadcasting, publishing and newspapers. These plans were subsequently holed below the water line by the phone-hacking scandal, the activities of journalists and management at the *News of the World* and the alleged illicit collusion between journalists and the police.

Table 3.1, for example, illustrates the oligopolistic nature of media ownership in the UK, with approximately 90% of the media market in the hands of five companies. Such concentrations of ownership reflect the imperfections of markets and pose a threat to the diversity and plurality of views. Narrowness and concentration in the ownership and control of the media poses additional moral problems to those found in other types of markets. The danger here is that limiting plurality and diversity may pose a potential threat to democracy by limiting the avenues by which free speech and criticisms of government may be articulated. In addition, the media scholar Cohen-Almagor (2014, p. 4) argues that:

> Free speech entails freedom to scrutinize the market, not to buy it. Liberal governments should not allow a 'free market' situation in which media barons may buy whatever they wish, thereby increasing their power and their maneuverability to promote partisan interests. ... Decentralizing ownership defuses potential threats to democracy.

We might also add that the existence of powerful public service broadcasting media provides a potential counterweight to the concentration of media in private or corporate hands.

Table 3.1   The UK media market 1997–2009

Title/Company	1997	2002	2009
News International	34.4	32.2	33.8
Trinity Mirror	23.9	20.2	16.2
Northern and Shell	14.3	13.8	13.5
Daily Mail and General Trust	13.6	18.5	19.9
Telegraph Group	7.7	7.3	7.3
Total of market	**93.9**	**92**	**90.7**

Source: Cohen-Almagor (2014, p. 14)

An Underlying Moral Argument

Two fundamentally different conceptions of the distribution of media goods and services emerge from this debate. In Murdoch's view, the production and distribution of media content should primarily be left to private and corporate ownership and the operation of markets. On the other side of the barricade, the defenders of public service broadcasting maintain the market is imperfect and the needs of many consumers and communities would just not be met. The same arguments apply, for example, to any subsidy for (high) cultural activities. Why ought we to subsidize public art galleries but not football? Murdoch claims that public subsidy and control, dominated by a particular cultural elite, dilute diversity in favour of a set of particular, preferred values. For the Murdochs it is the market which gives expression to the widest range of values.

3.2 A JUDGEMENT CALL
Choosing 'the public interest'

George Brock (2012, p. 4), in a paper on the UK Leveson Inquiry, argues there is a need to strike a bargain over regulation and media freedom. However, such a bargain may hinge on the ideas of public service and public interest. Brock identifies three schools of thought on the nature of public interest.

Firstly, there is a school of thought that is consumer-led. This effectively denies the distinction between the public interest and the interests of the public; what is to be preferred will be determined by the preferences of consumers, as expressed through the marketplace. Value is not the preserve of media practitioners, publishers, lawyers or regulators. Secondly, the appeal to the public interest as a justification for journalistic practice seems to beg 'insoluble' questions given the complexities of arriving at a definition of the public interest, as we saw in the last chapter. We should proceed on the basis that the function of journalism (and the media more generally) is the duty to tell the truth. While a host of factors (legal, commercial, social, conscience) may influence or constrain editors and publishers, there is simply no point in constructing elaborate arguments to justify the practice of journalism. The only thing that matters is: is it true? Thirdly, Brock argues that it is nevertheless imperative to come to a better understanding and definition of public interest. He argues that not everything that is labelled or calls itself journalism deserves that title and is entitled to a public interest defence. In order to separate what kinds of journalism ought to be protected from the kinds of 'journalism' that ought not to be protected, we need a public interest test.

Consider whether or not a consumer-led or market-driven approach is a reasonable guide to the public interest.

We can see that the principles underlying the Murdochs' case have much in common with those of Bentham. In an ideal market there are no privileged consumers (as long as one appears with the appropriate amount of cash or credit!). In buying and consuming media products, services and content, people express their preferences. In expressing their preferences, we are justified in assuming that that is what gives them pleasure rather than pain. It would be perverse of me to buy a download of

The Sound of Music if I just hate musicals. In contrast, public service broadcasting is predicated on the assumption that there are certain types of content which are intrinsically good (aesthetically and morally) whether or not the mass of people prefer them. A corollary of this is that there must be some special group of people who know – and, what's more, can and ought to decide – what they are. Hence the charge of elitism frequently levelled at the BBC.

Bentham, as we have noted, robustly denies any qualitative distinction between pleasures: 'The quantity of pleasure being equal, push-pin [a children's game] is as good as poetry' (quoted in Sandel, 2009, p. 52). Push-pin is, hypothetically, quite capable of giving pleasure across Bentham's seven dimensions – as much as anything else. The apparent advantages of Bentham's system are, to reiterate, its simplicity, its non-judgementalism and its inherently democratic nature. Remember, no one's pleasures or pains are given any special status in the calculation:

> Prejudice apart, the game of push-pin is of equal value with the arts and sciences of music and poetry. If the game of push-pin furnishes more pleasure, it is more valuable than either. (Bentham, quoted in Plamenatz, 1993, p. 255, fn)

It respects all preferences equally and in this way fits very well with contemporary ideas of the 'sovereignty of the market'. Given the money, we all enter the market as equals and we buy the types of media products and services we want. You may want to watch endless hours of Sky Sports while I am more interested in the latest movies on the movie channel. Who is to say who has the better or more superior taste? For Bentham, we need make no judgements regarding quality; only regarding quantity, in terms of the relevant dimensions of pleasure. This is all very well when it's a matter of sport or the latest movie. But suppose it was a case of a widespread preference for violent and pornographic movies. We could accuse, as many have, the Murdoch media empire of reaching out to 'the lowest common denominator'. As we saw briefly in the previous chapter, Bentham's hedonism is vulnerable also to the objection that to appeal to pleasure is also to appeal to something base, to appeal to 'the lower self' – it is a recipe for 'bread and circuses'. Might we not want to take the view that such content was base and degrading and should be highly regulated? If we take that view, allied to the criticisms made by Law (2007), we are introducing a qualitative element into the system. The concepts of 'baseness' and 'degradation' carry with them their own moral baggage.

Two Further Objections

The first objection to the kind of market philosophy propounded by the Murdochs is what Vardy and Grosch (1999, p. 261) have called the 'Rational Spectator Fallacy', although, more accurately, it might be referred to as the 'Rational Audience Fallacy' (see Box 3.3). The Murdochs, in their MacTaggart lectures, tend to assume that all media audiences – radio listeners, television viewers, readers of newspapers – are rational in the calculation of their interests. The assumption is that what is in their interests is simply what may interest them, interpreted as what may bring them most pleasure. They assume that consumers come to the market-place in full knowledge of their own preferences and how to choose what they want. Audiences, as simple consumers, on this model can make sensible and balanced judgements about their media purchases. This fails to take into account the extent to which media audiences are vulnerable to the massaging of their emotions and the manipulation of their innermost desires and wishes. If nothing else, media studies in the late twentieth century and in the early 2000s has revealed the extent to which audiences are precisely and frequently not rational.

The second objection, the 'Neutral Media Fallacy', is related to the first. This fallacy is that the media are merely neutral conduits in the delivery of media content. But, as we can see in considering the Murdochs' own business empire, corporate institutions have their own interests and agendas. They are as much interested in shaping markets as they are in delivering content in line with audience preferences. Such corporations assert their power, again, as we have seen in the Leveson Inquiry, to achieve their own goals. They are far from neutral. The attack on the BBC in the MacTaggart lectures is clearly motivated by a desire to create more space for the expansion of News Corp at the expense of the BBC and the public service remit. The Murdochs' motivations for their attacks, of course, don't necessarily undermine the validity of their arguments. However, it must give us every reason for a close scrutiny of those arguments.

3.3 SUMMARY OF OBJECTIONS

The quantity/quality distinction

It seems simplistic to fail to recognize that pleasure has a qualitative as well as a quantitative dimension. In fact, we do have an extensive vocabulary for differentiating certain forms of pleasure as more refined and more significant than others. We may prefer the more visceral and bodily sensations of pleasure to the cerebral and sophisticated, but that does not mean we ought not to prefer so-called 'higher' pleasures.

The Rational Audience Fallacy

The Murdochs assume that all media audiences (spectators), radio listeners, television viewers, readers of newspapers, are rational in the calculation of what may bring them most pleasure. They assume that consumers come to the marketplace in full knowledge of how to choose what they want and can make sensible and balanced judgements about their media purchases. This fails to take into account the extent to which media audiences are vulnerable to the massaging of their emotions and the manipulation of their innermost desires and wishes.

(Continued)

(Continued)

Neutral Media Fallacy

This fallacy is that the media are merely neutral conduits in the delivery of media content. But, as we can see in considering the Murdoch business empire, corporate institutions have their own interests and agendas. They are as much interested in shaping markets as they are in delivering content in line with audience preferences. Such corporations assert their power, as we have seen in the Leveson Inquiry, to achieve their own goals (see Vardy and Grosch, 1999, pp. 261–264).

HIGHER AND LOWER PLEASURES
Mill's Version of Utilitarianism

John Stuart Mill (1806–1873), although deeply committed to utilitarianism (see Box 3.1), recognized an important deficiency in Bentham's system. He wrote that: 'Man is never recognized by him [Bentham] as a being capable of spiritual perfection as an end; of desiring, for its own sake, the conformity of his own character to his standard of excellence, without hope of good or fear of evil from other source than his own inward consciousness' (quoted in Norman, 1991, p. 126).

For Mill there is a clear tension between his commitment to the principle of utility interpreted as happiness and the sense that human beings are progressive and ought to realize their potential for self-improvement. Mill argues for a version of utilitarianism that is more 'other-regarding' than 'self-regarding'. In other words, we should be more attentive to the happiness and progress of others than to ourselves. He was educated at home by his father James Mill, a prominent utilitarian and social reformer and friend of Jeremy Bentham, beginning with Greek from the age of three and Latin from the age of eight. The intensity of his early education led to a nervous collapse in his late teens. It is this breakdown, it has been argued, that led to Mill's more nuanced version of utilitarianism, which recognized not only quantitative but also qualitative differences in the nature of pleasure or happiness. Mill spent most of his adult life working for the East India Company. He was a prolific author, polymath, social reformer and, briefly, an MP (1865). In 1830 he met Harriet Taylor, who was then a married women. They were only able to marry in 1851 on the death of her husband. Under Harriet's influence, he was an early champion of the cause of the emancipation of women. Mill wrote an important and influential set of works on a wide range of subjects, including: 'System of Logic' (1843); 'Principles of Political Economy' (1848); 'On Liberty' (1859); 'Utilitarianism' (1861); 'Considerations on Representative Government' (1861); and 'The Subjection of Women' (1869).

In Chapter II of his essay, 'Utilitarianism' (1861), Mill deals with contemporary (religious) critics who had seen the full secular implications of Bentham's system: 'To suppose that life has (as they express it) no higher end than pleasure – no better and nobler object of desire and pursuit – they designate as utterly mean and grovelling; as a doctrine worthy only of swine' (Mill, 1964b, p. 7). Mill goes on to reject this description of utilitarianism by making two moves. Firstly, he denies the comparison between 'swinish' pleasures and human pleasures; secondly, and more importantly, he introduces a distinction between 'higher' and 'lower' pleasures. He says the characterization of utilitarianism 'as a doctrine worthy only of swine' is 'felt as degrading precisely because a beast's pleasures do not satisfy a human being's conception of happiness. Human beings have faculties more elevated than animal appetites, and when once made conscious of them, do not regard anything as happiness which does not include their gratification' (Mill, 1964b, p. 7).

He 'corrects' Bentham by arguing that pleasures (and pains) differ from one another in quality as well as in quantity. In effect, Mill accepted the force of the argument we earlier saw demonstrated in the case of 'the Pleasure Machine' (see Box 2.7). But he had to reconcile the utility principle with his notion of human beings as somehow fundamentally committed to progressive self-improvement in their culture as well as in material circumstances. This, of course, implies that there is something 'base' to leave behind and something more 'noble' to aspire to and achieve. This idea of self-realization was also a widely held ideal in nineteenth-century thinking about culture (Skorupski, 2006, p. 25). What Mill rejected was the idea that all pleasures were 'swinish' pleasures.

Self-improvement

Mill, like philosophers before him, believed that we have to look at what is specific to human beings (what distinguishes them from other species) to determine what constitutes full and *genuine* happiness. But Mill, unlike Aristotle, for example, is not arguing that because certain activities are essentially human they therefore constitute the natural and proper purpose of human life. His argument is a psychological one. He is not saying that because human beings do in fact have certain characteristic capacities they therefore ought to (or are intended by nature to) seek their happiness in the exercise of those capacities. But from a psychological point of view, we will not be 'fully satisfied' by a pleasure that is not produced by their exercise (see Norman, 1991, p. 128).

But is Mill right to make this claim? The evidence is perhaps to the contrary. Television schedules are packed with trivial game shows, soap operas, and so on. Many people seem relatively content with mindless entertainment or relatively undemanding reporting of the news. This is part of the strength of Bentham's philosophy; it was entirely neutral in its method of judging between 'push-penny' and poetry. Mill's reply is that if your experience has been confined to trivial and mindless pleasure, then of course you may not recognize the claims of 'the higher pleasures'. People need to 'properly experience' the widest possible range of pleasures in order to be able to identify the higher ones. The transition to an appreciation of higher pleasures from lower ones requires 'education' feelings. Mill believed that the enjoyment of the higher pleasures was synonymous with living a happy and worthwhile life.

3.4 A JUDGEMENT CALL
Distinguishing higher or lower pleasures

Imagine we sat down in front of the television and watched three shows. The first show, say, is a football match between Manchester United and Barcelona. Football is, of course, often referred to as 'the beautiful game' and is immensely popular, and Manchester United in particular has a global following. The game will no doubt be enthralling and exciting. Our second programme is an entertainment show, an episode of *The Simpsons*. Again, it is an immensely popular show with a global following and is particularly noted not only for its humour, but also for its irony and satire. Our third show is an excerpt from a famous play by the great modern dramatist, Samuel Beckett, *Waiting for Godot*. Now Beckett is also noted for his humour but, more importantly, for his deep and insightful commentary on the human condition.

Consider the following questions:

Firstly, which of the shows did you enjoy the most, and by enjoyment here we mean which gave you most pleasure? Secondly, which of the shows would you rank highest, in the sense of which is the highest or worthiest? Finally, in answering the previous question, did you mean that the show was higher or more worthy as measured by the quality of the pleasure which it gave or according to some other standard?

Adapted from Sandel (2009, pp. 54–57)

If we consider the exercise of judgement in Box 3.4, what would be the likely outcomes? It is possible that either the football match or watching *The Simpsons* would be voted the most pleasurable. We might want to say, however, that watching football gives us a more visceral kind of pleasure – an emotion response that Mill would identify as a 'lower pleasure'. But at the same time it is likely that we might agree that the Samuel Beckett play offers a different kind of pleasure – a 'higher' order of pleasure. But some might argue that *The Simpsons*, with its blend of humour and social commentary, can compete with Beckett in the kind of experience it offers. Mill would argue that the 'higher pleasures' contribute to our self-improvement, giving us a deeper understanding of what it is to be human. It is for this reason that our comparison of the shows is more than an aesthetic judgement (which it may also be), it is also a moral judgement.

Criteria for Higher and Lower Pleasures

How does Mill distinguish 'higher' from 'lower' pleasures? What are these higher and lower pleasures? Mill argues that the more 'cerebral' a pleasure is, the relatively higher it is in the scale of pleasures. Such pleasures are those of thought, feeling and imagination. The higher pleasures are the pleasures of artistic, literary and creative work and the pleasures of intellectual enquiry. They are the kinds of pleasures that may not yield themselves on initial acquaintance but require application and commitment. It is these types of pleasures which should be given greater weight than those pleasures which are purely of the body and the senses.

It is crucial to note that higher pleasures are intrinsically higher, and not simply higher because they are preferred by some social or cultural elite.

Mill never seemed to have considered that certain kinds of physical activity that require skill, energy, care, commitment and intelligence might also constitute higher pleasures. For example, high levels of craftsmanship may require the exercise of all these capacities and yield pleasure to the craftsperson. Similarly, food, sex and drink are also not considered to be higher pleasures. However, again, we might want to argue that these are pleasures that, if pursued in the right way, may enrich human life. Mill does not dismiss them and certainly acknowledges that that life without them would be poorer.

We can also see how this distinction of higher and lower fits in with Mill's defence of liberty of thought and expression (see Chapter 4). Mill has in mind that freedom is exercised in order that we become more rational, progressive beings with a greater understanding of both the world and ourselves. But this comes perilously close to abandoning the pleasure principle at the heart of utilitarianism. Remember the radical simplicity of Bentham's appeal to pleasure and pain as our governing principles. But Mill's argument, according to Skorupski, is that 'Activity A can be more valuable pleasure-wise than activity B, because though it gives less pleasure, the pleasure it gives is of a higher quality. All that hedonism requires is that the only things that make a pleasure valuable are its characteristics as a pleasure' (2006, p. 32).

So I may get a lot of pleasure watching *Sex and the City* and relatively less pleasure watching *Romeo and Juliet*. After all, I may have to struggle with understanding some of Shakespeare's language and following the complex plot line. But in the end this will mean I will be rewarded by a higher quality and more valuable pleasure. This also, of course, implies that there is a standard of judgement operating that is not simply the sum total of our preferences or aversions, pleasures or pains. We are, as Mill acknowledges, often subject to the temptation of the lower and more visceral pleasures. But this does not alter the case. It still means that we can recognize the qualitative difference between Ingmar Bergman's *The Seventh Seal* and Tony Scott's *Top Gun*. In a much-quoted passage, Mill writes: 'It is better to be a human being dissatisfied than a pig satisfied; better to be Socrates dissatisfied than a fool satisfied. And if the fool, or the pig, is of a different opinion, it is because they only know their own side of the question' (Mill, 1964b).

3.5 A JUDGEMENT CALL
Who judges?

In Bentham's version of utilitarianism, as we discussed in the last chapter, there was a democracy of pleasures. For Bentham, no one's pleasure was necessarily more valuable than another's. The differences between pleasures according to his calculus could be measured purely quantitatively. Mill introduces the idea that certain pleasures were qualitatively

(Continued)

(Continued)

superior or 'higher' than other pleasures. This was Mill's response to the criticisms made of Bentham's system – that, in effect, it had produced 'a doctrine worthy of swine'. However, this introduced a layer of added complexity. For Bentham, working out which policy led to the most happiness was simply a mechanical one of calculating the relative pleasures generated. If I take action X, it will produce this amount of happiness or pain; if I take action Y, it will produce this amount of happiness or pain. Simplistically, if I broadcast this show, it will satisfy a larger audience than if I broadcast this one. Working out which is the best action to take is therefore purely arithmetic; it involves no specialized knowledge. If we adopt Mill's distinction between 'higher' and 'lower' pleasures (higher pleasures being those primarily of the intellect and the arts and the lower pleasures being those of the body and the emotions), we may have answered the jibe about a doctrine worthy of swine, but we have a difficulty. We have abandoned the strict notion of utility and introduced an element of judgement. Some people's preferences count for more than other people's.

Who is fit to make the judgements about which pleasures are higher and which are lower? Does this notion of an elite who knows what is good for us sit easily with democratic societies?

Who is Fit to Judge?

If we are to abandon the spontaneous operation of the market and the administrative calculation of the 'felicific calculus', then a number of implications follow. Firstly, it implies that some group must be fit to judge which are higher pleasures. Secondly, it implies that there is an elite who knows what is good for us. Thirdly, it implies that if a majority of people prefer the so-called lower pleasures rather than the higher pleasures, then their judgement is less reliable and may perhaps be overridden. Mill is elitist in the sense that those who prefer the lower pleasures are simply not competent judges: ' … the test of quality, and the rule for measuring it against quantity, being the preference felt by those who in their opportunities of experience, to which must be added their habits of self-consciousness and self-observation, are best furnished with the means of comparison' (Mill, 1964b, p. 8). We become a competent judge by the cultivation of feeling: the careful comparison, criticism and appreciation of different types of pleasures.

Mill claims then that, firstly, only those who have experienced the higher pleasures are competent to judge; and that, secondly, those who have experienced both the lower and higher pleasures tend to prefer the higher. The extent to which the second claim is an empirical one and is open to refutation. There may be highly educated people, familiar with the Shakespearean canon, who nevertheless consider *The Simpsons* to be of equal value. Or, of course, we may be prone to pay homage to 'high culture', but when no one is looking we bunk off to watch *Sex and the Vampire* (Sandel, 2009, p. 54).

If we accept Mill's argument, then in answer to our earlier question about who should be responsible for determining standards, the answer is 'those who have experienced both higher and lower pleasures'. This is hardly a new argument. It is precisely the argument that Plato has Socrates develop in *The Republic*. 'The lover of wisdom' has the greatest range of knowledge and experience of all the pleasures in question; *The Republic* recommends a benign dictatorship of philosopher kings. We might want to acknowledge that there is a qualitative difference between Shakespeare and *The Simpsons* but the argument about higher and lower pleasures doesn't seem to do the job. We begin to see why when we consider John Plamenatz's counter-argument: 'No man has ever known the pleasures experienced by another; he can only say that, among his own, he prefers some to the rest' (Plamenatz, 1949, p. 136). There is something odd about the attempt to rank pleasures at all!

Mill assumes that comparing qualities of pleasures is not a dissimilar process from comparing quantities. But the problem is that if pleasures and pains are not homogeneous but heterogeneous, as Mill seems to accept, then how can they be compared? My experience of the pleasure of *Sex and the City* may be very different from yours. What Mill does is to challenge the central doctrine of utilitarianism and yet, at the same time, attempt to reconcile it with a more progressive view of human development. He writes:

> It is quite compatible with the principle of utility, to recognize the fact that some kinds of pleasure are more desirable and more valuable than others. It would be absurd that while, in estimating all other things, quality is considered as well as quantity, the estimation of pleasures should be supposed to depend on quantity alone. (Quoted in Skorupski, 2006, p. 32)

Nevertheless, Sandel (2009, p. 56) argues that 'Mill saves utilitarianism from the charge that it reduces everything to a crude calculation of pleasure and pain, but only by invoking a moral ideal of human dignity and personality independent of utility itself'.

Mill therefore attempts to save the fundamentals of the utilitarian theory of pleasure by introducing the distinction between 'higher' and 'lower' pleasures (Skorupski, 2006, p. 31). He still believes with Bentham that 'all desirable things are desirable either for pleasure inherent in themselves or as means to the promotion of pleasure and the prevention of pain' (quoted in Sandel, 2009, p. 53), and that the evidence that anything is desirable is simply the fact that people desire it. But given the progressive nature of human beings, there is such a thing as the education of feelings. It is in this perspective we can perhaps best understand Mill's introduction of the idea of 'lower' and 'higher' pleasures. We leave behind the pleasures of bear baiting in favour of an appreciation of Mozart. We can cultivate higher pleasures and have a need to cultivate higher pleasures in order to live a truly full life. If we accept Mill's arguments, then the function of the media must ultimately be to support the progressive development of human beings; entertainment and pleasure are not enough. Mill's distinction inevitably leads to the conclusion that the market is not enough.

CHAPTER REVIEW

What we have discussed in this chapter is the extent to which pleasure might be considered an ultimate good such that it forms the basis for judgements about what types of media content should be produced, distributed and consumed. According to Bentham's 'science of morality', the right thing to do is that which is likely to maximize happiness in terms of an overall balance of pleasure over pain (the principle of utility). Like the outputs of any other social institution, this must also be the basis on which media institutions should operate. Bentham's general prescription makes no demands about quality. This is a quantity theory of pleasure.

In the chapter we saw that Bentham's approach intersected with a debate about the extent to which media content should be delivered by relatively unfettered markets in contrast to the idea of a strong element of public service provision. In this debate we took as emblematic Rupert and James Murdoch, who have at different times argued that state support for public service provision stifles the freedom of the market to deliver diverse and innovative media content. An unregulated market allows the expression of public preferences and thus leads to a greater satisfaction of public pleasure. As for Bentham, the nature of the pleasures that are to be satisfied is a matter of indifference. Only in the manifest public harm should law or regulation have a place.

The Murdochs argued that public service broadcasting, in the UK for example, is underpinned by a form of elitism based on class. If you do not permit the spontaneous expression of audience preferences through the market mechanism, then some group must be deciding what they think is good for the public. We mentioned objections to the Murdochs' line of argument: the Rational Audience Fallacy and the Neutral Media Fallacy. For Bentham, regulating for 'the greatest happiness of the greatest number' is a purely administrative function because it involves simply the calculation of the overall quantity of pleasure that will be produced on balance. This is challenged by the distinction between 'higher' and 'lower' pleasures.

Mill argues that there is an important distinction between higher and lower pleasures. The higher pleasures identified by Mill tend to be the more cerebral pleasures of traditional forms of 'high culture', while the lower pleasures are more associated with bodily sensations. We saw that Mill's distinction could reasonably be pressed into the service of the defence of public service provision but also as a possible (moral) regulating principle in assessing media content. There are just certain types of media content which need to be protected and promoted irrespective of whether or not they are commercially viable. Mill provides grounds for such a belief and for making appropriate judgements about the regulation of media content. In doing so, he modifies Bentham's version of utilitarianism and invites us to see human beings as inherently self-improving and progressive.

FURTHER READING

Brock, G. (2012) 'The Leveson Inquiry: there's a bargain to be struck over media freedom and regulation', *Journalism*, 13(4): 1–10. A critical reflection on the outcome of the phone-hacking scandal and the subsequent Leveson Inquiry. In striking a balance between regulation and media freedom the author advocates the use of a more stringent public interest test.

Cohen-Almagor, R. (2014) 'After Leveson: recommendations for instituting the Public and Press Council', *The International Journal of Press/Politics*, 19(2): 202–225, and [Online], 15 January. http://hij.sagepub.com/content/early/2014/01/14/1940161213516680 (accessed 20 January 2014). The author analyses the Leveson Inquiry and the various dimensions of the unsatisfactory nature press self-regulation in Britain. He advocates the creation of a new independent regulator, the Public and Press Council, which will have greater and unprecedented authority and powerful sanctioning abilities. The general principles that should underpin a Code of Practice are proposed.

Gordon, A.D., Kittross, J.M. and Reuss, C. (eds) (1996) *Controversies in Media Ethics* (1st edn). White Plains, NY: Longman. See particularly Chapter 11, 'Media ethics and the economic market place' (pp. 219–240), for a discussion of market ethics, competition and, crucially, the public interest.

Mill, J.S. (1964) 'Utilitarianism', in A.D. Lindsay (ed.), *John Stuart Mill, Utilitarianism, Liberty and Representative Government*. London: Dent. pp. 1–60 (1st edn, 1861). This is a seminal essay defining the doctrine of Utilitarianism. Note particularly Mill's treatment of higher and lower pleasures.

Sandel, M.J. (2009) *Justice: What's the Right Thing to Do?* London: Allen Lane. See particularly Chapter 4, 'Hired help/markets and morals' (pp. 75–102), for a critical account of justice and markets in general.

Sandel, M.J. (2012) *What Money Can't Buy: The Moral Limits of Markets*. London: Penguin. This is a popular critique of the dominance of market values, emphasizing how markets may crowd out morals. It extends Sandel's analysis of the relationship between social justice and capitalism.

HOW TO USE THIS ARTICLE

Go to https://study.sagepub.com/horner to access the following free journal article:

Gaber, I. (2012) 'Rupert and the 'three card trope' – what you see ain't necessarily what you get', *Media, Culture and Society*, 34(5): 637–646.

Use this article to take a look at Rupert Murdoch's beliefs and presentation of himself. This is a polemical piece which argues that under Murdoch's populist appeal and market liberalism, discussed in this chapter, there has been a consistent pattern of undermining democracy in the interest of profit and power. Gaber charts Murdoch's relationship with the political class and the various guises (trope) he adopts. The first part of the trope is that of the simple newspaper man with a passion for newsprint. The second part of the trope is that Murdoch uses his media holdings to pursue his own right-wing political agenda, even if sometimes this may go against his corporate interests. Equally, he opportunistically may appear to adopt left-of-centre positions. The third part of the trope is his projection of himself and his media as representing the 'ordinary bloke', frequently in opposition to the Establishment. We have seen the in this chapter in his criticisms of BBC elitism.

4
LIBERTY

We take it as axiomatic that freedom of speech is fundamental to the operation of all media. However, few would want to argue that that freedom should be unfettered and absolute. The value of free speech is relative and contingent upon circumstances. There is broad agreement that there are grounds for the regulation of certain kinds of speech – hate speech, for example – and legitimate restrictions on the disclosure of certain kinds of information, such as information relating to national security. In this chapter we will consider the moral value of freedom of speech and publication. But equally, we need to consider where it may be legitimate to draw the line between free speech and restriction of free speech. What are the moral grounds on which it is proper to impose limits on free speech? For example, we will consider the principles relevant to defining the boundaries between the private and the public spheres. In trying to understand these questions, we will focus on a seminal text on individual liberty and freedom of the press by John Stuart Mill (1806–1873). Mill's essay 'On Liberty' is widely regarded as one of the definitive defences of individual liberty and freedom of the press. Mill is writing in the middle of the nineteenth century in the context of the growth of the modern state and the growth of the power of public opinion. Mill was equally concerned that both of these phenomena were potential threats to individual liberty. Broadly, Mill's main idea was that individual liberty and free speech (the two are inseparably connected) ought to be restricted only if my action or speech is liable to harm others, or is a failure to act in accordance with a duty to others, or violates the good manners required in a public place. Mill considers all other grounds for interference to be illegitimate. (Consider the example in Box 4.1.)

It is often useful to try to understand the significance of something by contemplating its absence. This technique is employed to great effect in George Orwell's novel *1984*, which depicts a totalitarian state in which not only is there total control and censorship, but also newspaper accounts of the past are constantly changed in the interest of the dictatorship. We briefly consider The People's Republic of China as an example of control over all forms of media, both internal and foreign media. With the example of censorship in China in mind, we will then examine Mill's argument for liberty of the individual. Mill, for his time, makes a radical distinction between the private and the public spheres. The private sphere is the bastion of individual liberty, where the state, or indeed the sanctions of public opinion, has no right to interfere. The contemporary relevance of this can be seen in contemporary debates on privacy and media intrusions. As we saw in the last chapter, Mill is a utilitarian and his interpretation of liberty and free speech is underpinned by his utilitarian theory. Ultimately, moral questions about free speech and media freedoms must be resolved by making reference to consequences. The test for the limits of free speech must be determined, all things considered, by that which produces the best outcome, weighing the costs and benefits of restriction against the costs and benefits of freedom: 'I regard utility as the ultimate appeal on all ethical questions; but it must be utility in the largest sense, grounded on the permanent interests of a man as a progressive being' (Mill, 1964b, p. 74).

4.1 A JUDGEMENT CALL
The London School of Economics (LSE) and the T-shirt ban

In October 2013 two students at the LSE wore T-shirts depicting Jesus and the Prophet Mohammad. The students were wearing the T-shirts to promote the Atheist, Secularist and Humanist Society at the LSE's Freshers' Fair. For Muslims, the picturing of the Prophet is blasphemous and offensive. Equally, Christians may be offended by inappropriate depictions of Jesus. Security staff at the Fair threatened the two students with expulsion from the event on the grounds that displaying an image of Mohammad is forbidden under Islamic law and may constitute the harassment of a religious group. The students agreed to cover up the offending T-shirts. However, they subsequently launched a formal complaint to the university authorities. The students argued that there was no evidence that any students had complained about the T-shirts and, on the contrary, on the day the response to the T-shirts had been very positive. The T-shirts did not offend or harass anyone. More importantly, the students were simply exercising their right to freedom of expression, to which they were entitled as much as religiously inclined students were entitled to wear religious symbols, or indeed T-shirts, to give expression to their faith. The students' complaint was upheld and the LSE authorities in a formal statement acknowledged that 'with hindsight, the wearing of the T-shirts did not amount to harassment or contravene the law or LSE policies'.

Was this the morally right outcome? Would it have made a difference if there had been actual complaints from offended students?

Source: Burns (2013)

RESTRICTING FREE SPEECH

The case of the London School of Economics and the T-shirt ban described in Box 4.1 may seem like a storm on a teacup (if not a T-shirt!). However, it does in its own way raise the complexities of when it may be right or wrong to curtail some aspect of free speech. Initially, the actions of the members of the university in threatening the T-shirt-wearing students had been upheld by the university authorities. However, the students won an apology from the university when their complaint was upheld. Professor Kelly, representing the university in a BBC interview, admitted that they had got it wrong but described the situation as a 'grey area'. He argued that the law in such matters was complex. The UK has no US First Amendment guaranteeing freedom of speech 'without qualification'. The university had to take legal advice on the Human Rights Act, the 2010 Equality Act and the 1986 Universities Extension Act, given that the case potentially cut across all these pieces of legislation. In addition, Professor Kelly stressed that the Freshers' Fair was a welcome event involving international students from 130 countries. The students maintained that the apology was insufficient in that it did not recognise the harassment they had suffered and the fundamental fact that this was a suppression of freedom of speech.

What this case also raises from a moral point of view is whether or not offending an individual or group is really sufficient grounds for restricting expression. It is clear, however, given that the range of what may offend us is very wide, ranging from mere irritations through nuisances to deep psychological hurts, that the category of offence needs close specification. Raphael Cohen-Almagor (2005, p. 22) argues that four elements ought to be considered to establish whether or not restriction of free speech on grounds of psychological offence is justified: 'the content of the expression; the tenor and manner of the expression; the intentions and motives of the speaker; and the objective circumstances in which the advocacy is to take place'.

In the case we have just been looking at there was a formal process in which the competing claims could be adjudicated. This is a characteristic of liberal democracies. But even in 2010 in many, if not the majority, of countries around the world this is not the case. For example, this can be illustrated by the fate of the 2010 Nobel Peace Prize winner Liu Xiaobo. In spite of globalization, one of the world's most dynamic and powerful societies, The People's Republic of China, remains committed to censorship and the centralized control of the flow of information. The scope of individual liberty and freedom of thought and discussion is highly circumscribed.

China's response to the awarding of the prize in Oslo on 10 December 2010 was to block BBC and CNN programmers (Mail Foreign Service, 2010). The Chinese government's Internet Censors did their utmost to delete any posts that referred to the Peace Prize Ceremony or Liu Xiaobo. China's media blackout was backed up by a diplomatic campaign to encourage other countries not to go to the award ceremony. Seventeen other countries were persuaded to stay away from the ceremony, including Russia, Pakistan, Iran, Venezuela and Cuba. At the same time, Liu Xiaobo's wife was under house arrest, as well as over 100 other prominent dissidents. China's state media dismissed the ceremony as a 'farce'. *The Global Times*, part of the group of newspapers which includes the Chinese Communist Party's paper, *People's Daily*, wrote that 'It's unimaginable that such a farce, the like of which is more commonly seen in cults, is being staged on the civilized continent of Europe' (quoted in Foster, 2010, p. 11).

The prize winner's chair at the ceremony was empty (Swami, 2010, p. 20). Liu Xiaobo was jailed for 11 years on Christmas Day 2009 for allegedly subverting state power and for being the leading author of Charter 08, which called for democratic reforms. Liu Xiaobo is a prominent campaigner for civil liberties in the People's Republic and had been a prominent leader of the Tiananmen Square protestors in 1989. From his prison cell Liu requested that the prize be dedicated to 'the lost souls from the 4th of June', the day of the massacre of student protestors. The Chinese government's treatment of Liu Xiaobo is a paradigm case of an authoritarian regime's repression of individual liberty and of the political control and censorship of news media. The actions of the Chinese government transgressed Mill's concept of the scope of individual liberty. But we must be clear that, for Mill, this would not be a question of 'natural' or 'human' rights. Mill believed in freedom of thought and discussion because that was ultimately the 'best' path for both individual and social development, defined in utilitarian terms. It may be a genuine belief on the part of the leadership of the Communist Party of China that unrestricted freedom of the media (and especially the internet) is likely to lead to social disorder and to damage the country's general development and overall welfare. However, for Mill, authoritarianism is simply antithetical to the progressive development of the individual and freedom of speech is a vital part of that progressive development.

Even in the face of civil disorder we may still argue that the curbing of free speech may not acceptable. The case outlined in Box 4.2 illustrates the question of limits in relationship to social media and political action. The positive role of social media had been exemplified in the Arab Spring and in response to the earthquake disaster in Japan in 2011 (Asai, 2011). Social networking had been used as a means of coordinating rather than replacing social action, functioning as an information hub and as a means of organizing and enhancing 'social capital'. But the social risks inherent in social networking were also exposed in the British riots of August 2011. In response to the rioting, David Cameron, the British Prime Minister, in an emergency parliamentary debate, said that the government, police and intelligence services were looking at whether there should be limits on the use of social media sites. Twitter and Facebook, or services such as Blackberry Messenger, were being used to spread organized disorder. Blackberry Messenger, in particular, was being used by rioters to mobilize and target specific areas (and shops!). The proposal, only briefly considered, was whether to turn off social networks or stop people texting during times of social unrest. The onus for the shut-down would have been on the internet service providers and clearly this would be a major restriction of freedom of speech. The fact that the social media were being used to inflict harm on communities and individuals would provide clear grounds for some form of restriction of speech. As we will see later in this chapter, Mill thought that incitement to violence was a legitimate ground for state interference.

4.2 A JUDGEMENT CALL
Social networking and freedom of speech

In August 2011 many of Britain's city centres witnessed nights of rioting and looting, largely perpetrated by young men and women, teenagers and even children. The looters came from a mix of ethnic and social backgrounds. Whatever the ultimate sociological explanation for these actions, it was the case that social networking played an important role in the looters being able to coordinate their activities and to target particular locations, primarily shops and shopping centres. This altogether negative use of social networking was in stark contrast with the widely praised positive use of social networking to help coordinate protest movements in the Arab Spring movement. In both cases, however, governments considered shutting down social networking sites. In either instance this would clearly have been a form of censorship.

In the British case, given the social harm and disorder, should service providers have been made, or encouraged, to volunteer to shut them down? What differentiates this case from the Arab Spring case?

THE PRIVATE SPHERE
The Importance of Mill's 'On Liberty'

Having looked at a number of examples where free expression is problematic, we will now go on to consider John Stuart Mill's ideas in more detail. As suggested, the arguments that Mill presented in 'On Liberty', first published in 1859, effectively created a framework for a continuing discussion of freedom of speech and the limits of free expression (Mill, 1964a; see also Cohen-Almagor, 2005; Skorupski, 2006). Mill makes no appeal to natural rights. Liberty, according to Mill, is not an intrinsic good but good in as much as it promotes happiness and the progressive development of human beings. He argues that freedom of thought and discussion must be presumed: the onus is always upon those who want to restrict the application of the principle to show good cause why this should be so. Still, he wants to derive the liberty of the individual from utilitarian principles. Mill's principle is that liberty may only be circumscribed to prevent tangible and demonstrable harm to others. The liberty of thought and discussion (including the 'liberty of the press') is a subset of Mill's general principle (see Box 4.3).

4.3 DEFINITION
The liberty principle

'The principle is that the sole end for which mankind are warranted, individually or collectively, in interfering with the liberty of action of any of their number, is self-protection. That the only purpose for which power can be rightfully exercised over any member of a civilized community, against his will, is to prevent harm to others. His own good, either physical or moral, is not sufficient warrant.'

Mill (1964a, p. 73)

The Private Sphere and Individual Liberty

Mill begins with a powerful statement of his fundamental principle:

> The object of this Essay is to assert one very simple principle, as entitled to govern absolutely the dealings of society and the individual in the way of compulsion and control, whether the means used be physical force in the form of legal penalties, or the moral coercion of public opinion. The principle is that the sole end for which mankind are warranted, individually or collectively, in interfering with the liberty of action of any of their number, is self-protection. That the only purpose for which power can be rightfully exercised over any member of a civilized community, against his will, is to prevent harm to others. His own good, either physical or moral, is not sufficient warrant. (Mill, 1964a, p. 73)

This principle demarcates the private sphere, where an individual has absolute liberty, from the public sphere. The private sphere, according to Mill, encompasses three elements. It consists firstly of our private thoughts and conscience. We have absolute liberty to believe, feel and speculate on whatever we wish. Secondly, we are free to pursue our own tastes, likings and dislikings, and are free to frame our plan for our life in accordance with our character and inclinations. We are free to do what we wish as long as we are not harming anyone, even though our conduct is foolish, perverse and wrong. Thirdly, out of this liberty of each of us we can also combine with other individuals as long as the same provision is met, that is, we are not harming anyone (Mill, 1964a, p. 75). Even a group of sadomasochists may get together and as long as the harm they inflict on each other is consensual and they do not inflict harm on anyone else, they must be free to do so.

It is in the realm of the public sphere where harm to others ('the harm principle') is the chief ground which justifies regulation or interference. In the private sphere, I am entirely at liberty to perform 'self-regarding' actions, even if those actions are self-harming. Consider the case of the pro-ana websites (see Box 4.4). Pro-ana organizations and websites differ widely in their outlooks. Some claim that they are there to provide non-judgemental environments for anorexics, to provide fora to discuss their illness, and to help those who choose to enter recovery. Many websites, however, deny that anorexia nervosa is a mental illness. What they aim to promote is anorexia as a 'lifestyle choice' that should be respected by doctors and family members. If I choose to harm myself, according to Mill, then that is my business. However, it is a different case if I'm actively inciting others to harm themselves. On the face of it, this may provide grounds for restricting the availability of pro-ana websites. If my actions – and making a website available is an action – are liable to harm others, then society may have a legitimate reason for interfering with my individual freedom of speech and action. In as much as what I do only affects myself, then society has no legitimate ground for intervention, even if my action is likely to harm myself.

However, this does not, for Mill, make the private sphere a morality-free zone. As we saw in the last chapter in the discussion about the higher pleasures, Mill believed that we all had an obligation to engage in self-improvement because only in that way can we fully realize ourselves and attain true happiness. I may be persuaded to take the path of self-improvement but not coerced. But in these self-regarding matters I must be entirely at liberty to pursue my own path.

4.4 A JUDGEMENT CALL
Should pro-ana websites be banned?

Pro-ana refers to the active promotion of the eating disorder anorexia nervosa. The lesser-used term, pro-mia, refers likewise to bulimia nervosa and is sometimes used interchangeably with pro-ana. There are many websites that style themselves pro-ana websites and promote anorexia. The information on anorexic practices on the pro-ana sites is, in effect, incitement to self-harm. Anorexics and bulimics who subscribe to such sites share among themselves crash dieting techniques and recipes; they share techniques on how to decline food in socially acceptable ways (for example, by adopting an extreme vegan diet); they generate solidarity among anorexics and bulimics through collective fasts or setting up competitions in weight loss; they commiserate with one another over the web after breaking a fast or a bout of binge eating; and the sites provide advice on how best to induce vomiting and how best to use laxatives and emetics. The sites also provide advice on how to hide weight loss from parents and doctors. Other kinds of information on the websites include methods to reduce the side-effects of anorexia, and the ways and means of suppressing hunger pangs. Finally, the web provides a means of soliciting affirmation and acceptance through the publication of individuals' weight, body measurements, diet regimen and often, most shockingly, pictures of their emaciated bodies.

If we adopt Mill's approach to individual liberty and the private sphere, should pro-ana websites be banned?

The Importance of the Liberty Principle

As we have seen, Mill places great emphasis on the liberty of individuals in the sense of being able to determine their own life plan. You ought to be able to live your life according to values you choose and identify with. This meant for Mill that your values and lifestyle should not be dictated to by others (particularly, in the context of the nineteenth century, religious institutions). Alternatively, you should not choose your values and way of life unthinkingly, according to some set of stale conventions. Mill believed that individual liberty benefits not just the individual person, but everyone. The pursuit of individuality expresses the ways in which people are different, and leads to diversity. The liberty of individuals requires diversity so that people can choose and develop their own lifestyles (Mulgan, 2011, p. 116). We will see later that this also requires, as Mill argues, the freedom of publication in order to make available to people information about those varieties of lifestyles.

Mill was concerned not only to defend the liberty of the individual against the power of government, he was also deeply anxious about the threat to individuality from social pressures to conform – 'the tyranny of the majority'. He believed that, at least in England, the threat to individual liberty came less from despotic government and rather more from a kind of tyranny of a public opinion that enforced a collective mediocrity. The perception of such a threat, a levelling down, explains the concern in his essay for the need to defend freedom as a social good and the ideal of progressive self-development. His subsidiary argument in Chapter II of the essay, 'Of the liberty of thought and discussion', maintains that freedom to express and publish diverse opinions and beliefs is essential to this process of the progressive self-development of individuality.

Actions and policies are to be judged, as we have seen, on their tendency to produce more or less happiness. Mill's problem was to connect or reconcile his commitment to individual freedom and the idea of happiness as the ultimate good for human beings. As we say in the previous chapter, Mill makes a distinction between higher and lower pleasures, modifying Jeremy Bentham's rather cruder characterization of the doctrine of utilitarianism as the goal to maximize pleasure. It was this distinction that allowed Mill to connect liberty and happiness. We might paraphrase George Orwell and say that 'all pleasures are equal but some are more equal than others'. For Mill, rather like Aristotle, self-development is the condition of the enjoyment of highest forms of happiness. Freedom of thought and discussion are conditions for this process of individual flourishing. Censorship and repression can only be an obstacle by keeping people in ignorance.

Mill concludes that the institutions of a democratic liberal state are those under which individuals may be happiest. Liberty of thought and expression in the nineteenth century essentially meant a free press and the ability to publish, without censorship, books and pamphlets. 'Other beings', he argues, might flourish under different institutions. But liberty is fundamental to enabling human beings to pursue 'personal objects within the limits consistent with the essential interests of others' (Mill, 1964a, p. 75). This is Mill's essential dialectic between 'self-regarding' and 'other-regarding' actions. Mill's notion of happiness is therefore something like self-fulfilment (but not at the expense of others), enabling the development of all our potential as human beings.

Limits of the Private Sphere

We have already suggested that the limits of the private sphere are defined by 'the harm principle'. The interpretation of 'harm', however, has been much debated (Ellis, 1998). For example, there are clearly physical harms but also psychological harms; there are tangible harms and intangible harms. There are harms arising from what I do and harms that may arise from what I fail to do, for example, warning of an unexploded bomb in the road. So while the statement of the principle is relatively straightforward the method of its application may be less so: 'As a utilitarian, Mill recognized no fundamental difference between doing and allowing. My duty to help others is as strong as my duty not to kill others. Because harm is comparative, a failure to assist is a harm. I have absolute liberty to read what I like. But if I keep reading while a child drowns at my feet, then I harm her' (Mulgan, 2011, p. 118).

Mill has a very broad notion of harm, with the implication that the private sphere is rather more circumscribed than it first appears. This is particularly the case where my private acts may harm others even though still within a physically private, domestic space. For example, consider domestic violence where women and children are abused by their husband and father. Even though children do not enjoy the same scope for liberty as adults because they are not reasonable judges of their own welfare, they should not be harmed. This was a more significant point to make in Victorian England when a man's private sphere was considered to include how he behaved towards his wife and children and, if he could employ them, his servants. Similarly, acts performed in private by consenting adults may also become of public concern if physical or psychological harm is involved. Again, this is because even adults are not necessarily the 'infallible' judges of their own welfare. Despite Mill's general principle, it may be justifiable to exercise power to interfere with harmful activities even if performed in private (Mulgan, 2011, pp. 117–118).

We can apply the principle to the consumption of media goods. For example, my 'absolute' liberty refers only to the consumption of content in whatever form. It does not cover the manufacture, distribution, or sale of that content. Commercial activities may harm consumers, competitors or others who may want the resources used for other purposes (Mulgan, 2011, p. 117). I might, for example, be psychologically susceptible to the portrayal of extreme violence and thus may be harmed by viewing films or videos with extremely violent content. Under these conditions Mill's principle would warrant intervention, not necessarily to prevent my consumption of the material, but intervention to censor the producers and distributors. This is recognized by laws in most states which either regulate or censor media content of extreme violence in general and sexual violence in particular. The various classification schemes for film and video reflect the view that it is right to control the distribution of goods to certain age categories on the grounds of the potential harm to those who are not psychologically mature.

Mill draws an important distinction between freedom of thought and freedom of speech. My thoughts are private to myself; they are absolutely private. My thoughts cannot harm others. However, the articulation of those thoughts in speech (or through any other medium) may harm others. We recognize this in the concept of 'hate speech'. If the expression of hateful sentiments is injurious to others, then it falls beyond the private sphere and this may give grounds for society to intervene to prevent harm. In this sense, speech is not private. Again, self-regarding behaviour in private becomes a public matter. If I *offend* you, then this may also be a genuine harm.

However, the fact that some private activity may lead to harm may not be sufficient in itself. Mill, as a utilitarian, always wants us to balance the potential cost of suppressing speech against the public benefit of freedom of thought and discussion, for example, in the case of giving offence. One of Mill's primary values is that of individuality, and although he clearly recognizes offence as a genuine harm, this can never outweigh the value of individuality. The progressive development of individuality needs diversity and even the offended person benefits from liberty. For the same reason, Mill prefers regulation to outright censorship or prohibition (Mulgan, 2011, p. 118).

A Test for Intrusion

Central to the Leveson Inquiry has been a debate about the grounds on which a person's private life, celebrity or not, becomes a matter of legitimate public interest and thereby a legitimate object of journalistic investigation. Remember, in this regard Mill makes no claims about some natural right to liberty. The question must hinge on the question of harm. We might paraphrase Mill's statement of the principle of liberty in the following way: 'The principle is that the sole end for which mankind are warranted, individually or collectively, in making public the private acts of one of their number, is self-protection. That the only purpose for which journalists can be rightfully intrude into the private sphere of any member of a civilized community, against his will, is to prevent harm to others' (Mill, 1964a, pp. 72–73).

Thus we can apply the principle to the question of press intrusions into the private lives of individuals (see Box 4.3). Even with the qualifications we have just discussed, the justification for press intrusion into someone's private life, whether they are a celebrity or not, can only be that the private behaviour of the person gives rise to some harm which puts it into the public sphere. If private behaviour does give rise to harm, then, on Mill's principle, it becomes a public matter and falls outside the private sphere. But there is a subsidiary question, even where harm has been committed: 'Is the cost of allowing press intrusion and public exposure less than the potential harm to the progressive development of individuality?'

THE PUBLIC SPHERE: FREEDOM OF THOUGHT AND DISCUSSION

Thinking whatever we want to think is a 'self-regarding' action and therefore ought, on the liberty principle, to be free from interference. When we publish our thoughts via the media, these are 'other-regarding' actions – they move from the private to the public domain. Nevertheless, Mill's presumption is that without a right to free speech the defence of free thought would be absurd (Ryan, 1974, p. 136). But the ultimate defence is not from the privateness of my thoughts, but – and here Mill is using a supplementary argument – the value of truth. This to some extent is a breach of the original principle. The harm that censorship does is that it hinders the testing and emergence of truth. According to Mill, 'The truth of an opinion is part of its utility' (Mill, 1964a, p. 84). Mill's argument against the suppression of the free circulation of political (and religious ideas) is based on utilitarian grounds that in the long run the costs of censorship outweigh the benefits. For Mill, as a social reformer, individual and social progress is grounded in the discovery of the truth. The sole rational attitude in confronting the world and trying to understand it is that of open-mindedness. And such openness should be reflected in our institutions.

Mill's Arguments for Free Speech

For Mill, the importance of free speech is grounded in the need to discover, as far as possible, truths about the natural and social world. He deploys four arguments.

Firstly, 'the fallibility assumption': human beings are notoriously fallible. Whatever we say or write may turn out to be wrong. Our opinions and beliefs are frequently shown to be mistaken (corrigible). Anything we can claim to know about the social and natural world at any specific time or place is contingent; that is, we may subsequently find that we were mistaken. But we must be free to say and publish in order precisely to discover our errors. Mill often contrasts this view with the dogmas of religion, which assume infallibility. In consequence, 'if any opinion is compelled to silence, that opinion may, for aught we can certainly know, be true. To deny this is to assume our infallibility' (Mill, 1964a, p. 111). Thus all authoritarian regimes and dictatorships, in repressing contrary views, implicitly, if not explicitly, assume their own infallibility. However, it is not clear that this conclusion follows. I can have reasonable grounds for believing what I do believe without assuming my infallibility. I can argue, for example, that given the scientific evidence it is likely, but not a certainty, that the Earth is subject to global warming brought about by human activities.

Secondly, 'the partial truths assumption': Mill believed that in order to arrive at truth, at least provisionally, there needs to be a diversity of opinions so that the collision of adverse opinions would lead to the production of truth. This is an essential idea in defence of the need for plurality and diversity of the media. We each may hold a portion of the truth:

… though the silenced opinion be in error, it may, and very commonly does, contain a portion of the truth; and since the general or prevailing opinion on any subject is rarely or never the whole truth, it is only by the collision of adverse opinions that the remainder of the truth has any chance of being supplied. (Mill, 1964a, p. 111)

However, Mill underestimates the extent to which much public discourse may be of a frivolous nature. The internet is packed with false and crazy ideas. Do all of these merit attention? Is the volume of material such that it might obscure the emergence of truth rather than provide a foil against which we might discriminate truth from error? For example, the documentary *Loose Change* (2006), which was globally available on YouTube, promoted the belief that the terrorist attack on the Twin Towers and the Pentagon on 9/11 was in fact a conspiracy by the US security services.

Thirdly, 'the requirement for testing assumption': established and received truths should be constantly tested, 'even if the received opinion be not only true, but the whole truth; unless it is suffered to be, and actually is, vigorously and earnestly contested, it will, by most of those who receive it, be held in the manner of a prejudice, with little comprehension of its rational grounds' (Mill, 1964a, pp. 111–112). All knowledge is provisional; there are no final answers. We progress by a constant process of argument and testing. Suppression or censorship of ideas clearly inhibits this process. Again, we might raise the problem of frivolous discourse, or even malicious discourse. Where it is expensive to collect, organize, process and evaluate information, it is simply not possible to consider every utterance (Mulgan, 2011, p. 120).

Fourthly, the need for active belief: practical rationality demands that we understand the grounds of our beliefs. To be rational, social and moral agents we must be capable of justifying what it is we do believe. This is essentially an argument about the psychology of belief. Mill writes that 'the meaning of the doctrine itself will be in danger of being lost, or enfeebled, and deprived of its vital effect on the character and conduct: the dogma becoming a mere formal profession, inefficacious for good, but cumbering the ground, and preventing the growth of any real and heartfelt conviction, from reason or personal experience' (Mill, 1964a, p. 112). Here Mill is arguing that we must be able to give good reasons for our beliefs. However, we may have reasons in a motivational sense that drive us to hold certain beliefs even though the reasons, as evidential grounds for belief, may be very weak. Open debate may be dangerous in that it assumes that the clash of beliefs and arguments will lead to the emergence of truth, if not immediately, then eventually. Conflict, on the contrary, rather than testing our assumptions may lead us to more intransigent positions. Mill defends his view with reference to history.

Mill's Historical Perspective

In the opening pages of 'On Liberty' Mill presents a brief and sweeping (but primarily Euro-centric) outline of human history which is characterized as the struggle between liberty and authority. This may be contrasted with Karl Marx's view of all history as the story of class struggle (Marx and Engels, 1976, pp. 477–519).

But what unites Mill with Marx is that, for both, human history has a pattern and develops in progressive stages through struggle. Although, for Mill, democracy is a desirable form of government, and an outcome of this progressive social development, yet there are signal dangers for individual liberty in the kinds of social pressures and conformity that may accompany it. Therefore, forms of institutional protection are required for freedom of thought and expression. Mill assumes that civilizations progress through the discovery of truth – truth about the natural world and about the social world. Laws and institutions must be founded on rational debate and evidence. It is partly the role of what we would now call media institutions to safeguard the liberty of the individual and restrain the authoritarian instincts of the state, on the one hand, and the tyranny of the majority on the other.

The progressive development of individuals and society, according to Mill, requires the growth of knowledge. The publication of ideas and freedom of thought and discussion are essential. History is the battle between authority and liberty, where authority constantly seeks to repress social progress. The truth is always vulnerable to the 'dungeon and stake'. Much of 'On Liberty' trawls the historical record for examples of persecution and the stemming of social progress through repression to support this view. A liberal society requires a free 'market-place of ideas', which will operate against an assumption of infallibility. Mill's opposition to censorship was firmly based on the idea, as we have seen, that (a) censorship and repression hinder progress towards truth; (b) truth needs to be tested; (c) without testing the rational grounds for truth claims cannot be established. This is not an argument suggesting that truth has an intrinsic value or is an intrinsic good. Repression leads to the promotion of dogma and not just for politics, but also for aesthetic and moral judgement (see Box 4.5).

4.5 A JUDGEMENT CALL
Should we restrict publication by climate change sceptics?

One horn of the dilemma is that the threat of climate change is such that our failure to moderate our ways of life now may lead potentially to significant catastrophic effects on future generations if not the potential of global extinction for the human race. If the arguments of the climate sceptics should persuade people to ignore the threat, and the threat is true, this would be disastrous. So we ought to ban climate change scepticism, but this would be to deny the fundamental freedom of thought and discussion.

The second horn of the dilemma is that if we ban or suppress climate change scepticism and the effects for global warming turn out to be greatly exaggerated or false, we will have hindered the emergence of truth through censorship and engaged in a range of unnecessary policies at the expense of the welfare of current and future generations.

If we adopt Mill's arguments for freedom of speech, which horn of the dilemma is more attractive?

Press Freedom and its Limits

Mill understands that there are legitimate areas for state or community intervention but such interventions must be justified by reference to the principle of harm. Incitement to violence would clearly be grounds for the restriction of free speech. He makes a distinction between opinions or beliefs, and actions. He gives the following example to illustrate what he means:

> No one pretends that actions should be as free as opinions. On the contrary, even opinions lose their immunity when the circumstances in which they are expressed are such as to constitute their expression a positive instigation to some mischievous act. An opinion that corn dealers are starvers of the poor or that private property is robbery ought to be unmolested when simply circulated through the press, but may justly incur punishment when delivered orally to an excited mob assembled before the house of a corn-dealer, or when handed about among the same mob in the form of a placard. (Mill, 1964a, p. 114)

There are two notable elements here. Firstly, the concept of incitement represents 'a positive instigation', an attempt to move people to 'mischievous' action. That is not simply giving information or establishing the truth, but the action being contemplated is violent and disorderly. Secondly, the point that the audience ('the mob'), by definition, is not in a rational state of mind means there is considerable importance attached to the context in which remarks are uttered or views disseminated. Mill thought that the liberty principle did not apply to those who are not capable of rational thought. So for those who could not rationally govern their own lives, it would be appropriate to intervene. On this basis, for example, public policy to protect children through mechanisms such as film classification is an appropriate policy. Children, by definition, are not in a position to make rational judgements about their own welfare.

The media therefore have a responsibility to consider the importance of the context in which reports are made. Thus actions are not as free as opinions! The press and broadcast media have a responsibility to consider the possible social costs of their reporting. Freedom is limited by the harm principle, although this again will have differential effects depending on whether we are talking about the private or the public sphere. If I rage and shout at the television screen in the privacy of my own house, no one has any justification for interfering. But if I do the same in the public road, then I can expect to be restrained.

4.6 EXAMPLE: Article 10 of the European Convention on Human Rights

'The exercise of [the freedom of expression], since it carries with it duties and responsibilities, may be subject to such formalities, conditions, restrictions or penalties as are prescribed by law and are necessary in a democratic society, in the interests of national security, territorial integrity or public safety, for the prevention of disorder or crime, for the protection of health or morals, for the protection of the reputation or rights of others, for preventing the disclosure of information received in confidence, or for maintaining the authority and impartiality of the judiciary.'

European Court of Human Rights (2010, Article 10)

We can see that the harm principle informs the way Article 10 of the European Convention on Human Rights has been framed (Box 4.6). Although apparently couched in the language of rights, it nevertheless may be interpreted in a utilitarian way with its emphasis on weighing the costs and benefits of freedom of expression against possible social harms. From a utilitarian perspective, there is no absolute right to freedom of thought and discussion. Article 10 makes it clear that there must be limits and those limits are determined by consequences in terms of general social well-being (utility). Firstly, the exercise of freedom of expression must take place within the existing legal framework since, in principle at least, our laws are framed in the wider interests of society. Secondly, we can see that the article's concern is with the harm that may be done to individuals through disclosure of information. Wider considerations of social and individual well-being are grounds for placing limits on media freedoms.

CHAPTER REVIEW

In this chapter we have been concerned with the liberty of the individual and the value of freedom of speech. Given that few would maintain that unfettered freedom of speech is morally permissible, we have been considering what the limits of freedom are. We have examined media freedoms from the perspective of utilitarianism. More specifically, we have drawn a distinction between 'self-regarding' actions and 'other regarding' actions. This distinction is fundamental to Mill's liberty principle, by which he seeks to prescribe the nature and limits of individual liberty and the freedom of thought and discussion. He argues that to the extent that an individual's actions affect only him- or herself ('self-regarding' actions), then those actions should be absolutely free from interference either by the state or society more generally. This sets boundaries between the private and the public. If an individual's actions are purely self-regarding, there can be no ground for intrusion or interference. But to the extent that our actions (including the activities of the media) impinge on others and lead to harm, then there may, but not necessarily, be grounds for intervention by the state.

Mill has two types of argument for his 'liberty principle' when applied to the freedom of the press. The first set of arguments concern the importance of free media as a means for providing the conditions under which truth may emerge and lead to the progressive development of individuals and society. For truth about the social or natural world to emerge it is vital to have the freest possible diversity of beliefs expressed and for these to be open to criticism. To foreclose a debate by censorship is to risk the hindering of progress. The second type of argument is historical. In his essay, 'On Liberty', he provides many instances in which the suppression of ideas and beliefs, especially by religious authorities, has hindered social progress. For Mill, social progress is defined in terms of the expansion of the liberty of the individual towards the greatest possible fulfilment and self-realization. If the media are useful in conveying information, educating the public and providing 'higher pleasures', they should remain unfettered.

Mill's 'liberty principle' is a touchstone of liberal thinking on the need for the liberty of the press, in particular, and the liberty of the media more generally (Box 4.6). According to this, in the public sphere the regulation or censorship of the media must be considered as a balancing of harms – the harm principle. Free speech may only be curtailed if the harm brought about by production, publication and dissemination outweighs the harm of censorship or regulation. For example, incitement to violence may be sufficient ground for censorship. But, for Mill, the presumption must always be in favour of freedom. A balance must be struck between media freedoms and the potential harmful and corrupt abuse of such freedom and the potential harm of state-controlled regulation, preventing the media from 'speaking truth to power'. The first qualification of freedom of speech is that it may be curtailed or restricted if it causes harm. We also introduced a related notion that there may also be grounds for restriction if speech or publication leads to offence, 'the offence principle', which we will explore in more detail in later chapters.

FURTHER READING

Asai, R. (2011) 'Social media as a tool for social change', in A. Bissett (ed.), *Proceedings of the Twelfth International Conference: The Social Impact of Social Computing, ETHICOMP 2011, Sheffield Hallam University, Sheffield UK, 14–16 September 2011*. Sheffield: Sheffield Hallam University, pp. 44–50. Useful as a review of recent cases where social media have been used in contexts of the struggle for social change.

Cohen-Almagor, R. (2005) *Speech, Media and Ethics*. London: Palgrave Macmillan. Chapter 1 gives a full account of the harm principle, the offence principle and hate speech.

Furedi, F. (2011) *On Tolerance: A Defence of Moral Independence*. London: Continuum. See particularly Chapter 7 for a useful critique of the idea of 'offence' as a sufficient ground for the curtailment of freedom of speech.

King, G., Pan, J. and Roberts, M.E. (2013) 'How censorship in China allows government criticism but silences collective expression', *American Political Science Review*, May: 1–18. Good for empirical examples of the scope and nature of censorship in action. The article analyses social media in China and the role of censorship. It shows that censorship is oriented primarily to forestalling collective action and protest.

Sanders, K. (2006) *Ethics and Journalism*. London: Sage. See particularly Chapter 6, 'Freedom's scope' (pp. 63–76), for a philosophical discussion of freedom in general and freedom of the press in particular.

Skorupski, J. (2006) *Why Read Mill Today?* London: Routledge. See particularly, Chapter 3, 'Liberty' (pp. 39–64), for an analysis of Mill's ideas on the nature of liberty in general and freedom of thought and discussion in particular.

HOW TO USE THIS ARTICLE

Go to https://study.sagepub.com/horner to access the following free journal article:

Dimbleby, J. (2013) 'On freedom of expression', *Index on Censorship*, 42: 142–144.

Use this article as an example of an impassioned defence of freedom of expression by a veteran broadcaster and journalist and a previous chair of the Index on Censorship. Dimbleby extols the virtues of freedom of expression as 'a precious human right' and 'a defining characteristic of a civilized society'. He places the origins of his commitment to freedom of speech precisely in the work of John Stuart Mill and Jeremy Bentham. He then briefly reflects on the fact that all the principles remain the same yet the context in which they need to be applied are in some ways radically different.

5
VIOLENCE

Popular criticisms of the media often suggest that they are addicted to sensationalism, trivialization and a general lowering of standards. Extreme representations of sexuality and violence are cited as evidence of these trends. The decline in media standards is a symptom or even cause of moral decline in society more generally. Media practitioners must take into account the social, cultural and moral contexts in which they operate in liberal-democratic states. Freedom of speech and publication, as we say in the previous chapter, cannot be treated like a blank cheque. The consequentialist approach, which we explored in the last chapter, maintained that the modification or restriction of free speech must take place on the grounds of the effects which media representations might have. We introduced two kinds of qualifications of free speech – the harm principle and the offence principle – which ought to inform decision making. In this chapter we consider the grounds on which it is right or wrong to restrict, regulate or control representations or reporting of violence. Primarily, we will concentrate on the principle of harm. The argument is that if it can be established that some representations of violence are harmful in some way, then there is a *prima facie* case for restriction or control in some form.

We begin with the concept of 'moral panic', a term introduced by the sociologist Stanley Cohen (1943–2013) to describe how certain types of events or persons might come to be construed by media and audiences alike as a threat to social and moral order. Important to Cohen's argument is that the media help to amplify the public perception of such threats. The phenomenon of moral panic is illustrated by reference to the case of the brutal murder of James Bulger. He was abducted by two older children from a shopping centre in northern England and murdered. 'Video nasties' were claimed to have influenced his two killers. This gave rise to a moral panic about the effect of children's viewing of violent material and led to a call for stronger control of violent films, video games and other forms of media content. The argument here is directly a consequential one and hinges on the idea of 'an emulation effect', that is, those violent actions represented in the media in some way *cause* others to copy or imitate those acts. It may then reasonably be argued that such depictions of violence ought to be banned, or at least more highly regulated. We consider a range of counter-arguments to such calls for greater regulation. We consider the nature of the responsibilities of media practitioners in the production of violent imagery. We will also examine other circumstances where judgements may need to be made to restrict depictions of violence.

DEPICTIONS OF VIOLENCE: ARGUMENTS TO RESTRICTION

There is a widespread belief among the public that media representations of violence and crime feed into the actual perpetration of violence and crime in society. In 2003 an ICM poll asked a cross-section of the British public 'Do you believe that on-screen violence (in the form of films, television and computer games) encourages violence in society or not?' The survey revealed that nearly three-quarters of respondents (73%) believed that on-screen violence did indeed encourage off-screen violence. The belief was even stronger among the older respondents (that is, those over 45 years of age). Similar results were also reported in a study in the United States (Cumberbach, 2010, p. 355). However, as always with surveys, one must examine the wording of the question carefully, and in this case it is important to point out that 'to encourage' is not the same as 'to cause'. Encouragement implies a rather weaker link than causation. Is 'encouragement' sufficient to warrant censorship? Similarly, the fact that some state of affairs is 'believed' to obtain does not make it a fact. To establish a causative link requires evidence to show that in fact some harmful representation can be linked directly to harmful behaviour.

Moral Panics

There is a fundamental and mutually reinforcing cycle between popular anxieties about levels of violence in society and media reporting (Box 5.1). This was demonstrated in empirical work on 'moral panics'. Stanley Cohen's original characterization of a moral panic in *Folk Devils and Moral Panics* (2002, first published in 1972), emphasized the role of sensationalism in reporting violent disturbances in British seaside towns in the 1950s and early 1960s. Cohen's original study had focused on clashes in 1964 between 'mods' and 'rockers' – a clash between the be-suited, moped-riding 'mods' and their opponents, the leather-clad, motorbike-riding 'rockers'. Cohen's research showed that reporting, particularly by local newspapers, greatly exaggerated the violence that had taken place. This was amplified by the national press to the extent that these disturbances appeared to threaten a wholesale breakdown of public order.

5.1 DEFINITION
A moral panic

'A condition, episode, person or group of persons emerges to become defined as a threat to societal values and interests; its nature presented in a stylised and stereotypical fashion by the mass media, the moral barricades are manned by editors, bishops, politicians, and other right-thinking people; socially accredited experts pronounce their diagnoses and solutions; ways of coping are evolved or (more often) resorted to: the condition then disappears, submerges or deteriorates and becomes more visible.'

Cohen (2002, p. 1)

But the media themselves have a double role in 'moral panics' in, firstly, sensationalizing violence and, secondly, seeming to the general public to be a causative force in promoting violence and the potential for breakdown in the social and moral order. Thus, the very reporting and depiction of violence have come to be seen as implicated in greater levels of social disorder. The media now often appear in the popular imagination as the 'folk devil', implicated as ubiquitous sources of representations that destabilize accepted values. In other words, the now greatly expanded range of media is *causative*; the very act of depiction becomes itself both morally reprehensible and the cause of reprehensible behaviour. The result is frequent calls for tighter controls, the abandonment of self-regulation and forms of censorship. The current concern about media threats to privacy in the UK in the Leveson Inquiry may be just such another cycle in the generation of a moral panic. In this case, the media themselves emerge as the folk devils that must be exorcised.

Moral panics have material effects. Cohen observed, for example, that the police became more sensitive to the groups that were demonized (the folk devils of Cohen's title) and reacted in a draconian manner to any hint of trouble. Arrest rates increased dramatically and magistrates handed down harsher sentences. Bill Osgerby (2010, pp. 476–477) observes that a whole series of similar 'amplification cycles' involving press sensationalism can be traced from the 1960s onwards. Subsequent 'folk devils', usually 'wayward youth', include the 'skinheads' of the 1960s, the 'punks' of the 1970s, the 'New Age travellers' of the 1980s, the 'acid house ravers' of the 1990s, with the latest recruits to the demonology being the 'hoodie' gangs of the 2000s. All these groups were, to a greater or lesser extent, presented and represented as threats to the social and moral order out of all proportion to their actual behaviours and effects.

The Murder of James Bulger

In the United Kingdom, one of the most well-known and terrible cases of what was claimed to be 'a media-inspired crime' was the brutal murder on 12 February 1993 of the 2-year-old toddler James Bulger. The toddler was killed by two 10-year-old boys on a railway line in Merseyside, northern England, having been abducted from a shopping centre two miles away. At their trial, an explicit link was made between their crime and the fact that they had watched violent video films. There was both a high level of media reporting of the crime and a very high level of public interest in the case. In particular, people were exercised by the problem of how young children could do such a thing and what was the role of TV, video and their parents in their conduct. In seeking to explain their behaviour, the presiding judge, Mr Justice Moorland, in sentencing the two boys, made the claim that 'exposure to violent video films may, in part, be an explanation' (quoted in Cumberbach, 2010, p. 358). Following the pattern of moral panics, the national newspapers in particular began to elaborate and amplify Mr Justice Moorland's remarks, for example, the idea that watching extremely violent videos 'may, in part, be an explanation' for the crime. The claim was made that *Child's Play 3* was the film that the boys appeared to have watched and then emulated. One of Britain's tabloid daily newspapers, *The Sun*, in the true tradition of combating 'folk devils', organized a public burning of the video (Cumberbach, 2010, p. 358).

The police investigation had specifically focused on the question of whether or not there was evidence of a link between the murder and various forms of media, including video films. The investigating police officer, Detective Superintendent Albert Kirby, had concluded that there was no evidence for any link. Neil Venables, the father of Jon Venables, one of the convicted boys, three months previously had indeed rented the film (probably the source of *The Sun*'s story). But at the time the video had been rented, Jon Venables was not living with his father and the investigating officer concluded that it was highly unlikely that he had the opportunity to see the video. This conclusion was corroborated by the fact that Jon was upset by depictions of violence in films and did not like horror films. Psychiatric reports subsequently confirmed that this was indeed the case. The campaign for more stringent controls on video films continued unabated despite the highly tendentious nature of the claim that some explanation of the boys' behaviour was to be found in the viewing of violent videos. Without evidence for a demonstrable link between the viewing of the violent video and the subsequent murder, there could be no grounds for censorship or the tightening of regulations on 'video nasties'. Note here that, again, facts may be decisive in settling a moral dispute.

What gave particular weight to this story was that both the victim and the perpetrators were all children at the time of the crime. And, of course, it seems intuitively right to suggest that the material to which children should be exposed should be more highly regulated and policed than that for adult audiences. This is reflected in the classification systems for film and video. It is important to note that much of the argument for regulation and censorship has drawn upon notorious cases involving children under the age of legal responsibility. From an empirical point of view, if we are going to find a link between exposure to the representation of violent acts and the actual commission of such acts, then, in a very real sense, children must be the test-bed for the proposition. Children are a special case as a media audience which is likely to be more easily influenced. But even if it was established that children are particularly vulnerable to the depiction of violence, this would not necessarily provide evidence for censorship of material destined for adult audiences.

5.2 A JUDGEMENT CALL
Banning video games

You suspect that a new video game, which is about to be launched onto the market, may have a bad influence on particularly vulnerable individuals (including children). The game allows the player to appear to participate in the wounding, disfigurement and ulti-mately the massacre of opponents. The game has been produced to a very high standard of graphics, giving a heightened sense of realism. Your problem, as a regulator, is that the possible effects on certain susceptible or vulnerable individuals are not known, but the evidence base for 'emulation effects' does seem weak. However, equally, the risk of the impact of the game is not knowable. This just might be the 'tipping point' at which we discover triggers for imitative, violent behaviour.

What ought to happen and why?

In considering the judgement call outlined in Box 5.2 it may be helpful to review the elements in moral decision making outlined in Chapter 1 (see Table 1.1: Elements of moral judgement). Our first element concerns the facts of the case. We need to consider whether or not there is evidence for a direct link between viewing images of violence and actual behaviour. There may be little evidence to show that normal individuals under normal circumstances are influenced by such images, that is normally people are well able to distinguish between the fantasy elements of a game and real-life situations. But it is likely that there may be some (weak) evidence on vulnerable individuals. We would need to address the evidence in terms of both adults and children. In addition to the evidence, we would also need to consider what moral principle is applicable in such cases. Clearly, what we are most concerned with is whether the video game will lead to harm. Such harm may be psychological harm on the individuals affected, and then the kinds of harm that might result if aspects of the game were acted out. Given that the social and psychological evidence is crucially lacking, we may need to exercise our imaginations as to future scenarios. The argument then might be that we need to exercise a 'precautionary principle' in the absence of definitive evidence. This principle is defined in the following way: 'If some action has a possibility of causing harm, then that action should not be undertaken or some measure should be put in place to minimize or eliminate the potential harm' (Tavani, 2011, p. 382). We may therefore, on this argument, ban the video. A less draconian strategy may be to restrict the distribution of the video to particular groups (e.g. excluding children) and make sure that it is issued with strict warnings concerning the nature of the content.

ANATOMY OF THE ARGUMENT FROM EMULATION

If certain kinds of representation may possibly cause social harm, then some kind of restriction or regulation to protect society is morally permissible. Here there is no necessary difference whether the depictions are factual or fictional. In the previous section we looked briefly at the case for restricting a potentially violent video game. In this section we will examine in more detail the nature and use of argument. An argument is logically a set of premises leading to a conclusion. For the conclusion to be necessarily true the form of the argument must be valid and the premises must be true. In Box 5.3 an argument for censorship or regulation is outlined based on a presumed tendency for audiences to emulate media depictions. In trying to get to the bottom of a moral argument, it is often useful to try to express it in this simplified form in order to establish the key elements of its structure. This is a valid argument form, that is, the conclusions 4 and 5, follow logically from the premises 1, 2, and 3, but if, and only if, those premises are true. However, if any of the premises are false, then the conclusions do not follow. This does not necessarily mean that the conclusion is false, just that the premises, as stated, do not give grounds for the valid deduction of the conclusions. Let's consider the premises of the argument.

Premise 1 is an empirical, factual claim about the (social) world. Either it is true to say that people (adults and/or children) are caused to emulate depicted actions or it is false. Given that this is an empirical claim, then it is capable, in principle, of being established one way or the other. In order for the argument to be valid its proponents must have good evidence for claiming that people are 'caused' to act by viewing and listening to some media representation. It is important, however, to be clear that to say an action is caused is to make a very strong claim. It is to say that what I might do is influenced in some way. It is to claim that I cannot have done otherwise. But the price for saying that I was *caused* to do something is to annihilate the idea of moral culpability. If I couldn't do otherwise, then I was not free to make a (moral) choice. To emulate someone or some action is not, in itself, to be caused to do something; it is fundamentally to choose to do something. Thus there must be sufficient convincing evidence that media depictions can *cause* (not merely encourage) the real occurrence of similar actions.

Premise 2 is also, I suggest, an empirical claim – whether some action is harmful or not is broadly true or false. There may be an argument about what we might mean by 'harmful'. If we have a broad consensus about what types of action are harmful, then whether or not any particular action is harmful is, again, an empirical fact. We can establish that social harm actually is the result of the action.

Premise 3 of the argument is partly a matter of fact in the sense that clearly laws do give the right to the police, for example, to restrain the activities of individuals and organizations. However, it is also a principle which is broadly in line with Mill's liberty principle, discussed in the last chapter. The fact that our actions may harm others gives the state or society a justification for intervention to prevent harm.

An example of the 'emulation argument' is that of the relationship between violent Rap music videos and violent behaviour. It has been claimed that certain kinds of Rap music, employing violent lyrics and imagery, provoke individuals to emulate such depictions and lead to violent behaviour. (Famously, Chris McDaniel, a Mississippi Senate candidate, once claimed that 'The reason Canada is breaking out in brand new gun violence has nothing to do with the United States and guns. It has everything to do with a culture that is morally bankrupt. It's called hip-hop' (Global Grind, 2014).) This corresponds to premise 1 of the argument – that certain kinds of musical depictions lead to certain kinds of behaviours. For premise 2, these behaviours are characterized as violent or aggressive. In other words, they are socially harmful. These are empirical claims. A psychological researcher, Eliana Tropeano, summarizes the empirical evidence derived from the work of various experimenters and concludes that 'It seems obvious that there is a significant relationship between listening to violent music and watching aggressive and violent music videos and one getting into fights, using inappropriate language, inappropriate gestures, and a tendency to think less of women' (Tropeano, 2006, p. 32). The operational definition of 'violent behaviour' here is physically and verbally hurting others. However, the overall claim established by the experimental work is that there is a direct correlation between violent music videos and people behaving violently. This is not as strong a claim as that of direct causation. Nevertheless, combined with premise 3, it would yield the conclusions (4 and 5) that society had a right to restrain the producers of violent music videos and those who might want to consume them. However, we have already seen other social and psychological studies that would contest the link (Cumberbach, 2010). We may therefore want to apply the precautionary principle.

5.3 EXAMPLE: Anatomy of the emulation argument

1. The media depiction of certain sorts of action causes people to emulate those actions.
2. The actions are of a socially harmful kind.
3. Society has the right to restrain the activities of individuals to prevent harm.

Thus:

4. Society has the right to restraint the activities of those who create, produce and distribute depictions that lead to socially harmful actions.
5. Society has also a right to restrain the activities of those who would view those depictions.

Adapted from Graham (1998, p. 153)

Calls for draconian measures against violent video films followed this pattern in the case of the killing of James Bulger. Similarly, concerns arose in the USA in 1999 following the Columbine murders when, in this case, violent video games were implicated in the actions of the teenage killers. And again, as Charles Ess (2009, p. 136) points out: 'Subsequent shootings – not only in the United States (e.g. the Virginia Tech killings in 2007) but also, e.g. in Emsdetten, Germany (2006) and Jokela High School, Finland (2007) – are likewise connected in media reports with a focus on the killers' favourite violent computer games'.

The challenge to this form of argument is simply the lack of agreed empirical evidence that a link can be made between specific media depictions of violence and specific cases of violent action. The argument largely hinges on matters of fact rather than of moral principle. There may be a correlation here, but the causation remains unproven. The types of children or adults who watch violent videos or play violent video games may just be the types of individual who are likely to commit violent acts. Reasonable judgements must be based on the balance of probabilities. An authority in the field (Cumberbach, 2010, p. 364) states that 'The most notable feature of the vast research literature on "media effects" is for strong conclusions to be reached about harm on rather weak data. The devil is in the detail and only close scrutiny reveals the inconsistencies in the findings'. In other words, there is no body of evidence that establishes a causal link for sure. And, as we saw above, the argument requires that premise 1 is shown to be true.

Emulation is Not Self-evident

A typical counter-move of proponents is the claim that the occurrence of imitative behaviour is simply 'self-evident'. For example, Graham (1998) quotes the veteran journalist Janet Daley to the effect that it is not necessary to establish a direct link between a particular act and the consumption of a piece of violent pornography. That there is such a link is a self-evident and commonplace fact of human psychology. Here, Daley represents a populist argument that stems from the phenomenon of moral panic. She writes, 'What is beyond dispute is that the saturation of popular culture with images of cruelty normalizes violence' (quoted in Graham, 1998, p. 154). The effects of representations may not be demonstrable in specific cases, but the overall effects of living in a media-saturated environment where extreme representations are commonplace, and are particularly available to children, are 'bound' to influence some members of society in a detrimental way. But the relative rarity of such actions, especially by children, tends to tell against this – if we are to take the claim of 'saturation' seriously.

Graham points out two mistakes with the 'self-evident argument': 'First, even if it is not possible to establish a direct mechanistic link between the watching of a particular film and the carrying out of a particular act, it may yet be possible to make general statistical connections between actions of those types' (Graham, 1998, p. 153). Extensive research has not been able to establish any such 'general statistical connections': 'Second, the fact that a statement by its nature is not *provable* does not release us from the obligation to believe it only if it has been shown to be *probable*' (Graham, 1998, p. 154, original emphasis). If we follow Mill's utilitarian logic, it must also be demonstrated that the immorality of harm resulting from media representations must be worse than the evil of living in a society with highly controlled media. The evidence of some social harm is not necessarily a sufficient justification for censorship or restriction. It may be, all things considered, that there are some social harms we have to live with because the alternative is worse.

Depictions of Violence are Cathartic

A further counter-argument to our specimen argument is that rather than being potentially damaging, depictions of violence may be morally beneficial. In considering premise 2, it may hardly be disputed that violence against another person must be, on the whole, immoral. However, the depiction of violence is altogether different. There is a categorical difference between fact and fiction.

The argument for censorship would have us believe that representations promote violence in society. Moral panics thrive on this assumption. But there is an alternative and long-standing argument that the dramatic representation of violence may forestall violent actions. For example, it was Aristotle's view that the effect of watching violent tragedy was less an urge to action and more a purging of emotions which, if really acted upon, would have been harmful. Aristotle's theory of catharsis asserted that:

> Tragedy excites the emotions of pity and fear – kindred emotions that are in the breasts of all men – and by the act of excitation affords a pleasurable relief. The feelings called forth by the tragic spectacle are not indeed permanently removed, but are quieted for a time, so that the system can fall back upon its normal course. The stage, in fact, provides a harmless and pleasurable outlet for instincts which demand satisfaction, and which can be indulged here more fearlessly than in real life. (Butcher, 1898, p. 241)

By 'the stage' in this quotation, we could substitute the contemporary range of media content displaying fictional violence.

DILEMMAS OF DEPICTION

Other Grounds for Restriction

There are other reasons, besides the fear of emulation and the commission of social harms, that might lead us to want to restrict free speech and certain kinds of fictional or factual representations of violence. In the first instance, we might wish to forebear from publishing details or pictures of the victims of violence. For example, we may wish to spare the relatives of a dead person the trauma of seeing their loved one as a mangled and disfigured corpse. Secondly, in considering fictional representations of violence, there may be an issue of decency. We need not assume that depictions of violence lead to replications of such violence in order to forebear from showing such violence. For example, we might consider it wholly inappropriate to show even fictional representations of sexual violence against children. Even though we have no strong evidence to show that such depictions may lead to such acts in reality, we may feel that such depictions are intrinsically immoral rather than simply immoral because of their consequences. In addition to social harm, Mill also recognized another category of harm, that of giving offence. However, the category of offence is a more narrowly defined one than (physical) harm.

In 'On Liberty' (Mill, 1964a, p. 153), Mill rejects the idea that simply giving offence to others' feelings and sensibilities constitutes sufficient reasons for inference or restriction of individual liberty or free speech. He illustrates this with the example that living in a Catholic society would by no means constitute grounds for restricting other forms of worship, or that the prohibition of eating pork in a Muslim society would justify a general prohibition on pork. Even though the sensibilities of Catholics and Muslims might be offended, this would not justify interference with my eating pork or adopting another style of worship. But Mill recognizes this as a reason for curtailing some behaviour because it is intrusive rather than because it is directly, physically harmful, and by 'intrusive' he means 'violations of good manners' or offences against decency (Mill, 1964a, p. 153). He does not elaborate on 'offences against decency', indicating that it would not be appropriate to write about them in any detail! What he seems to mean is not that they might harm others (like secondary smoking) or even that they are directly offensive, but that they are intrusions on other individuals in a public or shared space. For Mill, this constitutes 'a violation of good manners'. However, as with the category of harm, the trick is knowing when it is appropriate to use such a concept.

BOX 5.4 A JUDGEMENT CALL
Whether or not to release photographs of the death of Osama bin Laden

'A debate on whether the military photos should or should not be released to the public has taken place. Those supporting the release argued that the photos should be considered public records that the photos are necessary to complete the journalistic record, and that the photos would prove bin Laden's death and therefore prevent conspiracy theories that bin Laden is still alive. Those in opposition to a release of the photos expressed concern that the photos would inflame anti-American sentiment in the Middle East.

President Obama ultimately decided not to release the photos. In an interview set to air on May 4 on *60 Minutes*, Obama stated that "We don't trot out this stuff as trophies. We don't need to spike the football!", and that he was concerned with ensuring that "very graphic photos of somebody who was shot in the head are not floating around as an incitement to additional violence, or as a propaganda tool.

(Continued)

(Continued)

That's not who we are." Among Republican members of Congress, Senator Lindsey Graham criticized the decision and stated that he wanted to see the photos released, while Senator John McCain and Representative Mike Rogers, the chair of the House Intelligence Committee, supported the decision not to release the photos.'

Was it right to not to release the photographs? Is there a sense in which such a release would be, in Mill's phrase, a 'violation of good manners'?

Source: Death of Osama bin Laden (2012)

To Publish or Not to Publish?

Dilemmas in general usually involve a 'choice between options, each of which has unacceptable or unwelcome consequences or implications' (Black, 2012, p. 63). A moral dilemma involves a clash between different moral principles when those principles may equally be applied to the same situation. For example, a journalist may be in the position where the freedom to write and publish a story of public interest may be in conflict with some kind of harm that publishing the story may give rise to. On the first horn of the dilemma, if the journalist decides not to publish, then the act of self-censorship seems in conflict with the fundamental role of reporting the truth. On the second horn of the dilemma, publishing the story may create unhappiness or distress. In either case there are undesirable consequences. From a utilitarian point of view, the choice must be whichever option causes least harm.

Dilemmas arise probably most acutely in circumstances of natural catastrophes or war situations. For those who report or comment on such disasters there are frequent tensions between the imperative to report as truthfully as possible and the imperative to prevent harm and maintain a sense of decency. There are editorial codes which proscribe the showing of extreme images of violence on television. For example, the death of Saddam Hussein, although filmed, was not broadcast on mainstream TV in the United Kingdom. It could be argued that there was no direct social harm that might arise from showing the hanging of Saddam Hussain. It might provoke Saddam supporters to acts of violence, but equally, and with greater effect, it might convince his erstwhile supporters that he was indeed dead. Similarly, the US military filmed their assassination of Osama bin Laden. However, although much of the operation was made available to broadcasters, the actual shooting was not broadcast (see Box 5.4). Much of the debate about the release of the photographs of bin Laden's death revolves around the balance between the potential social and political harm of release versus the potential harm of non-release. However, there is the suggestion in President Obama's remarks that there would also be something *indecent* in their release.

5.5 A JUDGEMENT CALL
Publishing the photographs of war dead

In the first Gulf War, as the Iraqi army was expelled from Kuwait, columns of retreating Iraqi soldiers were heavily bombed by allied aircraft. Many thousands were killed in their vehicles as they fled the conflict. This looked very much like a massacre, particularly since these Iraqis appeared to have given up the fight and just wanted to go home. Subsequently, the bombed columns with their gruesome cargo of the dead were photographed by allied photojournalists. The scenes were horrific, with many corpses in terrible states of decay. The judgement here was should such photographs have been published?

The publishing of the photographs would have given a truthful picture of the consequences of the allied bombing of the retreating Iraqi army. However, the war was still continuing and the effect of publishing such shocking pictures, because they were so distressing, may have affected the morale of the civilian populations of the allied countries and weakened the political resolve (which was fragile) to continue to pursue the war. There was the potential distressing effect on the Iraqi population and, in particular, on the families of the dead of publication.

What would you have done and why?

CHAPTER REVIEW

In this chapter we have been exploring the limits of freedom of expression as these were conceived by J.S. Mill. According to Mill, the presumption must be that the press (now the media in general) must be free to publish and broadcast. Any constraint on the media must be justified by the authorities on grounds of social harm. However, we also noted a second potential qualification of free speech to do with the idea of offence. Certain kinds of speech may be so psychologically offensive to individuals or groups in the sense of their right to dignity and respect. In the chapter we focused on the extent to which the depiction of violence ought to be subject to regulation. We introduced the phenomenon of 'moral panic'. This term was introduced by the sociologist Stanley Cohen in an attempt to explain how certain types of events or persons and their representation might come to be construed as a threat to the social and moral order. Important to Cohen's argument is the role of the media in amplifying and exaggerating the public perception of such threats. The brutal murder of James Bulger was used to illustrate the way in which a moral panic functions to call for more stringent media regulation. In this case, there was a public perception that there was a connection between the viewing of particularly violent videos and the murder. The implication was that in some way the two young boys who had committed the murder were led to do so by their viewing violent videos.

We have laid out a general argument which tends to underlie calls for restriction of free speech and media regulation. The argument largely hinges on the empirical question of whether there is any truth to the idea of 'an emulation effect', that is, that violent actions represented on the media in some way *cause* others to copy or imitate those acts. If such an effect were proved, then such depictions ought to be banned or at least highly regulated on grounds of social harm. The question here is not a matter of principle but of fact. If we can agree on the facts, we can formulate appropriate policies. There are a number of arguments against the central 'emulation effect' claim. Firstly, the truth of the claim is not self-evident and needs empirical support. Secondly, the social and psychological research in the area tends to be divided on whether or not there is such an effect and whether or not the relationship between representations and behaviour is one of correlation or causation. Thirdly, the whole notion of being caused to do something is conceptually flawed. Fourthly, viewing depictions of violence, on the contrary, may have a cathartic effect. In the absence of definitive evidence, there may therefore be a case for applying 'the precautionary principle' when considering depictions of violence.

However, we also considered cases where emulation is not the issue. Rather, the issue is the distress caused by certain kinds of reportage or viewing certain kinds of images. The cases considered here tend to be less concerned with matters of fact and more with what are the relevant principles; where we might have a conflict between the imperative to represent the truth and the imperative to protect people against the distress that certain kinds of imagery may give rise to. Here the question may be less to do with physical harm and more to do with a sense of what it may or may not be decent to show. For example, the debate which arose following the assassination of Osama bin Laden about whether or not to publish film of his death.

FURTHER READING

Cohen, S. (2002) *Folk Devils and Moral Panics: The Creation of the Mods and Rockers* (3rd edn). London: Routledge (1st edn, 1972). The seminal account of the idea of moral panics and the role of the media in their generation.

Cumberbach, G. (2010) 'Effects', in D. Albertazzi and P. Cobley (eds), *The Media: An Introduction* (3rd edn). London: Pearson Education. pp. 354–368 (1st edn, 1998). This provides a good, introductory review of some of the psychological evidence for the emulation effect. Cumberbach concludes that there is no evidence for such an effect.

David, M., Rohloff, A., Petley, J. and Hughes, J. (2011) 'The idea of moral panic: ten dimensions of dispute', *Crime, Media Culture*, 7(3): 215–228. The paper reviews the history of the concept of moral panic. It discusses some of the disputes which have arisen about the concept over its history, for example whether or not there are positive as well as negative aspects to such panics. It makes the case for its continuing relevance.

Ellis, A. (1998) 'Censorship and the media', in M. Kieran (ed.), *Media Ethics*. London: Routledge. pp. 165–177. Discusses arguments on the restriction of free speech in relationship to blasphemy, profanity, obscenity, indecency and offensiveness.

Global Grind (2014) 'Well look at that: new study shows Rap music and violence are not linked' [Online], 7 January. http://globalgrind.com/2014/01/08/study-rap-music-violence-not-linked-details/ (accessed. 14 April 2014). An article giving an account of a study providing some empirical evidence for the lack of any direct link between Rap music and the occurrence of violence. The study is based on a comparison between FBI data on violent crime and the rise in the popularity of Rap music.

Graham, G. (1998) 'Sex and violence in fact and fiction', in M. Kieran (ed.), *Media Ethics*. London: Routledge. pp. 152–164. Provides an analysis of arguments about censorship and pornography.

Plaisance, P.L. (2009) *Media Ethics: Key Principles for Responsible Practice*. London: Sage. See particularly Chapter 5, 'Harm' (pp. 105–134), for an overview of the meaning and morality of harm in the media.

Tropeano, E. (2006) 'Does rap or rock music provoke violent behaviour?', *Journal of Undergraduate Psychological Research*, 1: 31–34. A useful introduction to some of the evidence that tends to show a link between aggressive music lyrics and videos and resulting behaviour. The paper also includes an account of an empirical study which tends to support previous research establishing a link.

HOW TO USE THIS ARTICLE

Go to https://study.sagepub.com/horner to access the following free journal article:

Maltby, S. (2014) 'Broadcasting graphic war violence: the moral face of Channel 4', *Journalism*, 15(3): 289–306.

Use this study to see how a major TV channel handles the broadcasting of graphic war violence. The paper is an empirical study which investigates how Channel 4, through a process of discretionary decision making, copes with the potentially conflicting and competing imperatives of commercial, regulatory and moral requirements in relationship to the broadcasting of violent imagery. The author claims that 'imaginings' are central to these negotiations between competing imperatives. These imaginings relate both to the nature of the audience and the organization itself: 'Put simply, in the process of negotiating commercial, regulatory and moral requirements, C4 utilize their own "imagining" of the C4 "face" as a guiding tool, a legitimation tool and a market strategy'. This is a close reading of how decisions come to be made about whether or not to broadcast potentially controversial images of violence and the effects of violence against a background of competing imperatives.

6
PORNOGRAPHY

Violence and pornography are frequently linked in debates about freedom of speech and censorship. Indeed, from a feminist perspective, pornography is talked of as a form of violence or an expression of an exercise of power by men against women. The pattern of argument deployed in relationship to pornography or explicit sexual material may be much the same as that employed in considering depictions of violence. Most societies have as a matter of fact legislation and regulations designed to control the production, distribution and consumption of pornographic material. As in the case of violence, concerns about pornography often take the form of moral panics in that obscene or explicit sexual material is perceived as a threat to the social order. What differentiates pornography from violence is that the kind of harm frequently referred to in the case of pornography is 'moral harm' rather than physical harm; pornography is seen as a form of corruption and a direct threat to public morality. In the 'popular mind', morality and sexual morality are almost synonymous. The philosopher A.C. Grayling (1997, p. 11) remarks 'As the notion now operates, morality applies just to parts of life, chiefly to interpersonal relationships; and it invariably concerns such matters as marital infidelity and malicious gossip.'

In the previous chapter we considered arguments and evidence that may justify restrictions on media freedoms to depict violence. In this chapter we must consider another perennial and contentious area of moral concern for the media which involves the principle of freedom of speech. No one would suggest that the production and dissemination of sexually explicit material in films, videos or television programmes ought to be completely unfettered. The situation has been made more acute by the vastly expanded scope for the distribution of sexually explicit material via the internet. Liberal-democratic societies regard freedom as a core value. It implies that individuals should make their decisions and choices regarding their lifestyles and inclinations as freely as possible. However, there is far from being a consensus on the moral boundaries for the creation and production of sexually explicit material. The focus of the chapter is on the morality of pornographic representation seen from three perspectives: conservative, liberal and feminist. We approach this largely from a consequentialist point of view (see Box 6.1). In other words, moral judgements about the regulation and restriction of sexually explicit material ought to be based on the consequences of the depictions for individuals or society. We locate the problem in an historical perspective because social and cultural attitudes to sexuality shift over time. The distinctions between material that is sexually explicit, erotic, aesthetic and pornographic are discussed. A broadly conservative argument for the prohibition of pornography is outlined, followed by the liberal counter-arguments. We then discuss feminist approaches to representations of sexuality and the prohibition of pornography.

6.1 DEFINITIONS
Consequentialism and utilitarianism

Consequentialism

A generic word for a group of ethical theories that appeal to the consequences, effects, outcomes or ends as the essential criterion, or standard, to be used to justify specific actions or policies. For consequentialists, the key question to ask when confronted by a moral decision is: 'What option offers the morally best outcome?'

Utilitarianism

A consequentialist ethical theory based on the principle that an act or a policy is morally permissible if it produces the greatest good, where 'greatest good' is interpreted as the greatest amount of happiness and the minimum amount of pain for the greatest number of people affected by it. The theory is particularly associated with Jeremy Bentham (1748–1832) and John Stuart Mill (1806–1873).

SEXUALITY AND PORNOGRAPHY
Historical Perspective

Social and cultural attitudes to sexuality are highly volatile and subject to the conditions of particular historical circumstances. Contemporary views of sexuality, for example in the United Kingdom, are highly influenced by those of the Victorian era but are very different in many ways. Sexual mores were radically transformed in the second half of the twentieth century. Attitudes to what might be discussed, written about and depicted have become ever more liberal or permissive; repressive attitudes have given way to liberty. However, this liberalization has consistently met with opposition. We have seen that John Stuart Mill detected in history a pattern of evolution based on an intrinsic struggle between authority and liberty. The philosopher A.C. Grayling similarly argues that the 'moral evolution' of societies, particularly with respect to sexual matters, has a cyclical character: 'Moral history can seem endlessly cyclical, with periods of austerity succeeding relative liberalism, which in turn liberalize after a time, only to retrench again. Sometimes there seems to be inertia in human affairs, reversing progress at every opportunity of war or disaster' (Grayling, 1997, p. 2). In this context, Grayling warns us of a danger of projecting present value judgements backwards into history.

Grayling argues that this historical flux represents a 'Heraclitean' struggle between the forces of conservative and liberal values; he speaks here primarily of the Western world, the world of European and Judaeo-Christian origin. He believes that we cannot predict the precise forms this struggle will take in the future, yet it will continue. For Grayling, as for Mill, what is at stake is the happiness of humankind. He, of course, lines up the liberties associated with liberalism with happiness. At a personal level, he remarks that we may hover between our liberal and conservative tendencies. With regard to our own conduct, we tend to adopt a liberal attitude, whereas to the conduct of others we adopt a more conservative one! He draws a distinction between situations where liberals prevail and situations where conservatives prevail. In particular, as Mill illustrates in his essay 'On Liberty', in periods when conservatives are in the ascendancy there tends to be active persecution and repression (Grayling, 1997).

6.2 DEFINITIONS
Pornography

'...obscene representations or display, especially of human sexuality, produced to provide an occasion for fantasy' (Blackburn, 2006, p. 283)

'...sexually explicit images and texts that are intended to be arousing' (Strangroom, 2010, p. 60)

6.3 A JUDGEMENT CALL
To censor or not to censor *Crash* (1996)?

In 1996 the film director David Cronenberg released the controversial film *Crash*. The film is based on a novel by J.G. Ballard. The plot hinges on a man and a woman (played by James Spader and Holly Hunter) who, after being injured in a crash, and in spite of being injured, find they are sexually aroused by the accident. They then become initiated into a group who make it a practice to seek out crashes in order to gain sexual gratification. In the film, explicit links are made between the violence of the crashes and the levels of sexual arousal. But importantly, the violence is self-inflicted – it is 'autoerotic'!

The film is described in its entry in *Halliwell's Film and Video Guide* (Walker, 2000) by criti-cal quotations from *Variety*, The British Board of Film Classification and the *Daily Mail* as: 'A compelling, not very likable movie that gives new meaning to autoeroticism in an account of technological fetishism that is stylishly made and seriously intended'. Todd McCarthy in *Variety* describes the film as: 'A forbiddingly frigid piece of esoteric erotica.' In Britain there was considerable controversy about whether or not the film should be released uncut. The British Board of Film Classification (BBFC) consulted an audience of disabled people, a forensic psychologist and a barrister. They concluded: 'Rather than sympathising or iden-tifying with the characters in this film, the average viewer would in the end be repelled by them, and would reject the values and sexual proclivities displayed.'

In contrast, a conservative newspaper, the *Daily Mail*, rejected this view, writing that: 'All the psychobabble in the world cannot refute the simple fact that: The film is sick. It should not be shown.'

Source: Walker (2000)

The BBFC decided to release the film uncut. Would this have been your decision? If not, why not?

A further aspect of historical change we should also bear in mind is the transformation of media technologies which to a large extent have aided and abetted the liberalization of sexuality in the last 60 years. These technological changes have enabled the 'democratization' of the making and publishing of sexually explicit material. The ability to create, record, reproduce and distribute sexually explicit material has been enhanced beyond all recognition. Waves of innovative media technologies, such as 35mm film cameras, video cameras and video-tape machines have broadened access to sexually explicit material. However, the rise of the internet, the World Wide Web and the smart phone has further amplified the availability of sexually explicit and pornographic material. It is a popular view (or misconception) that one of the main drivers of content on the internet is in fact pornography. But we must be cautious not to give technology too great a role since human history *before* radio, television, magazines, videos, the internet, etc. is replete with accounts of violence and depravity (for example, Gibbon's *Decline and Fall of the Roman Empire* [1930]). Technology has created a new battleground for the struggle between broadly liberal and conservative values.

Sexting

An example of the way in which digital technologies are being used to distribute sexually explicit material is 'sexting'. Sexting may be defined as 'the practice of sending sexually explicit text messages' using mobile phones (Lunceford, 2011, p. 99). Such texts include nude or semi-nude photos or videos. However, these photos and videos may become widely distributed, without the consent of the par-ticipant, and go on to be distributed over the internet. Clearly, this may become psychologically distressing. This has become something of a moral panic because it is a practice that seems to have been widely adopted by teenagers. A survey by the National Campaign to Prevent Teen Pregnancy and CosmoGirl.com found that 22% of teenage girls, 18% of teenage boys and 11% of young teenage girls (ages 13–16) 'have sent/posted nude or semi-nude pictures or video of themselves' (quoted in Lunceford, 2011, p. 101). The consequences of the wide circulation of images without consent can lead to tragic outcomes. For example, it was reported that 'Pat', a young woman from Ohio, sent nude photographs of herself to a boy who then circulated the pictures to others. The nude pictures were seen by some of her classmates at school and also by others in her local community. This led to Pat being taunted by some of those who had seen the photographs. The effect on Pat was distressing to the extent that in May 2008 she took her own life (Tavani, 2011, p. 285).

Can we argue that sexting is not pornographic and should not be treated as such by the law (see Box 6.4)? Sexting, it can be argued, is simply the posting by adolescents of images of themselves for their own sexual 'fulfilment', and in that sense may be different from child pornography. It may be morally permissible if all sides in the exchange of images are consenting. The cases in which things go wrong, for example, for Pat and Bill (see Box 6.4), are less to do with the images themselves and more with a breach of trust. There is a moral risk in sending explicit images of oneself in that it relies on the receiver(s) of the text not to abuse that trust. In Bill's case, it is the fact that he distributed the photograph without Jane's consent that made prosecution the appropriate course of action, although there could be a further argument about the severity of the penalty. A further factor here may that of age. It seems more acceptable if those exchanging the explicit material are roughly the same age, although this doesn't automatically rule out the possibility of undue pressure and exploitation. But is a 16- or 17-year-old boy who takes and 'sexts' a photograph or a video of a 13-year-old girl really engaging in child pornography?

Raphael Cohen-Almagar (2005) argues that whether we are considering physical harm or a psychological offence that is caused to others, four considerations are pertinent: the content of the speech; the manner in which the speech is expressed; the intentions and motives of the speaker; and the circumstances in which the speech takes place. If we apply these conditions to sexting, then we can make a moral defence in the following way. Firstly, if the content of the explicit material is acceptable and not repellent to whoever receives it. Secondly, if the manner in which the texts are expressed is intimate and caring for the other person rather than being obscene and gratuitously titillating. Thirdly, if the intention and motives of the exchange of texts are to promote a caring relationship and not for the purposes of subsequent exploitation. Fourthly, if the circumstance of the exchange is an established and private relationship. However, as we have seen above, there is always a risk that a breach of trust is involved. And such a moral defence of freedom of speech may not be the attitude that the law takes.

6.4 A JUDGEMENT CALL
Is sexting a form of pornography?

'Bill', a resident of Florida, had broken up with his girlfriend, 'Jane', and without consent sent a nude picture of her to his friends and family. Jane was only 16 years of age whereas Bill was just 18. The police arrested Bill and charged him with sending child pornography. He was convicted of a felony offence and was required to register as a sex offender. His name will appear on an internet registry of sex offenders until he is 43 years old. As a consequence of this criminal record, Bill was expelled from college and was unable to find a job (see Tavani, 2011, pp. 284–286).

Was this an appropriate course of action to take against Bill? Should sexting be classified as child pornography?

Sexuality, Obscenity and Pornography

Pornography tends to be representations of sexuality that are obscene. Simon Blackburn, professor of philosophy at the University of Cambridge, makes a fundamental distinction between erotic art and pornography. Human passion is central to erotic art but is not obscene. If we were to lose this distinction, much of Western art and Oriental art might be classed as obscene! From a sexual point of view, Blackburn argues that, firstly, what characterizes obscene representation of sexuality is its tendency to display or represent the human body or parts of the body as abstracted from emotion or human relationships and commitment. But, secondly, neither are such representations objective or descriptive in the way you would find in medical or educational material. Thirdly, bodies or parts of bodies are reduced to the status of objects whose purpose is to service, 'more or less disgustingly', a single human appetite or function – sexual arousal. There may also be obscene representations of violence, eating, defecating, abuse of animals, and so on (Blackburn, 2006, p. 258).

6.5 A JUDGEMENT CALL
Is 'twerking' obscene?

Something of a moral panic has been provoked by the performances of singer Miley Cyrus, for example, on her Bangerz tour. Concerns were raised in the press and in the Twittersphere about the sexually explicit nature of her performances both in concert and on YouTube videos. However, it should be noted that her music videos exist in explicit and less explicit versions and frequently display a 'parental advisory' sign. The criticisms were that she had 'gone too far' in the skimpy nature of her costumes and the provocative

(Continued)

(Continued)
nature of her dancing. Her clothing is designed to emphasize her sexuality by displaying or featuring particularly sexual aspects of her body. Similarly, the presentation on her videos and her style of dancing are seemingly designed to explicitly emphasize her sexuality. Twerking is a type of dancing which is sexually provocative, involving thrusting hip movements and a low squatting stance. Much of the Miley fan base is predominantly teenage girls. Parents are concerned that celebrity performers like Miley Cyrus may encourage young girls to become obsessed with their looks and their bodies ('the emulation effect').

Would it be right to describe Miley Cyrus's performances as obscene and, if so, ought they to be restricted in some way? Or would that be an infringement of individual freedom?

Such forms of obscenity, it can be argued, constitute a specific form of harm often described as 'moral harm'. If we decide that a graphic representation is obscene, we are, by definition, suggesting that it is harmful. Of course, to say something is harmful is not necessarily to say that it should be proscribed. For example, consider the case of Miley Cyrus and 'twerking' (see Box 6.5). Elements of her performance could readily be characterized as obscene, given the definition discussed above. She explicitly displays or represents her body or parts of her body as sexually titillating and abstracted from emotion or the human relationship. Twerking, in particular, serves simply to emphasize the bottom in a sexual way. However, even if we accept that elements of her performance may be obscene, it does not necessarily imply that such performances ought to be restricted.

We may blame or morally censure the producers and users of pornography, but we might want to stop short of an outright legal ban. Is the moral harm sufficient to justify legal proscription? This is a major contentious issue; we come again to the point of balancing harms – the harm of the representation versus the harm of censorship. We have already argued that there is no necessary coincidence between acts that are immoral and those we may wish to make illegal. In the case of pornography there is a long history of debate, for example in the UK and the USA, about whether or not sexually explicit material, even when recognized as obscene, ought to be made illegal. In the UK, the Obscene Publications Act (1959) did make sexually explicit material illegal if it is 'taken as a whole, such as to tend to deprave and corrupt persons who are likely, in all circumstances, to read, see or hear the matter contained or embodied in it' (see Box 6.7). The focus in what follows is the key moral arguments about whether or not pornography should be censored.

CONSERVATIVE ARGUMENTS
Argument from the Intrinsic Immorality of Pornography

Moral conservatives tend to view pornography as morally wrong because it leads to a specific kind of harm, a moral harm. To be morally harmed in this sense is to be depraved and corrupted. 'To deprave' a person means to make them morally bad, to pervert and debase them; and to 'corrupt' is to render a person morally unsound or rotten, or to destroy their moral purity or chastity, to pervert them. We must have some moral standard by which we can 'measure' depravity and corruption. What is usually meant by this is that sexual explicitness and pornography fundamentally run counter to a wider moral order, often of a religious kind. The claim is that the morals of individuals will tend to be degraded by exposure to, and use of, pornography. This may mean that pornography tends to encourage behaviour that transgresses certain social or moral precepts. These include, for example, the view that sexuality *ought* to be expressed between married heterosexual men and women within marriage. Such views are usually held on religious grounds. Pornography may promote various forms of promiscuity, sexuality outside marriage, masturbation – forms of behaviour that are regarded as intrinsically immoral – against the moral order, which is somehow set into the very fabric of the universe by a deity or deities. This rests on a certain conception of the function of sexuality – that it is primarily concerned with procreation (Strangroom, 2010, p. 60). This may look to some extent like a consequentialist argument of the type we have become familiar with. But what is important here is that pornography is morally wrong because it encourages individuals to enjoy sexual pleasure as *an end it itself.*

Conservative Consequentialism

Conservatives, as we have seen, tend to be more concerned with the maintenance of moral and social order than with the protection of liberty. For example, in the USA liberal organizations, such as the American Civil Liberties Union (ACLU), have considered pornography on the internet as protected free speech. The ACLU successfully overturned the Communications Decency Act (CDA). The Act, in an effort to regulate the internet, aimed to 'criminalize the "knowing" transmission of "obscene or indecent" messages and pictures to anyone under the age of eighteen, and to prohibit knowingly sending or displaying to a minor any message "that in context, depicts or describes, in terms patently offensive as measured by contemporary community standards, sexual, or excretory or organs"' (Beauchamp, 2001, p. 348). On 26 June 1997, the US Supreme Court, by a unanimous vote, ruled that the CDA was unconstitutional.

For liberals, freedom is the greater value; the curtailment of free speech is to be opposed even in the case where the intention of the censorship is to protect minors. The concern is that the attempt to curtail access to pornography by minors would likely impinge on the rights of adults to free speech. For conservatives, however, liberty must be subject to a moral order.

The organization, Focus on the Family, for example argued:

> Behind the shelter of anonymity, millions of young boys, as well as older men, have viewed pornographic images. Not only can these stolen glances affect a male's ability to relate intimately with other women in the 'real

world,' but in some cases obscene online images, such as bestiality, bondage and child pornography, can create in males a desire to 'act out' in dangerous ways. (Beauchamp, 2001, p. 349)

Here the argument is that the consequences of viewing or reading pornography are morally degrading and have particularly morally bad social consequences. The effect of pornography may be to destabilize marriages, families and 'healthy' intimate relationships between the sexes. This again subverts the (moral) foundations of the social order, leading to social breakdown. On this basis there are, therefore, strong grounds for a stringent censorship and control of pornography. The state must have the right to prevent certain of its citizens from engaging in actions that undermine the social and moral foundations of society and pose a threat to established standards of morality and decency (Strangroom, 2010, p. 60). Such actions include all the stages in the production, distribution and consumption of pornography. However, as Grayling points out, in those jurisdictions with relatively liberal laws on pornography (for example, Holland and the Scandinavian countries) there has been no 'social implosion'. The social problems such countries have are more likely to be related to liberal policies on immigration than on liberal policies on sexuality. From a liberal, consequentialist perspective, if there is no demonstrable social harm, then censorship is illegitimate.

Argument from Offence

Perhaps a weaker, though frequently made, claim is that certain forms of media content should be banned because they are offensive in some way. The opera based on the *Jerry Springer Show*, for example, was criticized by Christian groups on the grounds that it was both offensive and blasphemous. The fact that people are offended by indecency may just not be sufficient to justify restricting free speech. To allow that anything that offended anyone would be grounds for restricting free speech would surely set the bar too low (see Box 6.6). It is necessary to define 'offence' more stringently. For example, Ellis (1998, p. 175) draws an important distinction between (a) offensive nuisances, such as smells, loud noises, assaults on the senses which have physical effects on the body, and (b) offensiveness to the mind, such as nudity. In the latter case, to be offended is simply to have an opinion or attitude that something is indecent. The argument that something should be banned merely because I or some group disapprove of it cannot be acceptable.

However, to be offended may be, in certain circumstances, more than a subjective feeling of disapproval. So, as Cohen-Almagor (2005, p. 22) argues, if the content and manner of a certain speech are designed to inflict psychological offence on a specific target group, then we have here something more than some generalized feeling of disapproval. This, combined with objective circumstances, where the target group is directly and inescapably exposed to that offence, does give us grounds for restricting that freedom of speech. An example here may be the Protestant Orange Order parades in Northern Ireland. These parades are explicitly triumphalist in character, celebrating the victory of the Protestant King William of Orange over the Catholic James II at the Battle of the Boyne in 1690. In the context of intense conflict between the Protestant and Catholic communities in Northern Ireland, and especially before the peace agreements, the parading of the Orange Order in Catholic areas and down Catholic streets clearly constituted an exercise of free speech which was directly threatening to those communities. In such circumstances, the authorities were, and are, justified in restricting that particular exercise of free speech.

LIBERAL ARGUMENTS
The Liberal Case

Mill's 'On Liberty' (1964a), as we saw in Chapter 5, mounts an essentially liberal defence of liberty. Ultimately, the happiness of humankind is best served by the widest possible liberty of the individual. For Mill, defence of the freedom of thought, discussion and expression is a support in the defence of the liberty of the individual more generally. Firstly, following Mill, the liberal might argue that the primary presumption must be that the state has no right to curtail individual freedom to *acquire* and *consume* pornography unless it is about preventing harm to others. Secondly, the state, given the primacy of freedom of thought and belief, has no mandate to police the behaviour of individuals in order to ensure some kind of 'moral rectitude' (Stangroom, 2010, p. 60). The state is not entitled to coerce someone for their own good. The principle of liberty specifically rules this out. Thirdly, we can view the production and distribution of pornography as a form of trade like any other media product. By analogy with free speech, pornographers must have the liberty to find an audience and to distribute their products to that audience. The defence of the liberty of publication and consumption of explicitly sexual material and pornography is that it is an exercise of 'free speech'. When Mill writes about freedom of the press, for example, he is writing about such freedom as 'one of the securities against corrupt or tyrannical government' (Mill, 1964a, p. 78). His concern was with the transparency, accountability and accessibility of the state to the people and ultimately to the individual. This now seems a world away from an assumed freedom to publish pornographic images without restraint. The general liberal argument about freedom of the press seems an inappropriate tool in this context.

6.6 DEFINITION
The offence principle

'Under the Offence Principle, when the content and/or manner of a certain speech is/are designed to cause a psychological offence to a certain target group, and the objective circumstances are such that make the target group inescapably exposed to that offence, then the speech in question has to be restricted.'

Cohen-Almagor (2005, p. 22)

Liberty of Tastes and Pursuits

It seems that the liberal needs to look to other arguments than simply that of the freedom of publication. Does my desire to acquire and consume pornography form part of that 'plan of life' that I may freely choose as a free individual? Mill argues that an essential part of the liberty of the individual is the freedom to frame the plan of our life to suit our own character. We may pursue 'personal objects within the limits consistent with the essential interests of others' (Mill, 1964a, p. 75). The limit of this freedom would be if the production of pornography involved the exploitation or degradation of others. Mill writes:

> desires and impulses are as much a part of a perfect human being as beliefs and restraints: and strong impulses are only perilous when not properly balanced; when one set of aims and inclinations is developed into strength, while others, which ought to co-exist with them, remain weak and inactive. It is not because men's desires are strong that they act ill; it is because their consciences are weak. (Mill, 1964a, p. 68)

Mill presumably would be concerned if these desires and impulses were unbalanced and took an 'abnormal' turn – the extraordinary, the abnormal and the pathological. And in that sense their exceptionality could hardly be the basis for a general case for the corrupting effects of media depictions of violence. The paedophile's obsession with pornographic representations of children is evidence of abnormality rather than the representations being the cause of it. What is striking is that the very oddness of the relationship between beliefs, desires and interests in pathological cases distances them from normal patterns of behaviour (Graham, 1998, pp.55–56).

Pornography as a Violation of Good Manners

Would, then, John Stuart Mill actually have countenanced the suppression of pornography? To the extent that the use of pornography may be an entirely private and self-regarding action, it is clear that he would have opposed censorship. Not because he might have any inclination to think pornography is in any way valuable to the development of truth or the progressive development of the individual, but simply because, in principle, he was in favour, as far as possible, of limiting the intervention of the state in relationship to the liberty of the individual. In addition, he would also have surely considered the consumption of pornography as a 'lower pleasure' concerned with the satisfaction of some of the more basic human appetites. The liberty principle applies to freedom of thought and discussion in the sense of the clash of views, opinions, beliefs, and so on. Pornography as such does not fall into that category of expression. He would not have seen it necessarily as part of a striving for the truth and the progressive development of human beings!

Even if the use or excessive use of pornography was harmful to the well-being of an individual, this alone would not be a sufficient ground for state intervention. Mill (1964a, p. 153) writes: 'Again, there are many acts which, being directly injurious only to the agents themselves, ought not to be legally interdicted.' However, it is quite another matter if such acts have a public face and impact. Mill goes on to argue that certain acts, when done publicly, are 'a violation of good manners' – a rather different principle from the harm principle. It's likely that Mill means that lewd and indecent acts done in public may justifiably be prohibited. The crux is that some acts may not be condemnable or prohibited if done in private but may be censored if done in public (Mill, 1964a, p. 153).

In this sense, on the question of public decency, Mill might tend to line up with the conservative arguments. Let's take the example of sexually explicit YouTube videos where individuals may make public certain kinds of private conduct. These clearly are public and may be obscene and indecent. But rather than harm public morals, it seems that Mill might be more inclined to put these in the category of 'a violation of good manners', and in that sense, as an offence against good manners, may then be construed as a form of harm to others which may warrant prohibition. But this may not be on the grounds of 'harm to public morals', which would be the conservative case. Manners are much more fluid and changeable, and the boundaries of what may be permitted may change.

An Aesthetic Defence

As we noted above, it is possible to make a fundamental distinction between erotic art and pornography. As Blackburn argues, human passion is central to erotic art but is not obscene. If we were to lose this distinction, then much of Western art and Oriental art might be classed as obscene (Blackburn, 2006, p. 258)! One of the frequent differences between liberals and conservatives is the argument over whether a particular work does or does not fall into the category of art with some erotic content or is merely pornographic. Can this distinction be made more than a matter of feeling or personal taste? This kind of debate was at the heart of the trial in both the UK and the USA of D.H. Lawrence's novel *Lady Chatterley's Lover*. The novel had been first published in the 1920s and banned. The ban was reconsidered in the late 1950s and early 1960s. The crux of the argument was whether or not the novel was a work of art (see Box 6.7).

The key to maintaining the difference between aesthetic and pornographic representations of sexuality lies in the way the sexual material was *treated*. The claim in the case of *Lady Chatterley's Lover* was that this was a novel of serious, and indeed moral, intent and the sexually explicit passages were an integral part of achieving its artistic purpose. Can we make the same claim for David Cronenberg's *Crash* (see Box 6.3)? A pornographic novel or film would use sexuality for purposes of mere titillation or sexual arousal. Such depictions would lack literary merit or artistic distinction. What is being suggested here is that claims for artistic status are more than just a matter of instinctive taste or preference and therefore of subjective judgement (for example, Mill's 'higher pleasures'). There are standards by which these distinctions can be made. To illustrate this point, Graham (1998, p. 160) uses the example of a music teacher and a pupil. The job of the teacher is not merely to train the musical abilities of the pupil, but also to educate that pupil's musical taste so that they come to know what is *worth* playing. The key point is that existing preferences are not sovereign; in the realm of art, particularly, it is not simply a question of satisfying pre-existing preferences but of developing new ones to appreciate and enjoy. Graham argues, 'The crucial point to be observed is that the pupil–teacher relationship is one in which it is the informed taste of the teacher, not the natural taste of the pupil, which is sovereign' (Graham, 1998, p. 160). By analogy, a distinction between the pornographic and the aesthetic is reflected in the difference between creating or educating an audience and pandering to an audience.

6.7 A JUDGEMENT CALL
Obscenity, art and *Lady Chatterley's Lover*

Whether or not to remove the ban on D.H. Lawrence's novel, *Lady Chatterley's Lover*, first published in 1928 (and banned!), was a touchstone of changing social attitudes about sexuality in both the United States and the United Kingdom in the 1960s. Very much the same arguments about the novel were deployed on both sides of the Atlantic. Was this an obscene book? If it was an obscene book, then the moral harm would be both to the individual but ultimately to society more generally, and a ban would be justified. In considering this question there was a subtle intertwining of moral, aesthetic and legal judgements. The key distinction, however, is that between explicit representations of sexuality which were obscene and representations which were explicit but could be justified on some other grounds as not obscene. Moreover, could there be representations of sexuality which not only were not obscene but also served some higher aesthetic or moral purpose? In the Lady Chatterley Trial in London, in defending Penguin Books, the publisher, against prosecution under the Obscene Publications Act, and defence witnesses (there were no witnesses for the prosecution) testified to the book's artistic merit, but also to the manifest absurdity of the claim that it could, and did, 'deprave and corrupt' (the legal test of obscenity).The publication of the book was a tacit recognition that the simple act of reading it would not tend to deprave and corrupt the reader. On that basis the argument for harm falls.

Does the claim that a work is a work of art provide sufficient grounds for not restricting it?

FEMINIST ARGUMENTS

So far we have polarized the debate about sexually explicit material and pornography according to liberal and conservative arguments. As Strangroom (2010, p. 132) remarks, the idea that openness about sexual matters or pornography undermines the moral fibre of society appears quaint and rather antiquated. However, such views are still strongly held by some religious believers. The fact that conservative arguments are weak does not automatically mean that the liberals are right. There have been other approaches to arguments about pornography, in particular those emanating from the work of feminists, writers and activists, although feminism presents a far from unified view (Cornell, 2000). Nevertheless, there may be other reasons altogether why pornography, or even a work of art, ought to be prohibited which go beyond liberal and consequentialist thinking (Dupré, 2013, p. 145).

Arguments for Prohibition

Feminist thinkers and activists Catherine MacKinnon and Andrea Dworkin, by no means friends of moral conservatism, in *In Harm's Way: The Pornography Civil Rights Hearings* (1997), have argued for the prohibition of pornography. MacKinnon and Dworkin have redefined pornography as part and parcel of the subordination of women in patriarchal society, and have argued that the practices of pornography should be 'conceptualized as sex-based discrimination' and subject to law (MacKinnon and Dworkin, 1997, p.7).

6.8 EXAMPLE: MacKinnon and Dworkin's characterization of pornography

'We define pornography as the graphic sexually explicit subordination of women through pictures and words that also includes:

i. women are presented dehumanized as sexual objects, things, or commodities; or

ii. women are presented as sexual objects who enjoy humiliation or pain; or

iii. women are presented as sexual objects experiencing sexual pleasure in rape, incest or other sexual assault; or

iv. women are presented as sexual objects tied up, cut up or mutilated or bruised or physically hurt; or

v. women are presented in postures or positions of sexual submission, servility, or display; or

vi. women's body parts – including but not limited to vaginas, breasts, or buttocks – are exhibited such that women are reduced to those parts; or

vii. women are presented being penetrated by objects or animals; or

viii. women are presented in scenarios of degradation, humiliation, injury, torture, shown as filthy or inferior, bleeding, bruised, or hurt in a context that makes these conditions sexual.'

MacKinnon and Dworkin, 1997, p.428

Pornography on these grounds appears both to have harmful consequences and to be intrinsically immoral. It is part of the structure of the male domination and exploitation of women. In other words, it is part of an unjust social order. It presents women in a dehumanized way, constantly subordinated to the desires and fantasies of men (see Box 6.8). It is the case, of course, that the majority of pornography is produced by and for men; it is an industry. MacKinnon and Dworkin's approach in effect treats pornography as a question of equality and hence as a matter of civil rights. If we accept that pornography is part of the machinery of the subordination of women, then pornography becomes a breach of civil rights and hence women must have rights against it (MacKinnon and Dworkin, 1997, pp. 3–24). On these grounds, MacKinnon and Dworkin have been involved in various campaigns to effect legal prohibition in a number of states in the USA.

Problems with a Feminist Approach

The problem with this quasi-civil right approach to pornography is the lack of agreement on the evidence that would support the case that pornography is primarily bound up with the subordination of women. Again, we might agree with MacKinnon and Dworkin in principle, but their argument also requires empirical support. The parallel case was our consideration of the explicit depiction of violence and the likelihood, or otherwise, of emulation effects. The problem is that it is claimed that pornography promotes or, rather more strongly, celebrates rape and battery of women. However, there is no evidence to show that pornography is a causal factor in sexual violence, although there are studies that show other social and psychological factors are evident in the case of sexual violence. If anything, evidence tends to point in the other direction. In countries where the regulations on pornography have been liberalized, such as Denmark, levels of violent crime have tended to diminish (Grayling, 1997, p. 34).

There is a fundamental methodological question to be surmounted here. There is an immense range and variety of sexually explicit material. As Strangroom (2010, p. 133) points out, it is unclear by what method we might be able to demonstrate whether a specific image or word ought to be categorized as pornographic in the sense defined by MacKinnon and Dworkin (1997, pp. 3–36). A more liberal feminism tends to shy away from an implied alliance with conservatives on the question of censorship of pornography. Such censorship is either argued to be illiberal or misplaced. It has been suggested that pornography can widen and enhance women's sexual experience. In this way, pornography can act 'as a counterpoint to traditional [conservative] conceptions of femininity and female sexuality' (Stangroom, 2010, p. 134). This would be the case if women are seen as active (equal) participants rather than subordinate objects.

Grayling imagines the following scenario: ' … if there were sexually explicit material made by happy people who grew rich providing a service to contented clients, it would be on this reasoning unexceptional. If pornography were legal, the likelihood of its being produced in an exploitative way diminishes' (Grayling, 2010, p. 33). His point, of course, is that pornography is objectionable where it depicts women (or anyone!) in an abusive way and where the pornography industry exploits the people who produce it. But the important moral point here is that the moral evils are the abuse and the exploitation and not because of the involvement of sexuality.

CHAPTER REVIEW

This chapter discussed three approaches to the moral judgements of explicit sexuality and pornography. We sought to unpack different lines of reasoning which lie behind a variety of moral views about sexually explicit material and pornography. These included a restrictive, conservative approach; a more expansive liberal approach; and finally, a feminist approach which identified pornography with the subordination of women in society more generally.

We argued that, historically, views about sexuality tend to oscillate between relatively liberal and relatively conservative periods in which attitudes to sexuality were respectively more austere or more open. We also made the point that in the second half of the twentieth century technology has tended to aid and abet a period of liberalization in what has become acceptable to say and display through old and emergent media. We defined pornography as 'obscene representations or display, especially of human sexuality, produced to provide an occasion for fantasy' (Blackburn, 2006, p. 283). We discussed a number of arguments mainly advanced by conservatives which favoured the censorship of sexually explicit and pornographic material. These arguments included the view that pornography tended to deprave and corrupt individuals; that in doing so it constituted a broader threat to the social and moral order of society and that for these reasons should be banned. We also saw that conservatives argue that certain depictions, performances or literary works should be banned because they create offence.

We considered some liberal arguments against prohibition based on Mill's view of the liberty of the individual and the limits that ought to be placed on the powers of the state. Pornography should only be banned if there is demonstrable harm. It was argued that the evidence for social harm seemed to be either equivocal or lacking. But we also questioned whether the argument about censorship of sexually explicit material or pornography was an argument about freedom of speech or publication at all. We could equally see this as a question of 'good manners' or 'decency'. However, even if we were to see it in this light, it would still be the case that we would want to see it as fundamentally a question of the freedom of the individual. A further liberal argument concerned the extent to which some explicit sexual material could be defended against the conservative impulse to censor on grounds of artistic merit.

Feminist approaches to the prohibition of pornography started from very different assumptions from those of the conservative view, although they have been conflated with them. The reasoning behind this feminist view was that pornography was part of the more general machinery of male oppression of women in society. It was part and parcel of a patriarchal subordination of women and ought to be prohibited on those grounds. A feminist definition of pornography saw it as 'the graphic sexually explicit subordination of women through pictures and words'

(MacKinnon and Dworkin, 1997, p. 428). Underlying this view was an idea of social justice. Pornography, to the extent that it subordinated women, denied their equality and hence their civil rights. This looks like an intrinsic moral wrong transcending the claims of a utilitarian, consequentialist approach to the control of representations of sexuality.

FURTHER READING

Dupré, B. (2013) *50 Ethics Ideas You Really Need to Know*. London: Quercus. pp. 144–147. A brief but useful discussion of censorship. See particularly the section on 'Porn wars' and 'Art and the censor'.

Ellis, A. (1998) 'Censorship and the media', in M. Kieran (ed.), *Media Ethics*. London: Routledge, pp.165–177. Discusses arguments on the restriction of free speech and in relationship to blasphemy, profanity, obscenity, indecency and offensiveness.

Gordon, A.D., Kittross, J.M. and Reuss, C. (eds) (1996) *Controversies in Media Ethics*. White Plains, NY: Longman (2nd edn, 1999). See particularly Chapter 10, 'Violence and sexual pornography' (pp. 199–218). This chapter discusses the question of whether or not representations of violence in media content are causative in promoting violence in society more widely. It also presents opposing libertarian and communitarian arguments for and against control and prohibition.

Graham, G. (1998) 'Sex and violence in fact and fiction', in M. Kieran (ed.), *Media Ethics*. London: Routledge. pp.152–164. Analyses arguments relating to censorship and pornography.

Mill, J.S. (1964) 'On Liberty', in A.D. Lindsay (ed.), *John Stuart Mill, Utilitarianism, Liberty and Representative Government*. London: Dent. pp.78–113 (1st edn, 1859). See Chapter II, 'Of the liberty of thought and expression', which is the seminal source for arguments on freedom of speech and freedom of the individual.

Plaisance, P.L. (2009) *Media Ethics: Key Principles for Responsible Practice*. London: Sage. See particularly Chapter 5, 'Harm' (pp. 105–134), for an overview of the meaning and morality of harm in the media.

 ## HOW TO USE THIS ARTICLE

Go to https://study.sagepub.com/horner to access the following free journal article:

Hasinoff, A.A. (2013) 'Sexting as media production: rethinking social media and sexuality', *New Media and Society*, 15(4): 449–465.

Use this paper to explore an alternative take on sexting. The author argues that many current approaches to sexting are ineffective and unjust for a number of reasons. Authorities go wrong in blaming the victims of nonconsensual sexting, use inappropriate and harsh child pornography laws against minors and give teenagers the unrealistic advice to simply abstain. The paper particularly focuses on girls' use of social media and concerns about their use of these to create and share sexual content. The author argues that viewing sexting as a form of media production creates the possibility of shifting the research focus onto the opportunities it provides as well as the risks. Consensual sexting should be seen as a creative act of media authorship. This may give rise to a better understanding of those who create media content, of sexual discrimination, of the nature of consent and of the need for online privacy.

PART III
OBLIGATIONS

7
TRUTH

In previous chapters we have looked at Media Ethics through the lens of consequentialism, the view that an action or a policy is right or wrong depending on its effects or outcomes. If, on balance, the good consequences of our actions outweigh the bad consequences, all things considered, then that action or policy is the morally right one. This presupposes we have an ultimate value or goal which defines what is good. In the case of utilitarianism the idea of individual and collective pleasure, happiness or welfare is 'the good'. Thus when confronted by situations in which moral choices are demanded, in our case, media practitioners or policy makers should make decisions which maximize happiness. In this chapter I want to focus on a different sort of moral theory that puts obligation at the centre of moral judgement. In this context, we will pay particular attention to truth-telling as a fundamental duty of the media and media practitioners.

This alternative approach is referred to as 'deontological ethics'. On this view, in contrast to consequentialism, actions are not justified by their consequences or effects, but by whether or not they are in accordance with moral norms or laws which define particular duties. Deciding what to do, whether an action is right or wrong, depends on whether or not it conforms to what in any particular situation you are obligated to do. (Many actions, or course, may be just neutral and have no moral significance.) What follows from a deontological view of morality is that we, as moral agents, are bound by a duty to obey a moral norm and do what is right. And this 'doing what is right' is largely *irrespective* of consequences. A deontological approach is suggestive of a much more dramatic and perhaps familiar experience of moral choice, in which we experience conflicts between our inclinations (desires) and our knowledge of what we *ought* to do. For example, although a journalist may obtain a good story by deception, our duty is to tell the truth; lying is intrinsically wrong and therefore we ought not to practise deception. We may have to forego a good story in order to do the right thing. From a deontological perspective, this is not an act of calculation, or balancing one good against another, but of an absolute imperative.

In the next section we explore contemporary criticisms of journalistic practice in relationship to accurate, balanced and objective reporting. The award-winning journalist Nick Davies (b. 1953) has labelled the widespread failure of print and broadcast news media to maintain a high standard of news reporting as 'flat earth news'. Davies argues that truth-telling must be fundamental to the practice of news reporting. His argument leads us into a discussion of a deontological approach to ethics in general and to truth-telling in particular. We analyse the dominant and widely influential moral theory of Immanuel Kant (1724–1804). Kant sets out a view of morality that is in opposition to that of consequentialism in its insistence on the performance of our moral duties irrespective of particular consequences. We discuss Kant's categorical imperative, 'the supreme principle of morality', and its application as a test of the morality of the maxims we generate to guide our moral decision making. Media practitioners frequently justify apparently immoral (and sometimes illegal) actions on the grounds that they are necessary to reach a 'higher truth', to expose corruption or call power to account. Finally, we explore a duty-based response to the question 'Is it ever right to tell a lie for some perceived greater good?'

THREATS TO TRUTHFULNESS

Nick Davies, in *Flat Earth News* (2009), presents a searing critique of contemporary journalistic practices for promoting a culture tending to produce falsehoods, distortion and propaganda rather than truth. Davies, as a renowned investigative journalist, is in a good position to know. (Davies has won awards as Journalist of the Year, Reporter of the Year and Feature Writer of the Year.) In answering the question 'What is reporting for?', he defines the work of journalists as fundamentally about truth-telling:

> You could argue that every profession has its defining value. For carpenters, it might be accuracy: a carpenter who isn't accurate shouldn't be a carpenter. For diplomats, it might be loyalty: they can lie and spy and cheat and pull all sorts of dirty tricks, and as long as they are loyal to their government, they are doing their job. For journalists the defining value is honesty – the attempt to tell the truth. That is our primary purpose. All that we do – and all that is said about us – must flow from the single source of truth-telling. (Davies, 2009, p. 12)

Davies believes current journalistic practices represent a fundamental threat to truth-telling through the production and reproduction of what he calls 'flat earth news' in the press and broadcast media. He defines flat earth news in this way: 'A story appears to be true. It is widely accepted as true. It becomes heresy to suggest that it is not true – even if it is riddled with falsehood, distortion and propaganda' (Davies, 2009, p. 12). Davies goes on to show that there is, in effect, a constant subversion of the maxim to tell the truth in favour of a set of other self-serving maxims or 'rules of production' (Davies, 2009, pp. 109–154). These 'rules of production' include, for example, 'run cheap stories', 'go with the moral panic', 'increase revenue by giving them what they want'. This amounts to a collapse in global news-gathering and truth-telling. Davies charges that some, but by no means all, journalists are failing to discriminate between truths and falsehoods in stories. Fundamental assumptions go unquestioned and unresearched. A paradigm case, according to Davies, was the coverage of the so-called 'Millennium Bug' (see Box 7.1). He argues that journalists had simply failed to find out the truth of the matter and had been content to recycle and elaborate other similar accounts. Journalists had failed to carry through on a fundamental obligation to gather and test information and question key assumptions.

7.1 A JUDGEMENT CALL
The Millennium Bug story – a case of 'flat earth news'?

In the run-up to the year 2000 there was a widely held belief that major computer systems would be unable to deal with the date change from 1999 to 2000. This story had begun to circulate in the early 1990s, originating with a brief report in the *Financial Post* (May 1993, p. 37) in Toronto, Canada. It originated from a technology consultant, Peter de Jager, and appeared under the headline 'Turn of century poses a computer problem'. The story gathered momentum throughout the decade to the extent that as the millennium approached the press and broadcast media ran increasingly apocalyptic stories about the possible end of civilization, of communication systems collapsing, of aeroplanes falling from the skies, of records systems of all types, from banking records to government databases, ceasing to function, and so.

Once this story got going, it spread in a viral way with little or no close scrutiny of its basic assumptions. Governments and major corporations were swept up and spent many billions of dollars on supposedly checking and rectifying systems. In the event, the threatened apocalypse did not materialize; nothing happened! Now this might have been because remedial action was taken, but there appeared to be no difference in consequences for those countries that had spent many millions on 'solving' the problem and those that had not. And yet this had been a major news story in which the vast majority of reports had promulgated the idea of disaster.

The original speculations of some computer specialists suggested there may be a problem, but they simply did not know the scope of the problem or how serious it was actually going to be. However, some specialists did maintain that there was a set of limiting factors which would be likely to vastly reduce the impact of the supposed problem. For example, 'they knew that the problem would occur only in computers which had internal clocks (most desktop computers do, but most "embedded systems", on which big organizations rely, don't), but only if those clocks calculated time by using a calendar rather than by simply

(Continued)

(Continued)

measuring the gap between two dates, and only if those calendars use only two digits to register the years, rather than four, and only if the computer was being used for programs which had to calculate time across the boundary between 1999 and 2000' (Davies, 2009, pp. 24–25). In addition to these limiting factors, many systems, even before the millennium, had been making calculations across the 99/00 boundary without problems. For example, such calculations were made by information systems dealing with pensions, life insurance, mortgages and similar arrangements which involved long-term calculations. Such problems as had already arisen had been dealt with relatively easily.

What was the fundamental moral failure in the reporting of this story?

Source: Davies (2009, pp. 9–45)

What Davies is suggesting is that the moral imperative to tell the truth is not a matter of calculation but a fundamental moral duty. This is essentially a deontological approach: the response to the question 'What is the right thing to do?' must be decided by reference to what my obligations are. A deontological view of ethics is reflected in, for example, journalistic ethical codes in that they lay out a set of professional obligations. For example, the Society of Professional Journalists' Code of Ethics in America directs its members to 'Seek truth and report it. Journalists should be honest, fair, and courageous in gathering reporting, and interpreting information' (quoted in Plaisance, 2009, p. 30). Similar injunctions may be found in the code of the British National Union of Journalists. Now this way of thinking about morality is a particular kind of moral reasoning. Codes of ethics set up norms and rules which seek to determine the duties of media practitioners. 'Doing the right thing' means recognizing a duty to follow and obey the rules. But why should this be the case and what is the test for a true and valid moral rule?

A DEONTOLOGICAL PERSPECTIVE

Notions of duty are not simply restricted to what may or may not appear in a code of practice; they are more deeply felt and embedded in human relationships. The scenario in Box 7.2 illustrates the limitations of a consequentialist approach to ethics and exemplifies the idea of making a moral choice on the basis of a notion of duty.

7.2 A JUDGEMENT CALL
Is it always morally right to look at your own photographs?

'Venus Titian was 18 when she allowed her then boyfriend, Milo Reuben, to take photographs of her naked. Her decision was not coerced in any way, and the photographs were "artistic" in style rather than pornographic. A few years later, Venus and Milo split up, and Milo offered to destroy the photographs. Venus said she was happy for him to keep them on condition that he never showed them to anyone else. He agreed, and they went their separate ways.

Twenty years later, Venus is now a minor celebrity, about to appear on a sheep-pursuit reality show, *I'm a Celebrity Shepherd*. Milo still has the photographs, but has started to worry that there is some moral wrong in his looking at them. He would never show them to anyone else, and has no particular reason to think that the celebrity Venus would object (though given her public profile he knows that this is a possibility). Nevertheless, he still wonders whether he ought to destroy them. He can't help but think that it might be immoral for a man in his forties to be looking at naked photos of an ex-girlfriend that were taken 20 years previously when she was only 18.'

Would Milo be wrong to look at the photographs? What would you do in Milo's situation? How would making the photographs publicly available alter the moral quality of the situation?

Strangroom (2010, p. 14)

The scenario in Box 7.2 is not so fanciful given the contemporary ubiquity of our ability to take and reproduce digital photographs. Imaginary though the situation is, it does seem genuinely to conjure up a situation of moral choice. Milo's experience is a moral one in that he needs to decide on the right action to take. He can look at the pictures or destroy them. However, the story points up some of the inadequacies of a consequentialist view of morality. It's not clear that what Milo should do can be resolved by weighing consequences in that his moral concern is not with any immediately tangible effects. Looking at the photographs in private, for example, would not seem to produce any harm. Nevertheless, he experiences this position and his possible actions as having a moral dimension. He has a sense that looking at the photographs now would be morally wrong; he feels he has a duty not to look at them and maybe a duty to destroy them. A second problem in trying to look at this scenario from a utilitarian point of view is that neither Milo nor Venus could have made a calculation as to the relative good or harm of taking the photographs in the first place. They lacked crucial information, they could not know the future, they did not know that they would go their separate ways and they did not know what trajectories their careers would take. More particularly for Venus, when she consented to the photographs the consent could not really be characterized as 'informed consent' because she couldn't know the future course of events. Predicting consequences is a fundamental problem for consequentialist theories. Venus could not really know when she gave her consent what her feelings would be 20 years later when a 40-year-old man is looking at pictures of her naked body. If through some miraculous time travel she could have met Milo as his middle-aged self, when she originally gave her consent for the pictures not to be destroyed she might have chosen differently (Strangroom, 2010, p. 72).

At least some of Milo's sense of moral unease might stem from the realization that Venus was simply not in a position to have given informed consent in the first place. The evidence of consent now looks very different 25 years on and given how things turn out. We can never know certainly that an action or a policy is right or wrong by reference to *expected* consequences. We may never have enough evidence about what may happen and what evidence we have is always subject to interpretation. The great German philosopher Immanuel Kant (1724–1804) argued that the origin of morals cannot lie in the shifting sands of the empirical world, in the data interpreted by our senses. The starting point for morality must lie in our individual experience of moral obligation, although, as we will see, this is definitely not to relegate morality to the realm of the subjective (see Box 7.3). The experience of moral obligation is that very sense that when confronted with certain situations and choices (as in Milo's case) there is something we *ought* to do. As Mel Thompson puts it, ' … you do not find out first what is "right" and then decide you ought to do it; rather, that which you feel you ought to do is what you mean by right' (Thompson, 2000, p. 83).

7.3 DEFINITION
Deontological ethics

Deontological is derived from a Greek root that means 'obligation' or 'duty'; for deontologists, ideas of 'duty' and 'the moral law' are fundamental. In deontological approaches to moral decision making, the rightness of an action is determined by whether or not you have a duty, a moral obligation. Within this framework the consequences of actions are at best secondary, if not irrelevant. In other words, duty determines what is permissible and what is not permissible – the central question of ethics. Confronted by a situation which presents an ethical decision, the relevant question from a deontological point of view is 'What action am I morally obliged to take or desist from?'

THE SUPREME PRINCIPLE OF MORALITY
Kant and Moral Experience

Kant is generally recognized to have been the key figure in developing a systematic basis for deontological ethics. However, it is important to stress at that outset that in spite of the complexity of his thinking and the obscurity sometimes of his language, Kant was not inventing a set of new moral rules. His aim was to give an account of our everyday, ordinary moral concepts, for example keeping promises, not stealing, telling the truth, not committing murder, respecting other people, etc. His aim was to show that acting morally is to be explained as acting out of respect for the moral law. In acting out of respect for the moral law, doing our duty, we ought to act, to do what is right, again, not on the basis of the consequences. We simply have an absolute duty to tell the truth, keep our promises, and so on. The drama of our moral experience – and this seems at least intuitively right – is that of a constant struggle between our inclinations to satisfy our desires, to gain rewards, esteem, happiness, and the sense of doing what we ought to do.

Can Happiness Really be the Basis of Morality?

Kant firmly rejects happiness, pleasure, desire, or interests as foundational values for morality. Fundamental difficulties arise in trying to derive reliable maxims from unclear and often inconsistent goals. Firstly, there is a problem of defining solid and consistent notions of happiness. The satisfaction of one desire often means the frustration of other desires (opportunity costs), wants tend to multiply, and our inability to devise a 'calculus of satisfaction' demonstrates how recalcitrant desires can be. Secondly, different individuals (communities) manifest different desires. Conflict arises through the failure to agree on ends. Thirdly, obstacles to happiness are varied and many are social and natural. Fourthly, no matter how well we develop our skills and talents, 'nature' is simply not under control, and their fulfilment may in large part depend on accident. Changing circumstances may then falsify earlier maxims. Kant's conclusion is that there is no principle for deciding how to achieve lasting happiness in this world (Kant, 1965, pp. 41–43; Sullivan, 1997, pp. 35ff). This, therefore, disqualifies happiness as the possible basis for any moral system:

> If it were only equally easy to give a definite conception of happiness, the imperatives of prudence correspond exactly with those of skill, and would likewise be analytical. ... But, unfortunately, the notion of happiness is so indefinite that although every man wishes to attain it, yet he never can say definitely and consistently what it is that he really wishes and wills. (Kant, 1965, p. 41)

Morality is rooted in obeying 'the moral law' rather than calculating the 'best' outcomes of our actions. Similarly, morality is not rooted in traditional virtues, such as courage, nor in sentiment, that is, what we may feel. How we feel, particular personal virtues, are not central to moral evaluation. What really matters is that we do our duty and we can only know what that is, according to Kant, through Reason.

Kant presents the foundations of his moral system in the fearsomely entitled *Fundamental Principles of the Metaphysic of Ethics* (1965, first published in 1785). It is in this work that Kant expounds what became his most famous principle: 'the Categorical Imperative'. He describes this as 'the supreme principle of morality'. (He is not, of course, suggesting that we everywhere and always consult this principle in making our moral decisions, but what he is doing is providing the justification for why we ought to put duty at the centre of our moral life.) Kant undertakes to show that this principle, and its derivatives, underpins our everyday morality. Moral duties have 'a categorical form': 'Do this' or 'Don't do this'. They are prescriptive and universal. The basic form of the categorical imperative is 'I ought never to act in such a way that I could not also will that my maxim should be a universal law' (quoted in Sullivan, 1997, p. 29).

7.4 DEFINITIONS
Types of duty according to Kant

Perfect duties are the kinds of duties that others have a corresponding right to expect me to perform. For example, I have a perfect duty not to lie to people. Each and every person has a right not to be lied to by me.

Imperfect duties are the kinds of duties that I must perform but there is not some identifiable group or person to whom they must be performed and with a right to expect me to do so. For example, I ought to abide by the rules of my profession but I have some choice about how these should be followed in particular circumstances.

A Good Will

Kant germinates his system from the idea that a 'Good Will' is the only thing that is good in itself. He writes that:

> Nothing can possibly be conceived in the world, or even out of it, which can be called good without qualification, except a Good Will. Intelligence, wit, judgement, and the other talents of the mind, however they may be named, or courage, resolution, perseverance, as qualities of temperament, are undoubtedly good and desirable in many respects; but these gifts of nature may also become extremely bad and mischievous if the will which is to make use of them, and which, therefore, constitutes what is called character, is not good. (Kant, 1965, p. 10)

For Kant, the test of the moral worth (whether it is praiseworthy or blameworthy) of an action resides in our *intention* when we undertook it, regardless of whether or not the action succeeds in what we set out to achieve. Why is this plausible? We can imagine two kinds of cases. In the first case, I believe my moral duty is X and do the appropriate action Y. Things turn out badly but through no fault of my own. I am therefore, according to Kant, not blameworthy in this case. In the second case, I aim to do Z, which is the breach of a moral rule. In spite of bad intentions, things turn out well. But even if things turn out well by accident, we would still think, knowing the bad intent, that my action is not morally worthy. These intuitive assessments, common-sense judgements, would tend to show that we believe intentions to really count from a moral point of view – whatever the consequences. What is the right intention? For Kant to answer this question we must look to Reason.

Maxims

Kant argues that generally when we act we do so according to some rule or principle. These (subjective) rules of conduct he calls 'maxims'. The maxim is the reason for acting. Now, there is a distinction between acting according to a rule and acting by (consciously) following a rule. A maxim should be understood more often in the former sense rather than the latter. In other words, I don't constantly bring to mind specific rules. For example, a hedonist, someone who sees pleasure as the main goal in life, acts according to the maxim 'Always act to increase your pleasure'. A greedy person is acting according to the maxim 'Always act to maximize your wealth'. But these maxims are essentially subjective. However, when I come to justify my reasons for acting, I may then have to lay bare the maxim or rule which underpins my action. For example, those journalists who engaged in phone hacking were effectively acting on some maxim like 'Always steal personal information when it helps to get a story'. We will see why such maxims cannot be justified as moral principles.

Kant believes that because we are 'rational agents' reason determines that we have certain moral duties. Having a morally good intention is to act according to the motive of duty. These duties are categorical rather than hypothetical, and therefore apply irrespective of whatever consequences might follow from their performance. For example, with the duty not to tell lies, the imperative not to tell lies is categorical. What does Kant mean by this?

Why a 'Categorical Imperative'?

Grammatically, in the imperative mood, we command or advise some action or entreat someone to do the action. Mood is the form assumed by a verb to show the mode or manner in which the action denoted by the verb is represented. For Kant, therefore, an ethical system takes the form of a set of rules that are, in effect, a set of commands (imperatives). But not all commands are of the same type. Practical reasoning (that is, reasoning to decide what we ought to do) comprises both categorical and hypothetical imperatives. A hypothetical imperative is a guide or instruction as to what to do *if* you want to achieve some specific goal. It is instrumental. If you want to achieve Z, do A. For example, if you want to avoid being sued for breach of copyright, make sure you have the required permissions to use someone else's work (see Box 7.5).

7.5 DEFINITIONS
Types of Imperative

A hypothetical imperative takes the form: 'If you want to achieve X, do Y'. For example, 'If you want to be celebrity, appear on *Big Brother*'; 'If you want to increase the circulation of your newspaper, print more sensational stories'. It is conditional, therefore, on the end to be achieved.

A categorical imperative takes the form: 'You should do Y'. It commands absolutely, having no conditions attached to it. For example, 'You should report truthfully'. It is unconditional and without exception. Kant believed that moral rules must be of this type or they would not be strictly 'moral' rules; they would merely be rules to some other end.

Whether or not we act on a hypothetical imperative depends on what we want to achieve. If I take the view that all information should be free for anyone to use, I might ignore intellectual property rights altogether and just copy whatever I want – images, text, music etc. (We know that in fact unauthorized copying is widespread.) In contrast, a categorical imperative, simply formulated, just says 'Do A!' For Kant, all genuine moral principles are of this form. They are, in effect, categorical commands. So, for example, the categorical imperative is that 'Phone hacking is wrong' and not 'Don't hack into others phones because you may be found out and held to account'. All genuine moral imperatives instruct us in what we *ought* to do irrespective of the outcome or consequences we might in fact desire.

The Test of Universalizability

But how do we know what our moral duties really are? Kant argues that we can test whether or not a maxim we might adopt is hypothetical or categorical by using the test of one fundamental categorical imperative: 'Act only on that maxim whereby thou canst at the same time will that it should become a universal law' (Kant, 1965, p. 46). The categorical imperative is not in itself a new moral rule. For Kant, it is 'purely a formal and universal norm for the moral acceptability of possible policies' (Sullivan, 1997, p. 33). It is this principle which underpins what it means for our normal, everyday judgements to be genuinely moral judgements. In effect, moral judgements are both prescriptive – they tell us what we ought to do – and universal – they apply to everyone. I can't rationally adopt a maxim which is both prescriptive (moral) but true only for me. If those judgements don't conform to the categorical imperative, then they are not moral judgements in the true sense. They remain subjective maxims. In the *Metaphysic of Ethics*, Kant (1965) shows just why the duty to keep our promises, to tell the truth, not to commit suicide, and so forth is a genuine moral duty to be performed *absolutely*.

Logically, reason requires that, like laws of nature, the laws of morality must apply universally. Put simply, a law of nature would not be a law if it didn't apply uniformly and universally; that's just what it means to say Newton's laws of motion are natural laws. Kant thought that for an action to be moral, the underlying principle on which you act must be *universalizable*. It must apply to everyone and be a maxim that everyone can adopt. This seems intuitively plausible. We tend to believe anyway that genuine moral principles apply not only to ourselves or some particular group. They apply to everyone equally. Think here about slavery; it would be puzzling to say that before the emancipation of slaves in the USA it was morally right to enslave people. When we claim that it's a moral duty not to enslave people we are implying at any time and any place and for anyone. (See the discussion on Cultural Relativism in Chapter 1.)

Let's apply Kant's test. Suppose, as an investigative journalist, I adopt the maxim 'Always lie when it suits me'. I do not have a moral duty to tell the truth. But if everyone acted on this maxim and lied whenever it suited them, there would be no point in lying because no one would believe what anyone said. There could be no expectation at any time that we were being told the truth. Lying can only be effective if most people are honest most of the time. It fails the universalizability test. In contrast, 'Always tell the truth' passes the test. It's a maxim we can all adopt. If we adopted that maxim 'Always lie', this would in fact obliterate the concepts of truthful and lying. Lying is parasitic on the idea of truth-telling. A similar analysis can be applied to show why Nick Davies is right in his characterization that the 'rules of production' cannot be moral maxims for journalists to follow. For example, suppose we consider his Rule Nine, 'Go with the moral panic', that is, concentrate on running stories that tap into and reinforce in times of crisis the emotional state of the public (Davies, 2009, p. 142). You can't adopt this as a maxim without leading to a contradiction which undermines the very notion of reporting. You can't, logically, adopt a maxim like Rule Nine, which means that whenever you report anything, you don't give a truthful and balanced account, but set out simply to exaggerate and exacerbate the mood of your readers. This leads to a self-contradiction – rendering the very idea of reporting null. No one would have grounds for believing any reports that were made because they may very well be unreliable. If a source is untrustworthy in this way, who wants to listen?

In these cases, we are not talking about simply being mistaken, but about a deliberate intention to lie. Of course, if journalists are truly prevented from getting at the truth (that is, they genuinely have no choice in the matter), then they cannot be morally culpable. We can be held to be morally culpable only if we are able to tell the truth, as far as we can ascertain it, but then don't. Lying is characterized by 'the intention to mislead' (Bok, 1980, p. 80). I might inadvertently mislead you – there may be mistakes in this text – but if I haven't deliberately set out to mislead you, then I'm not lying. I might be guilty of other failings, such as laziness or inattention, but I would not have lied. Davies' charge is that journalists are culpable if they remain wilfully ignorant. In other words, what most of his 'Rules of Production' represent are avoidance strategies for not actually finding out the truth and publishing it. They are avoidance strategies which put the interests (usually profits) of the corporation or the individual journalists ahead of those of the public. It is clear that Davies' (ironically intended) rules of production would fail Kant's categorical imperative test. They couldn't be adopted as universal rules without falling into contradiction (see Box 7.6).

7.6 EXAMPLE: A thought experiment: On the necessarily universal nature of moral concepts

'Imagine a world in which you had no way of telling the time except by asking other people. In this world, other people (who *perhaps* know the time) answer at random, sometimes telling you the truth, sometimes telling you what they think *you* want to hear, and sometimes telling you what *they* want you to believe. In such a

(Continued)

(Continued)

world, you could never find out for certain what the time was. I think you would very soon give up asking! Now imagine if all information and all media channels operated on that basis. Communication, in the form of information-giving, would simply stop happening. There would be no point to it. Or it might be some sort of game, but it would not serve the purpose we usually think information-giving has, which is to change our responses to the world around us.'

Boyne (2008b)

Moral Character

In our moral life we face two types of challenge. The first type of challenge is to decide just what are the right moral rules or policies to follow. The second type of challenge is having the moral strength to observe and act upon the right moral rules (Sullivan, 1997, p. 29). We are always exposed to the tension of knowing what we *ought* to do and the temptation to take the often easier option of not acting morally. We often find it easier to lie rather than tell the truth and face the consequences. For Kant, to act morally is to act out of 'reverence' for the moral law. Our task in our moral lives is to cultivate that reverence and act upon it. This is true of our everyday lives as much as for our professional lives. Moral character is based on a disposition to dutifulness; the formulation of subjective maxims which express, and are in line with, universal principles. What determines the morality or otherwise of an action are not its consequences but the intention, the maxim, which is the general principle underlying the action ... if it is in alignment with the categorical imperative as a supreme test of moral principle:

> [A]n action done from duty derives its moral worth not from the purpose which is to be attained by it, but from the maxim by which it is determined, and therefore does not depend on the realisation of the object of the action, but merely on the principle of volition. (Kant, 1965, pp. 18–19)

It is your intention that counts. Thus to be a conscientious media professional must be to cultivate a disposition to dutifulness. To have a moral character is to act always out of a sense of duty and in doing so cultivate 'a good will', since we know that the only truly good thing is a good or pure will. Even if my actions fail, for example, I've written a truthful story but my newspaper won't print it, I will have done my duty and therefore acted morally.

IS LYING EVER PERMISSIBLE?

Kant's doctrine is criticized for being far too rigorous and impractical (Thompson, 2000, p. 92). Is he really saying that we can never have moral justification for telling a lie? Are there no motives or grounds which would support some deception for beneficial ends?

Can We Trade off Truth against Lies?

We are tempted to believe that in order to achieve a good end I may be permitted to break a few rules along the way. We can judge whether or not a lie is justified by balancing the relative harms and goods that may be caused by either telling the truth or telling a lie, which is a consequentialist approach. I may have a range of motives to lie and deceive. As a journalist, I may lie to protect my sources, I may lie in order to expose corruption, I may tell a relatively harmless (white) lie in order to dramatize a story, and so on. This certainly seems to have been the culture at the now defunct *News of the World*, as revealed by Lord Justice Leveson's Inquiry.

7.7 A JUDGEMENT CALL
Lying for a good purpose

Suppose I'm an investigative reporter and I am investigating possible corruption at a high level in some lucrative international sport. Now, I might pose as a wealthy gambler who wants to bribe a sportsman to do something at a certain stage in a game. I meet with the sportsman and offer money while secretly filming. Clearly, I am lying in the sense that I'm not who I claim to be. The moral reasoning here is consequentialist; I justify the breach of the rule because it brings about good consequences. By lying I can expose corruption and help to clean up the sport and, ultimately, this would be to the general good. Remember that, for a consequentialist, the test of a moral action is 'the greatest happiness of the greatest number' and in that context there are no absolute rules. My action is a good one for, if I'm successful, then I will expose wrong-doing, which will be in the public interest (defined as the greatest good of the greatest number), helping to rid the world of sport of corruption. But of course my motives are not entirely unmixed. I also want a good story and I want to improve the circulation of my newspaper. In that sense, I have also a duty to satisfy my employer.

Is lying justified in this case?

Even where corruption may be exposed, as in the case outlined in Box 7.7, Kant would always find lying unacceptable. Firstly, for reasons we have already discussed, our moral duty is not to tell lies and this is an absolute, categorical moral duty. I can't simply tell the truth when it suits me and tell lies when it suits me. This, according to the first formula, leads to a logical contradiction. It fails this formal test. Secondly, by setting up the pretend scenario I am using the victim of my 'scam' purely instrumentally. By using a trick, I am using the person as purely an object, a means to an end, to get what I want. To lie is also to treat someone instrumentally; it is a failure to respect their dignity as a centre of moral agency themselves. This respect is due to the wrong-doer as much as to the person of good character. The fact that I claim I might achieve a good end is not the point, for what

I do in constructing my web of pretence is to deny respect to my target by denying his status as a free and rational agent. The alternative is to confront the sportsman honestly, with whatever information I might have. This course of action may be the less effective but, from a Kantian point of view, effectiveness is not the issue. What is at issue is conformity with the moral law.

'On a Supposed Right to Tell Lies from Benevolent Motives'

But the absolute prohibition on lying that Kant advocates again seems much too rigorous. Surely a lie that is told from good intentions must be morally acceptable? We are all probably, at some time or another, 'guilty' of using a 'white lie', but for a good motive – to avoid hurting some one's feelings. More significantly, in the public realm a deception which is ultimately in 'the public interest' would seem to be a reasonable justification. Critics pursued this line of argument even during Kant's lifetime. In 1797, the French philosopher Benjamin Constant criticized Kant's absolutism. Kant responded in a famous paper entitled: 'On a supposed right to tell lies from benevolent motives' (Kant, 1923).

At the centre of the discussion was a hypothetical case. Suppose a killer comes to your door in pursuit of your friend to murder him. You are hiding your friend. The killer confronts you and demands to know where your friend is. A natural response in such a situation would be to lie and save your friend. Benjamin Constant's reasoning was that where there are no rights, there can be no duties. You only ought to tell the truth to those who have a right to it. No one who is going to commit harm can claim a right to the truth. Certainly, you can have no duty to tell the truth to someone who is intent on murdering your friend. But Kant was adamantly absolutist. Even in the case where my telling the truth to the murderer may lead to my friend's death, my duty is, nevertheless, to tell the truth. Why did he think this? Remember, always in moral reasoning, the purity of the intention, acting out of duty for duty's sake (the good will), is key rather than consequences.

Kant has three objections to Constant's arguments. Firstly, in responding to the proposed maxim that 'It is a duty to speak the truth, but only to him who has the right to the truth' Kant thinks the meaning of this is obscure but, in so far as it means anything, it must be wrong. This is because the truth is just not something which is a (subjective) possession, the right to which can only be granted to one; truth is a universal property. This is, of course, the implication of the categorical imperative. Secondly, he argues that a falsehood for altruistic reasons is not a wrong with regard to the particular culprit in the case, the potential killer; it is a wrong to humanity in general. It subverts the very basis of all duties in the sense of a social contract between all members of society. In the case under discussion, if I tell the truth I can be sure that I have done my duty and am not responsible for the consequences that follow. If I lie and my friend escapes through a window but is caught and killed by the murderer, I would then in some sense be responsible because I lied. Thirdly, Kant argues that to lie is to be unjust; it is an infringement of the principle of justice. It must be intrinsically unfair to lie (Kant, 1923, p. 365).

Table 7.1 Summary: variant formulations of Kant's categorical imperative

Basic Formula	Instruction	Brief explanation
I The Formula of Universal Law; the supreme principle of morality	'Act only on that maxim whereby you can at the same time will that it should become a universal law.'	The general conditions (or test) which a moral rule must meet; a formal and universal norm for the moral acceptability of possible moral actions and policies.
Variant Formulations		
Ia The Formula of the Law of Nature	'Act as if the maxim of your action were to become by your will a universal law of nature.'	This asks us to imagine the question for any moral rule (maxim) 'What would happen if everyone refused to do it?' For example, if everyone was prepared to disobey the rule to tell the truth.
II The Formula of Respect for the Dignity of Persons; the end in itself	'Act so that you treat humanity, whether in your own person or that of any other, always as an end and never as a means only.'	Whereas Formula I forbids us to discriminate between persons in an arbitrary or unfair way, this instruction enjoins us to respect each person as such. Every person is an end in themself in a twofold sense. They have their purposes (desires) and are also moral agents (rational beings).
III The Formula of Autonomy	'So act that your will can regard itself at the same time as making universal law through its maxim.'	This means that 'a rational will' (of a moral agent, a rational being) in effect makes or gives itself laws which it itself obeys and this constitutes its autonomy. We are all in that sense moral legislators.
IIIa The Formula of Legislation for a Moral Community	'So act as if you were always through your maxims a law-making member of a universal Kingdom of Ends.'	The most comprehensive of the formulations in that it brings together the form (universal law) and the content (ends in themselves) of moral action. 'The kingdom of ends' is the whole or system constituting everything humanity ought to seek.

Sources: Kant (1965, pp. 20–38); Paton (1971, p. 129); Sullivan (1997, pp. 28–45)

CHAPTER REVIEW

In this chapter we have contrasted a picture of moral decision making derived from consequentialist principles with one derived from deontological ethical thinking. For the consequentialist, reaching a decision is about weighing the effects of the different options; the key question is 'What consequences will my decision have?' On balance, the right action or policy must be the one, all things considered, of which we can say the good consequences outweigh the bad consequences. A picture of moral decision making from a deontological perspective is quite different. The key question when confronted by a moral choice is 'What is my duty in this situation?' In the consequentialist picture it is the effects that count, while for the deontologist it is the purity of the intention to do one's duty. The consequentialist is taken up with issues of calculation and balance, the deontologist with those of moral law and duty. Kant presents us with a drama of moral experience in which our inclinations or desires are in constant conflict with our rational appreciation of the need to fulfil our responsibilities, whether doing so is in our interests or not. The moral life on this account is one in which we may frequently have to make difficult choices.

But how do we know what our moral duties really are? Kant argues that we can test whether or not a maxim we might adopt is genuinely a moral one or not by using the test of one fundamental categorical imperative: 'Act only on that maxim whereby thou canst at the same time will that it should become a universal law' (Kant, 1965, p. 46). This 'categorical imperative' is not in itself a new moral rule. For Kant, it is ' purely a formal and universal norm for the moral acceptability of possible policies' (Sullivan, 1997, p. 33). It is this principle which underpins what it means for our normal, everyday judgements to be genuinely moral judgements. In effect, moral judgements are both prescriptive – they tell us what we ought to do – and universal – they apply to everyone. I can't rationally adopt a maxim which is both prescriptive (moral) but true only for me. Table 7.1 gives a summary of Kant's various and related formulations of his fundamental moral principle and their scope.

We have been concerned in this chapter with the question of telling the truth and its centrality to media practice. On Kantian presuppositions, it has been argued that truth-telling is an absolute duty. We used the work of Nick Davies, ironically characterized as 'Rules of Production', to illustrate how a set of maxims that is endemic in contemporary journalistic culture must be intrinsically morally wrong. In one way or another, such maxims as 'the bias against the truth' (report sensational events in a way that supports popular assumptions without appropriate context) fall far short of the journalistic duty to tell the truth. As we saw in our discussion of Kant's essay 'On a supposed right to tell lies from benevolent motives', the duty to tell the truth is absolute and cannot be a matter of compromise, even for the best of motives let alone the worst! The duty to tell the truth is compromised by instrumental and prudential considerations. For example, Davies' Rule Six – 'increase revenue by giving them what they want' – is an injunction to publish stories merely to increase the audience or readership rather than because of their intrinsic value as news. To the extent that Davies is right about the prevalence of such 'rules of production', whether implicit or explicit, it is to that extent journalism fails in a core function.

FURTHER READING

Alia, V. (2004) *Media Ethics and Social Change*. Edinburgh: Edinburgh University Press. See particularly Chapter 3, 'Lies, truth and realities: the search for a responsible practice' (pp. 36–51), for a good discussion of deception in gathering and reporting news.

Bell, M. (1998) 'The journalism of attachment', in M. Kieran (ed.), *Media Ethics*. London: Routledge. pp.15–22. This is a war reporter's view of the problem of objectivity and detachment in war situations.

Dear, J. (2014) 'A country where the truth can kill', *British Journalism Review*, 25(1): 50–55. A salutary account of the hazards of truthful reporting. The paper describes violence against journalists in Colombia, including threats, attacks and killings. The effect of this has been a tendency to practise self-censorship in an attempt to stay safe and in work.

Gordon, A.D., Kittross, J.M. and Reuss, C. (eds) (1996) *Controversies in Media Ethics*. White Plains, NY: Longman (2nd edn, 1999). See particularly Chapter 4, 'Manipulation by the media: truth, fairness and objectivity' (pp. 81–100). This chapter focuses on news media practitioners from journalists to those in public relations and their relationship to truthfulness. The authors suggest there are different methods of defining and operationalizing truth. They also debate whether other ethical concepts may be more important on occasions (e.g. fairness).

Kant, I. (1965) *Fundamental Principles of the Metaphysic of Ethics* (10th edn). Trans. T.K. Abbott. London: Longmans (1st German edn, 1785). There are many editions available of this fundamental text. Abbott's translation is one of the first English translations, published in 1873 (and republished many times), and for that reason it sometimes uses rather archaic language, but is nonetheless reliable.

Keeble, R. (2001) *Ethics for Journalists*. London: Routledge. See particularly Chapter 8, 'Battling for news: the dilemmas of war reporting (and not just on the frontline)' (pp. 97–109). This chapter discusses, with many examples, important dilemmas confronting journalists in war. These include: Should journalists automatically give their support to their government in wartime? Do mainstream journalists succumb too easily to agendas set by government, for example, during the Gulf War? What, if any, restrictions should journalists accept when reporting from 'enemy' countries? Do mainstream media reports sanitise war? What ought to be the role of journalists in alerting politicians and the public to human rights abuses?

Sanders, K. (2006) *Ethics and Journalism*. London: Sage. See particularly Chapter 4, 'Lying to tell a story' (pp. 40–52), for a discussion of the relationship between truth and lies in journalistic practice.

Shin, W. (2014) 'Being a truth-teller who serves only the citizens: a case study of *Newstapa*', *Journalism* [Online], 24 March. http://jou.sagepub.com/content/ear

ly/2014/03/18/1464884914525565 (accessed: 25 March 2014). An interesting account of the Korean independent newsroom Newstapa and its efforts to break away from the logic of mainstream journalistic practice. The aim is to combine the core of professional journalism with participatory (citizen-based) journalism.

Sullivan, R.J. (1997) *An Introduction to Kant's Ethics*. Cambridge: Cambridge University Press. See particularly Chapter 2, 'The categorical imperative: the ultimate norm of morality' (pp. 29–46), for an account of Kant's reasoning in deriving his categorical imperative – 'supreme principle of morality' – and its significance as a test for what constitutes a genuine moral law or rule.

 ## HOW TO USE THIS ARTICLE

Go to https://study.sagepub.com/horner to access the following free journal article:

Blaagard, B.B. (2013) 'Shifting boundaries: objectivity, citizen journalism and tomorrow's journalists', *Journalism* [Online], 3 February. http://jou.sagepub.com/content/early/2013/01/15/1464884912469081 (accessed: 13 February 2013).

Use this article to examine the relationship between citizen journalism and professional journalism. The paper contains a theoretical discussion of the practice of journalistic objectivity and the struggle to maintain this aspect of professionalism. It discusses the implications of the technological advances that increasingly support citizen journalism for objectivity. The empirical aspect of the paper consists of interviews with journalism students and investigates their understanding of the tension between standards of professional journalism and the growth of citizen journalism and the implications of user-generated content (UGC). The results of the interviews highlighted the extent to which students pitted their profession against citizen journalism, seeing it as a form of 'parajournalism': 'Citizen journalism is not seen to be useful to the public sphere beyond its connection to professional journalism'.

8
IMAGES

It is frequently asserted that we live in a visual age. One commonly held view maintains that 'one picture is worth a thousand words' and a privileged status is frequently attributed to images as evidence. This chapter explores the ethics of truth-telling in media imagery. In the previous chapter we were concerned with the morality of truth-telling through what we may say or write and publish. This chapter extends the discussion about the morality of truth-telling to visual imagery. There are good reasons to concentrate on this aspect of media imagery. Firstly, visual images are deemed to have a particular authority in the representation of reality, a particular property of literally showing the truth. Is this really the case? Secondly, we are in a period of rapid technological change where the creation, distribution and consumption of images are being rapidly transformed. What are the moral implications of this technological transformation? Thirdly, it may be the case that, as a consequence of technological change, the status of still and moving images is being radically transformed. At one pole we have the concentration of media ownership by mega-corporations pursuing monopoly ownership and control of images and at the other pole we have the rapidly increasing individual production and distribution of image-based artefacts.

The authority invested in images seems to transfer ethical significance from the intentions of their creators to the object itself. The sources of this belief in the authority of the image are discussed in the next section. We then analyse ways in which that supposed authority is subverted. Firstly, the artifice involved in media imagery necessarily subverts the authority of the image. Secondly, any selection represents 'a point of view' and necessarily falsifies and subverts the truth value of images. Thirdly, selection is also ineluctably bound up with evaluations of what is, or is not, important, further questioning the credibility of the image. Fourthly, we look at whether the new ways of taking, processing, manipulating and publishing images also contribute to subverting their authority in new and morally significant ways. Drawing on the discussion about lying in the previous chapter, we consider whether or not it may be legitimate to fake images for some putative moral good. We explore the analogy between truth-telling in textual and visual forms from the point of view of Kantian moral theory. The decay of the evidentiary authority of images seems to threaten the duty of photojournalists, for example, to tell the truth in visual form. Is it permissible to use fakery to tell the truth or manipulate images to achieve better effects?

8.1 DEFINITIONS
Types of duty according to Kant

Perfect duties are the kinds of duties that others have a corresponding right to expect me to perform. For example, I have a perfect duty not to lie to people. Each and every person has a right not to be lied to by me.

Imperfect duties are the kinds of duties that I must perform but there is not some identifiable group or person to whom they must be performed and with a right to expect me to do so. For example, I ought to abide by the rules of my profession but I have some choice about how these should be followed in particular circumstances.

THE AUTHORITY OF IMAGES
Trusting Images

There is a tension between the claim that, on the one hand, images are uniquely authoritative (derived from a belief that photographic images directly represent reality) and, on the other hand, that this authority is subverted by the very artifice and selectivity involved in the production of images. Trust seems to lie in the object itself rather than in the intentions of the producer of the object. There is a common-sense belief in the peculiar authority of images to portray reality. Dona Schwartz, a visual communications scholar, writes that historically:

> Publishers have deployed the evidentiary status attributed to the image as part of the larger attempt to assert the nonpartisan, objective view offered by the fourth estate, thereby positioning newspapers as consumable objects that transcended political, social or cultural affiliations. (Schwartz, 2003, p. 28)

She goes on to assert, however, that the arrival of the digital image has undermined the trust of the public in photography. But it has always been the case, since the advent of photography, that images can be manipulated and fabricated, and yet the myth of the evidentiary status of photography has persisted.

The case of 'the disappearing nipples' in Box 8.2 illustrates in a minor way some of the moral problems with the manipulation of imagery. The manipulation may be justified, if not on the grounds of truth-telling, then on the grounds that it is necessary so as not to offend the viewers. This, of course, would be a classic consequentialist type of defence when changing an image is justified on the grounds of its likely effect. In contrast, as we saw in the last chapter, Kant argues that the duty to tell the truth is an absolute and 'perfect' duty and thus anything which might constitute a lie would be impermissible (see Box 8.1). We might argue, however, that the kind of manipulation in this case is not straightforwardly a lie.

8.2 A JUDGEMENT CALL
The case of the disappearing nipples

Kate Moss, the supermodel, was pictured on the front cover of a special issue of the magazine *American Photo* (January/February, 1994). The model was pictured in a tight-fitting gauzy top. The editors had her nipples 'removed' digitally as 'a matter of taste'. In a response to a letter to the editor, it was subsequently disclosed that that was what had happened. However, there had been no indication or disclosure at the time of publication that the photograph had been altered in this way.

The dilemma here seemed to be as follows. To publish the original photograph would have been the honest action to take but, as it was originally (with nipples), might have offended at least some of the readership of the magazine. But to doctor significantly the picture (and we might say this was significant, for if not, why do it?) is to falsify the picture, to lie.

If you were the picture editor of the magazine would you have approved this alteration? Should we ever manipulate photographs in the (presumed) interests of our viewers? Was the action in this case unprofessional?

Source: Wheeler (2002, p. 57)

The moral concern about images, whether moving or still, arises especially from their very authority and persuasiveness. We tend to accept an intimate connection between 'seeing' and 'believing', more so than, say, hearing and believing or smelling and believing. Sight is the dominant sense. Sanders (2006, p. 54) points out that 'The truth of an event cannot be gainsaid if we have seen it with our own eyes. Pictures presented in news, current affairs or documentary context have traditionally had this special kind of authority. We believe what we see to be true'.

We can extend this argument beyond that of reporting. We are more persuaded, even in the presentation of dramas and soap operas, by the apparent degree of verisimilitude. This is beautifully captured in the film *The Truman Show* (1998). The fact that the eponymous hero of 'the show' (and the film) is unaware that he is part of a soap opera lends truth to the show, capturing an enrapt global audience. Life and television are ironically merged. The audience within the film believes in the 'reality' of Truman even though this is, in itself, an artifice created by the television production company. The film is an ironic commentary on our relationship with television images generally and the 'reality' of soap operas more particularly. The audience are engaged because it appears that they are watching something 'real'.

A Physical Basis for Trust

The authority of the image is at least partly grounded in the very nature of the traditional or analogue photographic processes. Warburton (1998, p. 128) points out that trust in the truth of photography rested on the idea of there being a direct and traceable (physical) causal link between the image and its source. Early techniques of photography depended on the light from objects making physical changes to the chemistry of film. There was a physical, causal chain running from an object or state of affairs embodied in a photographic image to the viewer. As a form of testimony, this appears to be stronger than that of a witness to an event. Contrast this with a simple illustration or even photographic illustration. In the case of the illustration, you may argue that there is still a link in the sense that the creator causes the production of an image based on his or her perception of an object or state of affairs. But the creator mediates and there is no direct causal connection between the depiction and what is depicted.

On this view, the veracity of the meaning of an image depends on what it is of or what caused it. But meaning also will depend on what it looks to be of and how it is used in a particular context (Warburton, 1998, p. 128). The meaning of an image is related (but not always) to the idea of its information content. For example, there are certain kinds of images whose importance rests on a direct 'one-to-one mapping' between the representation and what it represents. For example, the medical use of x-rays relies on the images produced having one-to-one mapping to the physical structures they picture. Our trust is here reposed in the technology; we rely on the intrinsic nature of x-rays, for example, because of what they are and can do. We trust them, assuming appropriate competence in the radiographer. Compare the example of the x-rays with the idea of reconstruction to produce a representation of a news event. In this sense there is a clear and tangible distinction between the documentary photograph and the photographic illustration. We might say that the authority of the image is established through its informational content.

Thus, on this view, the belief in photography as evidence is founded on the assumption of reasonably direct and traceable causal links. In traditional analogue photography, what is on the negative is a result from what is before the lens. Even with some distortions, if you know the conditions you can interpret the photograph. Again, consider the cases of a horse-racing photo-finish or aerial photography used in map making, and so forth. Truth here is invested in the very nature of the image and the means by which it is produced. The intentions of the creator or producer seem to slip into the background. This contrasts with Kant's view that in any situation what counts morally is the intention of the agent that our actions are moral because they arise from a 'good will'. But as we will see in the next section, the idea of images as mirrors of reality is not as straightforward as suggested. And this, as we see, raises questions not only about the veracity of the images, but also about their moral status.

SUBVERTING THE AUTHORITY OF IMAGES

Here we examine four threats to the authority of images and their implications. These are, firstly, 'the artifice problem', secondly, 'the point-of-view argument', thirdly, 'the threat from relativism', and fourthly, 'the threat from technological change'. The argument leads to the conclusion that we ought not to repose our trust in images *per se* and that we are inevitably drawn back to questions of intention and to the context in which images are produced.

The Artifice Problem

'The artifice problem' is the belief that images are artificial constructions rather than simply transparent representations of what happened in front of a lens. As Karen Sanders points out 'the grammar of pictures and especially of television, is shot through with artifice. Photographs are regularly cropped, documentaries use reconstructions and news programmes employ nodding shots' (Sanders, 2006, p. 54).

The implication here is that 'seeing may no longer be believing'. There are distinct categories of artifice. To begin with there are, and have always been, post-production techniques of image manipulation. But there is a distinction between legitimate editing and intentional or unintentional misrepresentation. We might make the case that 'touching up' a photograph to remove blemishes in a female model's complexion is something akin to a 'white lie' and justifiable on aesthetic grounds. There must be moral limits for post-production editing. In the scenario depicted in Box 8.3 we might, charitably, represent the dilemma for the university concerned in the following way. There was a benevolent motive in suggesting that the university student body was more diverse than it actually was. The idea might have been inspirational to attract more black students to come to the university. But at the same time this was clearly a misrepresentation of the university as it was. This might then be presented as a clash between the duty of the publications' director to improve the recruitment of black students and a duty to present the nature of the university honestly.

8.3 A JUDGEMENT CALL
Is political correctness a sufficient reason for manipulating a photograph?

'In the fall of 2000, the University of Wisconsin manipulated the cover of a brochure by inserting the image of a black student into a crowd of white football fans, so as to suggest racial diversity in the student body. The University's publications director admitted that the move was "an error of judgement".'

Wheeler (2002, p. 58)

Do you agree that this was an error of judgement?

Firstly, in post-production editing or 'picture manipulation', for example, the techniques involve working to change or modify in some way the nature of how the content appears. In the days of chemically-based photography, such manipulation involved intervention on the negatives to change the image once captured. For example, these techniques included the deliberate re-touching and airbrushing of pictures to produce particular effects. Celebrated examples include photographs of the early days of the Russian Revolution where subsequently 'old' Bolsheviks were airbrushed out of pictures to emphasize the role of Joseph Stalin. Here we are again on familiar Kantian territory where intentions count rather than the image itself. Without some earlier photograph or testimony it would not be obvious, for example, that the revolutionary Bolshevik leader, Leon Trotsky, had disappeared from the podium in a photograph of Lenin making a speech. Similarly, but perhaps less controversially, in the days before colour photography, photographs were often tinted to give the effect of colour. In the context of the contemporary digital production of images, the range of manipulation has been much enhanced in scope and ease.

Secondly, there has, and has always been, artifice in the construction of images. Even in the case of reconstructions, it can be argued that there is some relationship between the image produced and the real event. Staged shots and reconstructions are a means of constructing artificial images in the process of production itself. For example, there is the case of the famous radio and film series, *The March of Time* – a weekly news magazine, sponsored by *Time* magazine. *The March of Time* broadcast news of important political events throughout the 1930s and 1940s. However, the shows included a blend of reporting, on-location shots, and dramatic re-enactments. Characteristically, each of its weekly shows included a dramatized presentation of the week's major stories, mixing actual clips of newsmakers' voices (when available) with sounds and pictures of actors re-creating events through imitations of the actual newsmakers. This was done when authentic voice cuts were unavailable. So, for example, there were dramatic re-enactments of the negotiations leading up to the Munich Agreement of 1938 in which actors played the parts of the major political figures – Hitler, Mussolini, Chamberlain and Daladier.

Would we now say that such reconstructions are 'truthful'? In answering this question, the UK's Independent Television News Guidelines state, 'The reconstruction or restaging of events in factual programmes can be a great help in explaining an issue. It must always be done truthfully, with an awareness of what is reliably known. Nothing significant which is not known should be invented without acknowledgement. Reconstructions should not over-dramatise events in a misleading or sensationalist way' (quoted in Sanders, 2006, p. 56).

This implies that an image may be 'truthful' even though there is no direct physical connection (light rays transforming chemicals on a negative) between the events depicted and the event itself. What counts is that my intention in creating a reconstruction is not to deceive but to create an accurate account. In the USA the National Press Photographers Association (NPPA), in a statement of principle drafted in November 1990, emphasizes the belief in the evidentiary nature of photographic images as truthful reflections of reality:

As photojournalists, we have the responsibility to document society and to preserve its images as a matter of historical record. It is clear that the emerging electronic technologies provide new challenges to the integrity of photographic images. This technology enables manipulation of the content of the image in such a way that the change is virtually undetectable. In light of this, we, the National Press Photographers Association, reaffirm the basis of our ethics: Accurate representation is the benchmark of our profession. (Quoted in Schwartz, 2003, p. 34)

The Point-of-view Argument

One more radical threat to the veracity of imagery is the idea that images, rather than being faithful representations of reality, are always interpretations – they present a point of view: 'All pictures are interpretations of reality: they squeeze a slice of life into a small piece of celluloid or television screen' (Sanders, 2006, p. 55). The claim is that the distortion of 'how things are' is not a matter simply of deliberate manipulation, but is something intrinsic to the very process of image creation and publication. Since there can be no independent point of view, there can be no 'objective' truthful point of view. The very act of selection somehow vitiates the authority of the image.

The taking and processing of photographs are only two stages in a larger process, moving from an event to its visual portrayal. Photographers encounter a flood of facts and images – only a tiny portion of which can ever be recorded, processed and eventually published. The point-of-view argument suggests that 'subjectivity' must mediate and affect which facts and images are viewed as significant and which are to be ignored. Subjectivity further affects the process of constructing a story (or documentary) for publication. Story editors and photo editors revise, recast and rearrange, etc. All moments are decisions. In Box 8.4 we have three similar scenarios, each with a different moral status. It is clear that the first scenario represents the benchmark for accuracy. In scenarios 2 and 3 we have a sliding scale of reconstruction where the filming does not directly record the event as it happened.

8.4 A JUDGEMENT CALL
Three scenarios – spot the moral differences

Imagine three scenarios in which a photograph appears in a daily newspaper's 'City & Neighbourhood' section:

Scenario 1: The photographer 'sees two men piling sandbags on a makeshift flood levee and captures their activity on film'.

Scenario 2: The photographer 'sees them engaged in the activity and asks them to repeat it to allow time for loading the film and positioning the camera'.

(Continued)

(Continued)

Scenario 3: The photographer 'asks the two men to pose by the levee; they stand shoulder to shoulder and look into the lens as the shutter snaps'.

For scenarios 1 and 2, when published the photograph and the caption ('Local residents help out in the face of advancing flood waters') are identical. For scenario 3 the caption reads 'Biff Jones and Bob Smith were among volunteers who worked on a levee in the face of advancing flood waters'.

How would you characterize the ethical differences in the photographer's decisions?

Source: Wheeler (2002, p. 90)

The further, and morally significant, step in the argument is that any selection from 'a point of view' necessarily falsifies. This is akin to a more general argument that it is impossible to report or portray 'the whole truth'. However, the moral requirement is not necessarily for the whole truth. Two things may be said here if we approach this from a Kantian perspective. Firstly, we are only required to do those things which we are able to do. This is encapsulated in the phrase 'ought implies can': I am only morally obliged to do things which I can practically accomplish. Secondly, the focus of Kant's moral philosophy is on the intention with which we do things and not on the consequences, effects or outcomes. Photojournalists, of course, must operate in often murky and complex situations, but what counts here morally is the intention to show the truth accurately as best one can.

'Point of view' is a metaphorical expression and it is a useful metaphor. For example, when I'm climbing a mountain it looks very different from the way it looked when seen from a distance across a bay. Similarly, consider Hans Holbein's painting of 'The Ambassadors', which hangs in the National Gallery in London. Looking from a point of view which is to the centre of the picture there appears to be, between the ambassadors' feet, an elliptically shaped blur. However, by moving the point of view to the right the blur begins to reveal itself as the image of a skull. Holbein places a *memento mori* amid the sumptuousness of the Ambassadors as a reminder of the fragility of human life. At the same time, Holbein demonstrates his knowledge of perspective by painting an object that is only fully recognisable from one position, one point of view. The viewer must be in a unique position to make sense of the blur in the context of the rest of the picture. Since there are many other positions in which the onlooker can stand, it is natural to say that it is 'curious'.

In as much as we are all different from one another, we do literally see things from different points of view. There is a literal, non-metaphorical use of the phrase 'point of view'. Literally, you must see only from your point of view and I from mine. But it is nevertheless the case that people's points of view overlap and intersect. If this were not the case, there could be no communication. In the case of Holbein's painting, if I could only see the skull as a smear and you could only see it as what it is, we would have difficulty in coming to an agreement. But even so, it would not be impossible to work out what was going on and why we have these different perceptions. But because our points of view can overlap, we may more easily come to an agreement. There is, after all, a common world in which we each find ourselves. Similarly, we can bring about a big change in someone's (metaphorical) point of view by giving them evidence and using argument: 'But such an alteration is possible in so far as one person can make another adopt his own standpoint' (Stebbing, 1939, p. 34).

The Threat from Relativism

The threat from relativism (see the discussion of relativism in Chapter 1) is both a moral issue (the claim that there are no 'objective' values) and an epistemological one (the claim that there are no 'objective' or privileged standpoints for knowing the world). According to this account, the authority of images is subverted because, it is claimed, there can be no objectivity, moral or otherwise. All depictions of the world are in some sense value-laden. And values are always, and only, subjective. The sources of these values can be wide and varied, and are derived from the litany of social categories which are said to define us, for example, class, ethnicity, gender, culture, education, etc. The point is that our values will shape our decisions about what images to create and how we choose to do so, presenting a picture of the world based on our sensibilities. Far from images being reliable, objective and direct recordings of the world, they are more or less subjective interpretations. Seeing is no ground for believing (Kieran, 1998b, p. 24).

But while it must be the case that our interpretations and evaluations must have their origins somewhere, it does not follow that moral judgement is equivalent to a statement of preference, as we saw in Chapter 1. From the fact that we discriminate in our choice of shots when taking a photograph or making a video, it just doesn't follow that our take on the world is essentially subjective and relativistic. As Wheeler argues, even in the case of a manipulated photograph the ethics of media images cannot be judged apart for their use. It is the decisions we take about the composition, the set-up, and the method of processing that are moral or immoral, good or bad, appropriate or inappropriate. In addition, sound moral judgement must be exercised not only in relationship to the treatment of content, 'but also in what might be called its larger meaning' (Wheeler, 2002, p. 102).

If we were to take this claim about values and subjectivity seriously, we would expect that the visual output from Al Jazeera would be markedly different from that of other news media. But this is not the case. Al Jazeera's staff aspire to provide a professional and detached view of events. It presents a rather different perspective on Middle Eastern events, from an editorial point of view, but again this is within the recognizable bounds of editorial independence. It provides a vehicle for dissenting views – which are often unpopular with many of the elite rulers of the Arab states. Notably, it was the only channel to cover the allied invasion of Afghanistan from its office in Kabul. The very fact that we can draw a valid distinction between what is editorial comment and what is straight reporting demonstrates that the claim that in one way or another selection is always prejudicial is false. We can say that the aspiration to make decisions according to a set of professional values can hardly be described as 'a threat'. Rather there is a moral obligation always to mark the distinction between editorializing and reporting.

The Threat from Technological Change

Nigel Warburton (1998) argues that digital photography marks a qualitative change, potentially establishing a new relationship between the object, the image and the viewer. He argues that photographic conventions are transformed precisely because of the loss of the direct, physical, causal connection between object and image. He acknowledges, of course, that manipulation and fakery have been around since the dawn of photography, but he suggests a number of reasons for believing that the moral questions are now posed more acutely. In other words, we now have even stronger reasons for being sceptical about the claim that 'seeing is believing'. The physical, causal link in analogue photography between events and the recording of events no longer obtains. The new ways of taking, processing and publishing (digital) images have therefore greater moral significance.

Firstly, it is now the case images can be altered relatively easily. As we have already acknowledged, it has always been the case that such techniques as cropping, dodging, burning-in, air-brushing, composite printing, and the like have been in the toolbox of the photographer throughout photography's history. An important change, however, is that whereas in the past such manipulative techniques were largely the province of the professional or the talented amateur, now they are within the capabilities of even the most inexpert of photographers, given the right software and computer.

Secondly, it is also characteristic of the transition from analogue to digital that changes can be made seamlessly, leaving no physical trace. The implication is that no evidence of alteration is left. The notion of having an 'original' photograph is increasingly meaningless. With analogue forms of photography you could at least, in principle, refer to an original negative against which to check any subsequent changes. An edited electronic file need not reveal that it has been edited. To counteract the possibilities of misrepresentation, Ofcom, the British regulatory authority, requires that where material has been edited from interviews the points at which sections of an interview have been edited out must be visually indicated. The relative ease of changing the 'original' images and the undetectability of the changes do appear to widen the scope for the abuse of still and video images. YouTube is replete with both crude and sophisticated examples of the manipulator's art. This does seem to be a genuinely new development and one that has moral implications.

Thirdly, not only has the ease of fakery and manipulation been enhanced, but with it the ease of transmission has also been enhanced beyond all recognition. I have already mentioned YouTube. Similarly, the creation of digital platforms means *convertibility* between media. The physical photograph album is now all but redundant. We can carry around our archive of photographs and video clips in our mobile phones, laptops, tablets, etc., or simply store them in 'the cloud'. Ease of manipulation and reproducibility is linked to transmissibility. All these features – ease of manipulation, undetectability, transmissibility and reproducibility – raise more sharply the question of trust. Can we really trust that what we think we see in a photograph or a video represents what it claims to represent? But is this the right question? After all, many images are not always about depicting the truth of events.

Fourthly, consider, for example, the use of illustration in advertising. Still and visual images perform many functions from the kinds of literal representations we have been discussing to fictional storytelling, propaganda, advertising, and so on. No one conversant with media conventions is likely to think that an advertisement actually depicts a 'real' event. Similarly, many videos on YouTube are clearly 'fakes' of one sort or another done for comedic effect, such as the many comedy 'cat' videos we are familiar with. In the same way, we are unlikely to mistake a decoy duck for a real duck, or a mirage of an oasis, on close inspection, for an actual oasis. What kinds of obligations are relevant here? For example, in producing yet another adaptation of a Jane Austen novel, we might claim that there is some obligation to strive for truthfulness in the costumes worn by the actors and the everyday objects used in the dramatization. There may also be another level of truthfulness in the extent to which the representation of the novel is faithful or unfaithful to the original intentions of the author.

The characteristics I have briefly alluded to in this section have greatly enhanced the possibilities for the creation of images that cheat or lie in the sense that they just don't represent what they appear to represent. However, we must return to the question of intention. The changes brought about by digital, still and video photography do not, of necessity, create more mendacious images. In that sense, the technology is neutral. We can imagine a virtuous community in possession of such technology. If the practice of that community was, by training and habit, always to tell the truth, then the presence of the technology would make no difference. If it did seem to make a difference, then we would have to suspect that some members of the community had decided to kick over the traces but not that the technology had *caused* them to do so.

From the point of view of Kant's moral theory, there is a categorical duty to tell the truth. This applies equally to images as it does to text. It must be an (absolute) duty to be truthful in the creation and publication of still and moving images. This Kantian position is reflected in the Code of Practice produced in 1990 in the USA by the National Press Photographers Association (NPPA). Its statement of principle reads:

> As journalists we believe the guiding principle of our profession is accuracy; therefore, we believe it is wrong to alter the content of a photograph in any way that deceives the public … altering the editorial content of a photograph, in any degree, is a breach of the ethical standards recognized by the NPPA. (Quoted in Wheeler, 2002, p. 77)

This statement of principle was followed up in 1991 in the context of the then emerging 'new' media technologies with a reaffirmation that 'accurate representation' was 'the benchmark' of the photographic profession. Similarly, the Society of Professional Journalists contains the following imperative in its Code of Ethics:

> Never distort the content of news photos or video. Image enhancement for technical clarity is always permissible. Label montages and photo illustrations. Avoid misleading re-enactments or staged new events. If re-enactment is necessary to tell a story, label it. (Quoted in Wheeler, 2002, p. 77)

However, even given these injunctions, we might ask 'Are these absolute or relative obligations?' It may be a *prima facie* moral obligation but, in some circumstances, the truth-telling duty may be overridden. For example, in some situations may I not take, or produce, a 'lying photograph' if it is for a 'benevolent motive' or with the intention of telling the truth of some event?

CAN THERE BE LEGITIMATE FAKERY FOR A 'BENEVOLENT MOTIVE'?

In the last chapter we considered the question of whether or not it was right to tell a lie for benevolent motives. The corollary for images might be: 'Can it be legitimate to fake images'? Box 8.5 provides an example where a photograph was altered for a benevolent purpose. The idea was presumably to spare the feelings of offence that might have been experienced by Native Americans. Here there is clearly a clash of values between the universal imperative to tell the truth and a duty of benevolence towards another group of human beings. In the example, the judgement that was made put the value of benevolence above that of truth-telling. This might lead us to suppose that there may be something like 'legitimate fakery'. However, it could be argued, as Kant does, that truth-telling is so fundamental that it would be better not to have made the alteration. Visual lying, as with lying speech, fundamentally subverts communication. If lying became a routine practice so that we didn't know when people were lying or not, communication would become impossible.

8.5 A JUDGEMENT CALL
Of mascots and caps

Before publishing three photos of baseball caps, the *Seattle Times* deleted the Cleveland Indians' mascot, 'Chief Wahoo', a grinning caricature of a Native American Indian which was considered by many to be offensive. In admitting that the alteration was an error, Managing Editor Alex MacLeod explained 'The photo manipulation was well intentioned; the result was a visual lie'.

Was the alteration really an error?

Source: Wheeler (2002, p. 59)

A reconstruction (or manipulation) may be legitimate if it is clearly referred to as such. An important factor here must be the expectations of the viewer. If the intention of the producer of the image is not to deceive, and I do not expect that the image I am viewing to be an untouched, pristine, direct representation of its subject, then is there no lie perpetrated if the image is manipulated? In early 1996 a five-member committee appointed by New York University's programme on 'Copyright and the New Technologies' recommended a system of labelling for manipulated images. The marking of images with appropriate labels would be a direct method of shaping the viewers' expectations (see Table 8.1). This is one strategy adopted by newspapers to avoid confusion when photographs have been manipulated. However, this is not always successful in that readers may fail to find or recognize the appended label. For example, *Time* magazine used on its cover a digitally altered mugshot of O.J. Simpson, but readers would have had to find the label on the contents page. A second and more extreme strategy is to take the position that if a photograph has to be digitally altered, then it must be obvious that it has been so altered. In other words, the image must look so implausible to the viewer that it cannot be mistaken for an accurate portrayal (Schwartz, 2003, p. 38).

Table 8.1   Recommended ethical labelling for different types of image

Label	Description
'photo-reportage'	Unaltered photographs
'photo-portraits'	Posed photographs
'photo-illustrations'	Pictures in which elements were arranged
'photo-opportunities'	Pictures taken under imposed restrictions
'retouched'	Cosmetic alterations
'composite'	Pictures with objects that are added or subtracted
'computer-generated-image'	Non-photo-based computer illustrations

Source: Wheeler (2002, p. 167)

8.6 A JUDGEMENT CALL
Does it matter if the *Daily Mirror*'s weeping child is a lie?

The UK's left-leaning tabloid newspaper, the *Daily Mirror*, ran a campaign to point out the disparity between the fact that recent statistics had shown that the UK had more millionaires than ever before, while at the same time perhaps a million people were now regularly using free food banks. The target of the campaign was the government's new

(Continued)

(Continued)

benefit reforms, which, it was claimed, were increasing poverty in Britain. The *Mirror* reported the claim from the Trussell Trust that 330,000 children went hungry last year. The front page had the headline 'Shame of Condem Cuts', referring to the Coalition government. However, the majority of the front page was taken up with a 'poignant picture' of a weeping child. Unfortunately, the weeping child in question was not from Britain at all. It was a picture of a child taken in San Francisco in 2009. In that sense, it was not a fake – it was a real child and a real child weeping. It illustrated the story, but there was no intrinsic connection between the child and the story as such.

Was the use of the photograph tantamount to a lie and therefore should the newspaper not have used it?

Source: Brown (2014)

In the case outlined in Box 8.6 we may be inclined to question if it matters whether the child is or is not authentically British and the subject of the government's welfare cuts. The picture is true in the sense that it is a child and that child is weeping. The responses may depend on attitudes to the benefit reforms. If you agree with the reforms, then the lack of a direct connection between the picture and the story will reinforce a feeling that the story is bogus. If you are morally outraged by the cuts, then you are likely to feel that the picture is 'true' in every way that matters (Brown, 2014). We might, on instrumental rather than moral grounds, regret the use of the picture because it detracts from the focus of the campaign and gives fuel to those who reject the impact of the cuts. But morally, of course, we have to say that it is a lying picture because it purports to be something it is not. The implication here must be that the *Mirror* ought not to have used the photograph. This conclusion is strengthened by knowledge of its origins. The photograph was actually taken from a Flickr page. The little girl is the photographer's daughter. She is not crying because she is hungry but because an earthworm she had made 'friends' with had wriggled away and left her.

Box 8.7 illustrates a scenario in which a certain amount of fakery is used to tell what is, in fact, a true story. The analogy here is with lying for a benevolent purpose. In examining this case, we may have to decide the logically prior question as to whether or not this invasion of the privacy of the princess can be justified from a public interest point of view. Warburton's scenario well illustrates the contrast of older and newer media technologies. The scenario tellingly depicts the issues arising from the use of digital technology, discussed above. It illustrates the ease of manipulation of digital imagery, the production of a composite image, and the ease of reproducibility and transmission. Finally, it shows how the publication and reception of the image trades upon the expectation of verisimilitude that viewers think only pictures give. This is the function of 'the photograph as evidence', invoking the older model of there being a physical (causal) link between the image and what is depicted.

Did the photojournalist act unprofessionally? Did he lie? It is clear that the image sent down the wire was not photographic evidence for what occurred. The viewer did not have the right information regarding the photograph as evidence. What was disguised was how the image was made and what was suggested, implicitly, was that causal link between image and event: what the photograph looks to be of has, in some sense, 'caused' it. There are a number of lines of argument to be considered here. Firstly, the photojournalist could argue, in his defence, that he didn't lie because the events happened and his photograph, 'composited' as it was, nevertheless illustrated the truth. So he could deny that he had done anything wrong. However, we could respond that this leaves out the fact that the photograph was highly manipulated, if not actually faked. In addition, he did not inform his editor, lying by omission, so the paper published the image in a misleading way.

8.7 A JUDGEMENT CALL
Image manipulation in the interests of truth

'You pick up your morning tabloid on the way to work. On the front page is a photograph of a member of the royal family, a married princess no less, topless and in a compromising position with her bodyguard on a public beach. The picture is not in any way ambiguous. You can see who is involved and precisely what they are doing: no innocent explanation would be in the least bit plausible. The photograph is proof of what they did.

'We assume that the photograph really is a photograph of whoever the caption claims it is; we assume that what looks to be happening really was happening; we assume that the image is a photograph and not a skilfully executed painting, and so on. We might exercise a little healthy scepticism about how representative the depicted scene was of what was actually going on on the beach, but, as newspaper readers who have grown up with the conventions of photojournalism, we do not expect anything but a documentary photograph to accompany a news story. The photograph gives us convincing evidence of a special kind about what happened.

'Now consider how the image was made. The photographer climbed a tree with his camera and hung around for several hours until the couple emerged. He could scarcely believe what he was seeing through his telephoto lens. He shot a roll of film, then sneaked off to have it developed confident that he'd just made a year's salary in a few hours. To his dismay a fault in the film meant that only half of the shots had come out; none of the more compromising ones were printable. But all was not lost; he scanned the photographs that had come out into his computer and within half an hour he had produced a composite picture showing more or less what he had seen through the telephoto lens. He felt justified in what he had

(Continued)

(Continued)

done because he knew that the photograph was not misleading in any important way. He was committed to revealing the truth, and what better way to reveal the truth than with this striking image.

'He sent the image electronically to the picture editor of his newspaper, who decided to make it the lead story. However, just to cover himself, the picture editor telephoned back to check that the photograph wasn't misleading. He asked the photographer whether it showed what really happened; the photographer answered, honestly, it did. So the photograph appeared on the front page of the newspaper the nest day. None of the newspaper readers were aware precisely how the photograph had been made, nor was the picture editor. Consequently, they took it as incontrovertible evidence of the princess's misdemeanours.'

Is it morally right to manipulate images if the events depicted actually happened? Did anyone do the morally right thing?

Warburton (1998, pp. 126–127)

Secondly, the photojournalist could acknowledge that he had indeed transgressed the spirit, if not the letter, of the professional codes of practice. But the transgression was justifiable when set against the fact that he was publishing in the public interest. In other words, the duty to tell the truth to the public outweighed a professional duty to produce images which were truthful in the sense that the portrayal was faithful and accurate to the objects portrayed. (The analogy with analogue photography is that the image is directly caused by the objects photographed.) The key passage is this one:

> …he scanned the photographs that had come out into his computer and within half an hour he had produced a composite picture showing more or less what he had seen through the telephoto lens. He felt justified in what he had done because he knew that the photograph was not misleading in any important way. He was committed to revealing the truth, and what better way to reveal the truth than with this striking image. (Warburton, 1998, p. 126)

But thirdly, a 'slippery slope' argument might suggest that any deception, even if a minor one, may ultimately lead to wholesale deception, undermining the trust we might place in photojournalism. This is an argument about consequences. But slippery slope arguments are notoriously flawed because it is always possible to create a line of demarcation, to draw a line in the sand, by convention, by regulation, by law, which says for any particular slope: 'So far and no further!'

Fourthly, as we saw in the last chapter, for Kant, it must always be immoral to tell a lie even if we feel the lie will have more beneficial consequences than telling the literal truth. Therefore, as in the case of the supposed right to tell a lie for benevolent purposes, the photojournalist behaved immorally. He did not make clear how the image was produced and he did not inform his editor about how the image was created.

In effect, the photojournalist was adopting a subjective moral maxim of the form *'I will fake images that do not harm anyone and may have good consequences, and I will accept a world in which everyone is permitted also to fake images on these grounds.'* However, this fails the categorical imperative test as to whether or not this can be a legitimate moral rule. Remember that Kant argued that lying only makes sense if the aim of at least some kinds of speech, and by extension some kinds of imagery, are about the communication of information (Sullivan, 1997, p. 58). The problem with our photojournalist's maxim is that it leads to a logical contradiction if we try to universalize it (and remember moral rules, according to Kant, must be universalizable). The logical upshot of the maxim is that everyone will use the same kinds of images in order to communicate both truth and falsehood. Adopting such a maxim would mean we would never know whether or not an image was truly an informational image, an image that constituted direct evidence of what happened, or not. There would then be no such thing as a truthful image.

CHAPTER REVIEW

In this chapter we have seen that the truthfulness or otherwise of images is not necessarily dependent on the particular medium in which they are created or published. Trust in the truthfulness of images cannot be based on any assumed causal links between the image and the object or state of affairs which it depicts, but on the intention of the creators to produce a truthful image. In this way images are no different from our use of natural language. There must be a presumption of truth-telling for the lying or faked image to make sense. For, as in the case of truth-telling more generally, lies are parasitic on the moral duty of truth-telling. However, images like language are not solely or necessarily concerned with depicting events in a literal way. Not all still or moving photography is about providing evidence of events. Images can be used for telling jokes, telling fictional stories, reporting events, giving warnings, and so on. Our reception of images is tied up with expectations, conventions and context. To the extent that, as viewers, we are conversant with conventions, the genre of photographs and so on, we will not confuse an image intended to inform and one intended to perform some other social or aesthetic purpose.

FURTHER READING

Fishman, J.M. (2003) 'News norms and emotions: pictures of pain and metaphors of distress', in L. Gross, J.S. Katz and J. Ruby (eds), *Image Ethics in the Digital Age.* Minneapolis, MN: University of Minnesota. pp. 53–69. This chapter considers ethical questions concerning photographing the dead as part of news stories. It is partly based on interviews with 'news workers' in the USA and their attitudes to 'the corpse photo', and (distressing) impacts on the public from a moral point of view.

Gross, L., Katz, J.S. and Ruby, J. (eds) (1988) *Image Ethics: The Moral Rights of Subjects in Photographs, Film and Television*. Oxford: Oxford University Press. See, in particular, Chapter 1, 'Introduction: a moral pause' (pp. 3–33). A good introduction from a US perspective of ethical questions about still and moving images against a background of changing technology.

Sanders, K. (2006) *Ethics and Journalism*. London: Sage. See, in particular, Chapter 5, 'Faking it' (pp. 53–62), for an analysis of image manipulation and trust.

Schwartz, D. (2003) 'Professional oversight: policing the credibility of photojournalism', in L. Gross, J.S. Katz and J. Ruby (eds), *Image Ethics in the Digital Age*. Minneapolis, MN: University of Minnesota. pp. 27–51. This is a very good account of professional responses to ethical uncertainties in photojournalism. It examines the crisis in the evidentiary status of images under the impact of digital photography and the strategies being used to recoup the integrity of photojournalism.

Sullivan, R.J. (1997) *An Introduction to Kant's Ethics*. Cambridge: Cambridge University Press. See particularly Chapter 4, 'The formula of autonomy or universal law' (pp. 46–64), for an explanation of the first formulation of the categorical imperative, focusing on why moral principles, concepts and rules must be both universal and prescriptive. The form of a moral law (logically) must be that it holds universally and without exception.

Warburton, N. (1998) 'Ethical photojournalism and the electronic darkroom', in M. Kieran (ed.), *Media Ethics*. London: Routledge. pp. 123–134. An analysis of the moral dilemmas about the manipulation of digital images. The paper focuses on new questions arising from the change from analogue to digital photojournalism.

Wheeler, T. (2002) *Phototruth or Photofiction? Ethics and Media Imagery in the Digital Age*. Mahwah, NJ: Laurence Erlbaum Associates. See, in particular, Chapter 5, 'Rationales and excuses: justifying staged and manipulated photos' (pp. 55–66). This chapter discusses various defences of the manipulation of images put up by professional magazine photographers. It goes on to explore proposed justifications for altered photography in the mass media more generally.

 ## HOW TO USE THIS ARTICLE

Go to https://study.sagepub.com/horner to access the following free journal article:

Kapidzic, S. and Herring, S.C. (2014) 'Race, gender and self-representation in teen profile photographs', *New Media Society* [Online], 27 January. http://nms.sagepub.com/content/early/2014/01/24/1461444813520301 (accessed: 26 January 2014).

Use this paper to consider the moral aspects of selecting and manipulating images from an altogether different angle. The paper is concerned with a situation in which the photographic choice is in the hands of the user. The article considers the ways in which photographs are selected to manage and enhance self-presentation in popular chat sites. The authors analysed 400 profile photographs, controlling for self-reported gender and the apparent race of the photographic subject. Significant differences were found in gaze, posture, dress and distance from the camera according to gender and race. The findings of the study reflect those of previous face-to-face studies. It is suggested that teenagers construe their profile images as invitations to interact with others online. Their selection of photos 'reproduces culturally dominant ideologies of gender and race as reinforced by mass media images'.

9
STEREOTYPING

The use of the concept of 'representation' in the literature of Media Studies signals that the media are not simply transparent windows on the world, but reconstruct or re-present persons, events and situations. Patterns are established, through the decisions that media practitioners take, of routinely representing persons on the basis of particular characteristics: ethnic origin, class, gender, disability, age, sexual orientation and 'looks'. Categorizing people in various ways may naturalize certain stereotypes. In this chapter we will be concerned with the ethics of stereotyping. We will identify ethical principles relevant to moral judgements about stereotypes and make the case that stereotyping is simply morally wrong. Some representations of particular groups may raise profound questions of social justice. Stereotyping is implicated in the perpetuation of discrimination, inequality and exclusion.

A moral analysis of stereotyping concerns media content from television programmes to newspaper reporting. However, another way of thinking about representation is not in this representational sense of images and stories, but in the sense of actual physical presence and representation in media institutions and in media production – for example, the extent to which women are employed in significant roles in major media institutions. We need to understand the extent to which this, let's call it 'physical representation', is morally significant. It clearly is important if there is a big disparity, for example, between men and women in positions of power in major media corporations. Such disparities may unduly shape the production agendas of media corporations to the detriment of other interests in society. These issues raise important moral issues relating to justice as fairness.

We begin this chapter by defining what is meant by 'stereotypes' and 'stereotyping'. What is important about stereotypes, from a moral point of view, is that they are not neutral descriptions or categories but are evaluative, usually in a prejudicial way. However, as we will show, the logic of stereotyping is fallacious in a number of ways. Firstly, there is usually a fallacious move from statements about the average characteristics of some group to statements about particular persons. Secondly, stereotypes are usually constructed on the basis of 'the naturalistic fallacy' (a logically illicit move from descriptive statements about a group to evaluative conclusions). The morality of stereotyping is then analysed in more detail. Here, we invoke Kant's principle that we ought always to treat other persons as 'ends in themselves' and never only as a means (see Box 9.1).

9.1 DEFINITION
The Formula of Respect for the Dignity of Persons

'Act so that you treat humanity, whether in your own person or that of any other, always as an end and never as a means only' (Kant, 1965, p. 56)

Whereas Formula I forbids us to discriminate between persons in an arbitrary or unfair way, this instruction enjoins us to respect each person as such. Every person is an end in themselves in a twofold sense. They have their purposes (desires) and are also moral agents (rational beings) (see Table 7.1).

STEREOTYPING: A MORAL ISSUE
What Do We Mean by Stereotyping?

It would be hard to deny that in the media the tendency to stereotype is ubiquitous. Of course, in one sense this is often rooted in the benign necessity simply to talk about particular social groups as collectives sharing similar characteristics (see Box 9.1 for a definition). It is an extension of basic cognitive processes by which we seek to make sense of persons, events, objects and experience. Stereotyping involves the reduction and simplification of complex social phenomena into general labelled categories. Such reductions tend to focus on a limited range of characteristics and properties. Thus stereotypes identify general categories of people in terms of some (often arbitrary) distinctive features. These include categorization according to nationality, race, class, gender, deviancy, and so on.

What becomes of moral significance is the evaluative baggage that comes along with such representations. Implicitly or explicitly such social classification are highly value-laden sets of assumptions about the general behaviour of the group in question. Stereotypes denote general categories of people by gender (women and men), ethnic origin (e.g. the Latin race), national origin (e.g. the Scots), classes (e.g. the working class), or deviancy (e.g. drug takers). The central assumption is that some features that are supposedly true of a paradigm example of the class apply to all its members: blond women are always dumb; Scots are always mean; Latins are always excitable; members of the working class are crude and uneducated; drug takers are threats to the social order, and so on (Branston and Stafford, 2007).

An important aspect of stereotyping is an apparent insulation from factual rebuttal. It relies on evoking in its audience deep ideological and/or emotional resonances. Stereotypes are embedded, and play an important role in organizing every-day, common-sense discourse. It avails little to say 'Yes, but Marilyn Monroe was highly intelligent; many Scots of my acquaintance are extremely generous; many people who take drugs do so harmlessly on a purely recreational basis'. Stereotypes operate to construct mythical collectives of sets of people who may be alike in some ways, committed to and characterized by certain values, moved by the same goals, and who share similar personalities. Stereotypes link seamlessly with certain conventions and codes of media production. They provide a shorthand in which to organize stories quickly under the pressure of deadlines.

9.2 DEFINITIONS
Stereotype and stereotyping

'The social classification of particular groups and people as often highly simplified and generalized signs, judgements and assumptions concerning their behaviour, characteristics or history.'

Characteristics of stereotyping include:

'...both a categorization and an evaluation of the group being stereotyped; emphasis on some easily identified features(s) of the group being stereotyped; an evaluation of the group is often, though not always, a negative one; an insistence on absolute differences and boundaries where the idea of a spectrum of difference is more appropriate.'

Branston and Stafford (2007, p. 142)

Examples

Researchers in Media and Cultural Studies have analysed the political and social role of stereotypical representations in the mass media and, more specifically, on media representations of class, race, gender, disablement, and various forms of 'deviancy'. This research indicates the ways in which practices, conventions, and codes in news production promote specific forms of stereotyping. The use of stereotypes is the outcome of the ways in which news values arise in particular contexts. Important organizing values are those of dramatization, exaggeration and the search for 'extraordinariness'. The dominant news values and creation of stereotypes have important moral consequences in bolstering forms of discrimination, such as racism, sexism and ageism.

Here are just two examples of empirical studies drawn from the extensive literature on stereotyping and discrimination. Firstly, Karima Laachir (2010) provides an account of media representation of social class in France. She analyses how social class is represented in a number of 'media texts', including film and magazines, and concludes that the working class continue to be the subject of negative representations in the media. Laachir argues that 'it is important to examine the ways in which social class is portrayed in the media because the latter have a crucial role in maintaining, perpetuating or challenging social divisions' (Laachir, 2010, p. 427). This account of the representation of social class goes beyond simply describing the facts, mechanisms and impacts of the ways in which social class is portrayed. There is a moral assumption that social class divisions in themselves are unjust.

Secondly, Charlotte Ross's article from the same introductory volume on Media Studies discusses 'Sexualities'. Ross's article is an investigation of sexual stereotypes and media constructions of sexuality. Ross writes that:

> Articles in women's and girl's magazines turn predominantly around the issue of physical attractiveness: what exercises can be done, what clothes can be worn, make-up applied, and sexual techniques mastered in order to emulate the ideals of female sexuality promoted in their pages? This type of advice can be analyzed as a way of regulating female sexuality by indicating clearly how, and how *not* to behave and present oneself, which reinforce social norms. When you look through magazines, think about how stereotypes of sexuality feature in them. Quizzes and 'how to' articles often assume that all readers will want to achieve the same end result, for example that all women are predominantly concerned with pleasing and keeping their man, rather than experiencing pleasure themselves. (Ross, 2010, p. 401)

Ross identifies a set of norms which inform magazine articles for women and girls. But it goes beyond this in that it passes judgement on these norms. We have in the passage quoted a combination of factual statements about the content of magazines and an evaluation of the norms that are said to attach to such content. It is clear that the author thinks that 'pleasing and keeping their man' is not a worthy goal for women, or that 'physical attractiveness' is not a good that ought to be cultivated; that the values promoted in such magazines are bad. So this passage is itself a kind of moral critique: it identifies and rejects one set of values – of 'how, and how *not* to behave and present oneself' – and implicitly, if not explicitly, suggests an alternative set of values and norms that women and girls *ought* to pursue (see Box 9.3 below).

The question 'Should we discriminate in favour of unattractive people?' (see Box 9.3) is not a facetious one. We can, by analogy, see that attractiveness may be an attribute of a person in much the same way as age or race, and might need protection from discrimination in the same way. There is plenty of evidence to suggest that looks play an important part in selection for jobs. Evidence suggests that unattractive people are clearly at a disadvantage (Strangroom, 2010, p. 124). If we believe that appointments should be made on merit alone, then clearly there is a problem here. It would therefore be reasonable to suggest that positive discrimination would be justified as a means of redressing the balance in favour of the unattractive. Where two candidates for a role had the same qualifications, perhaps the selection panel should choose the less attractive of the two. However, a counter-argument here might be that attractiveness is not equivalent to the list of attributes singled out in the Equality Act (2010). The problem may be that it would be hard to get a consensus on what we mean by attractiveness. The idea of attractiveness is highly subjective and not an attribute at all.

In the following sections we will aim to do a number of things in deconstructing the concept of the stereotype. Firstly, leaving morality aside, we can show that the logic of stereotyping, that is, the stereotypical deductions made from the formation of categories, is simply fallacious. Secondly, we can argue from a moral point of view, on the basis of a Kantian analysis, that it is wrong. Stereotyping is always a moral offence to the dignity of a person. Thirdly, we might also add that in this context a consequentialist approach won't do. Utilitarianism, for example, has at its core the notion that moral judgements should be made on the basis of weighing the costs and benefits of an action. In other words, given that some might benefit from stereotyping, it isn't automatically ruled out. But as we will show, this must be morally wrong.

9.3 A JUDGEMENT CALL
Should we discriminate in favour of 'unattractive' people?

In the United Kingdom legislation exists to outlaw discrimination of various kinds. The Equality Act (2010) provides protection against discrimination on the basis of nine attributes: disability, age, race (including nationality), religious belief, sexuality, gender reassignment, sexual orientation, maternity and pregnancy, marriage and civil partnership. But what about discrimination on aesthetic grounds? There is plenty of evidence of media discrimination on the grounds of looks and attractiveness. This is especially the case for women and especially when it comes to who is in front of the camera! This discrimination on grounds of unattractiveness is also frequently linked to age. There have been a number of high-profile cases in which women news presenters, on reaching middle age, have lost their jobs or been sidelined in one way or another. Now this cannot be because women news presenters (unlike men) suddenly at a certain age lose their ability to effectively present the news or conduct interviews. In other words, there doesn't appear to be any rational ground on which such discrimination is made.

Should we therefore counteract this discrimination (as defined by some generally accepted standards) and positively discriminate in favour of the unattractive or downright ugly?

THE LOGIC OF STEREOTYPING

A classic example of stereotyping is the fictional and non-fictional representation of women as sex objects, defined by a dominant male view of what constitutes sexual attractiveness. A recent report into the status of women in Hollywood shows just how they are treated as 'second class citizens' (see Box 9.4). The treatment of women in film feeds into dominant stereotypes: ' … female stars are paid less, have fewer lines and spend more time with their clothes off' (Helmore, 2013, p. 36). Equally, women are massively underrepresented in positions of power in the film industry; most decisions about what ought to be produced are made by men. Women are stereotyped as suited to certain kinds of social roles, particularly associated with caring. Usually, such 'female' occupations or roles are perceived as inferior to men. Equally, the interests of women are less worthy of media attention than men, and so on. Consider the ways in which inordinate attention is paid to some 'male sports' (football or baseball, for example) compared to 'women's sports' (women's football, synchronized swimming, and so on). In addition, some forms of stereotyping intersect to reinforce negative effects. For example, older women may become socially invisible in a way that men don't.

9.4 EXAMPLE: Stereotyping and discrimination in Hollywood

A recent report has demonstrated the extent of stereotyping and discrimination of women in Hollywood. The report was sponsored by the New York Film Academy and authored by Dr Martha M. Lauzen of the Centre for the Study of Women in Television, Film and New Media at San Diego State University. The Academy claimed that 'By shedding light on gender inequality in film, we hope to start a discussion about what can be done to increase women's exposure and power in big budget films'. For example, a survey of the top 500 films produced between 2007 and 2012 found that only one-third of speaking parts were filled by women and only 10% of films were equally balanced in terms of role. The average ration of male to female actors is 2.25:1. In terms of production, of the top 250 domestic grossing films in 2012 women comprised only 18% of all directors, executive producers, writers, cinematographers and editors. This represented only a 1% improvement since 1998! The number of women directors remained unchanged since 1998 at only 9% of the total.

In analysing the content of films, the disparities between men and women are even more starkly apparent, revealing a pattern of stereotyping: 29% of women in the top 500 films wore sexually revealing clothes compared with only 7% of men; 26% of actresses appear partially naked compared with only 9% of men; and since 1997 the percentage of teenage female roles depicting nudity has risen by third. The ubiquitous sexual portrayal of women on screen feeds into dominant female stereotypes.

Source: Helmore (2013)

The Fallacy

Here we want to challenge the central assumption of stereotyping – that some features of a key example of a class apply to all its members. Leaving aside moral aspects for a moment, there is an immediate logical difficulty with stereotyping in that it is simply fallacious to ascribe characteristics from any collective description of a group to any one individual. On the descriptive side, we have a process of categorization, the grouping together by common characteristics. This in itself is an essential aspect of making sense of the world. Think, for example, if we didn't have a general word for the class of objects that are 'cups' and every cup had to have its own proper name. Referring to cups in general would not be possible and we would have to remember a separate word for every individual cup; this is literally unmanageable. We can apply this to persons – without the ability to classify, discourse would be impossible. We are all classifiable in a fairly neutral and descriptive way of a range of categories of people: lecturers, students, graduates, postgraduates; the under twenties, the over sixties, etc. So there are legitimate and morally neutral ways of categorizing.

Firstly, however, claims about groups are, by definition, claims about averages and ranges. We cannot, therefore, validly infer any categorical conclusion (the most it might be is probabilistic) about any particular member of the (stereotypical) set from a general statement of the average characteristics of that set (even if we were to accept the general characterization, which we may in fact want to deny). Secondly, a further fallacious move is the commission of what is called the 'the naturalistic fallacy'. This is the logically illicit deduction of value conclusions from statements of fact, moving from factual statements to evaluative ones. Being disabled may be a fact about a person's physical condition, but this does not (logically) entitle you to make value judgements as a person on the basis of those facts. Simply because foxhunting is an old, established tradition doesn't mean that it *ought* to carry on being practised.

Sexism and the Naturalistic Fallacy

Feminist analyses of sexual stereotyping emphasize the distinctions to be made between sex, sexuality and gender. Sex difference in this sense refers to a purely biological classification depending on physical characteristics: sex organs, secondary sexual characteristics, hormones, and so on. Sexuality or gender refers to people's sexual preferences and activities. Gender, it is argued, is socially and culturally formed. Social roles, although not independent of the body (as a biological entity, that is, being capable of child bearing), cannot be simply read off from the facts of biology. In this context an important aspect of stereotyping is its tendency to 'naturalize' certain attitudes through media imagery. In other words, certain specific roles are ascribed as 'natural' for men and women or certain characteristics may be 'naturally' ascribed to men and women.

Lest we think that such stereotyping is new or modern, consider this quotation from Aristotle's *Politics*:

> It is thus clear that there are by nature freemen, and that servitude is agreeable and just for the latter ... Equally, the relation of the male to the female is by nature such that one is superior and the other inferior, one dominates and the other is dominated ... Furthermore ... the poets say, 'It is just that Greeks rule over Barbarians' because the Barbarian and the slave are by nature the same. (Aristotle, 1960, p.16)

Aristotle's proposition and the logic of sexism are fundamentally mistaken. In both cases, the underlying argument is, firstly, that (non-social) nature determines our initial capacities and inclinations. Secondly, that these initial capacities and inclinations (defined by our biology) then determine not what our social roles are *in fact* but rather what they *ought* to be. Sexism stands for the view that men and women's places in the world are determined by non-social causes – the facts of biology and biochemistry. What is fallacious here is the move from statements about what *is* the case to statements about what *ought* to be the case.

We can accept that people vary greatly in their initial capacities and inclinations but none of this (logically) entails how things *ought* to be. Similarly, simply to state 'this is how things have been in the past' cannot (logically) mandate how things *ought* to be in the future. Conclusions about *rightness*, in a moral sense, cannot validly be deduced from propositions which only state what *is* the case. For a prescriptive 'ought' to appear in the conclusion and for the argument to be a valid, deductive one, then some value statement must occur in the premises of the argument. The naturalistic fallacy is the attempt to derive value-laden conclusions from purely factual premises (see Boxes 9.5 and 9.6 below).

9.5 EXAMPLE: The test of a valid, deductive argument

A test of a deductive argument is that it would be self-contradictory to assert the premises of the argument and yet to deny the conclusion.

So, for example:

1. If all human beings are mortal
2. And Marilyn Monroe is a human being
3. Then Marilyn Monroe is mortal.

In this very simple argument it would be clearly self-contradictory to hold (1) and (2) to be true and yet deny (3). If you did choose to deny it, this would only show that you hadn't clearly understood the meanings of the words and sentences making up the premises of the argument. Or, alternatively, you might be describing Marilyn Monroe as 'immortal' in some metaphorical sense about the continuing appeal of her major screen roles.

9.6 EXAMPLE: Applying the test to a case of the naturalistic fallacy, or why a woman ought not to be Director General of the BBC

Now apply a test of validity to some argument that purports to derive a prescriptive conclusion from purely factual premises. So, for example:

1. Marilyn is a woman
2. And no Director General of the BBC has ever been a woman
3. Therefore, Marilyn *ought* not to be Director General of the BBC.

(Continued)

(Continued)

This is not a validly deduced conclusion because it is not self-contradictory to hold both that 'Marilyn is a woman' and 'Marilyn ought to be Director General of the BBC'. This seems as obvious as to be barely worth spelling out. Nevertheless, the instances of such kinds of thinking are legion. The argument could be rendered valid (if repugnant) in the following way:

1. All women are naturally inferior
2. Marilyn is a woman
3. No one who is naturally inferior ought to be Director General of the BBC
4. Therefore, Marilyn ought not to Director General of the BBC.

However, the conclusion is only made valid by the inclusion of value-laden premises [(1) and (3)], premises we would clearly want to reject. In this case, the argument might be perfectly sound from a logical point of view, but the conclusion is in fact false because one or more of its premises is false. We would surely want to challenge, from a moral point of view, the idea of 'natural inferiority' in human beings.

The Paradox of Changing Stereotypes

Similar logic is at work in racial stereotyping and racism. Inherited and invariable characteristics are supposed to define a social category of people. However, if the categorization is meant to be based on some purely 'natural' attribute than it is hard to see how this can be used to define a 'social' category. Racial classifications are not neutral in that they smuggle in or even make explicit value judgements about the behaviour and the expected behaviour of the group and the individuals that make it up. Further, such behaviours are necessitated because they arise from non-social, biological, natural characteristics of genetic and psychological make-up. So, for example, Branston and Stafford illustrate this with the very particular ways in which black slaves before and during the American Civil War of 1861–1865 were subsequently represented in Hollywood movies of the 1930s, and most spectacularly in *Gone with the Wind* (1939). Black slaves were stereotyped as using 'a shuffling walk' and having 'musical rhythm with a tendency to burst into song and dance', and women house slaves were characterised by their 'bodily fatness, uneducated foolishness and childlike qualities' (Branston and Stafford, 2007, p. 143).

Interestingly, these stereotypes were deployed to imply that such characteristics were grounded in fundamental biological and genetic make-up, such that some groups were 'by nature' inferior, as Aristotle thought. What is interesting, but paradoxical, given the 'natural' claim, is that such stereotypes shift and change depending on social and historical circumstances. Contemporary stereotypes of 'blackness' stress the association of black youth with crime, especially gun crime, and an aggressive, 'drug-fuelled' gang culture. At the same time young black women are portrayed in a sexualized way and as being heavily influenced by the prevailing celebrity culture. What the paradox of changing stereotypes reveals is the ideological function of stereotyping. In other words, the supposed 'natural' basis of such representations is largely fictional. If stereotypes were truly grounded in some fundamental, unchanging, natural characteristics, then they would not so readily transform over time.

Similar representational processes are at work in the stereotyping of disability, gays and lesbians, and so on. Again, to explain something is not to show that it's necessarily morally wrong, as we saw above when we discussed sexism and the naturalistic fallacy. If we are arguing, as we are, that stereotyping is part of a fabric of social oppression, we need to show just why such oppression is fundamentally morally wrong. After all, historically there have been many societies, such as Greek and Roman societies, where it was perfectly acceptable to own other human beings. A further argument for a deeper moral view is the claim that there are also benign or positive stereotypical representations of social groups. The imagined scenario in Box 9.7 proposes that we might generate new stereotypes and at least one of these seems to be a benign stereotype, that is, that of 'the virtuous, environmentally aware homeowner'. However, this, we may say, suffers from the same fallacious logic we have been discussing. It's not the case that only negative stereotypes are wrong. I want to show that stereotyping is just as morally wrong in itself as it is logically fallacious.

9.7 A JUDGEMENT CALL
Generating a stereotype

In this time of debate about global warming, imagine the emergence of possible new stereotypes as follows.

For example, there is a group of homeowners who are installing solar panels on their homes. This installation of solar panels is both subsidized by the UK government and also allows the homeowners to profit from selling electricity to the national grid. In this case, we might imagine the potential emergence of two competing media stereotypes: (a) 'the self-interested, energy advantaged homeowner'; and (b) 'the virtuous, environmentally aware homeowner'. It is the case that the take-up of the government scheme is predominantly by more well-off, middle-class homeowners. In effect, it could be argued that the government scheme is a subsidy for the already wealthy.

Are these characterizations (a) and/or (b) really stereotypes? And if so, why?

THE IMMORALITY OF STEREOTYPING
Natural Rights

We have seen that stereotyping is based on certain fallacious ways of drawing deductions and inferences. However, we now also need to consider the principle on which we might want to reject stereotyping on moral grounds. One influential strain of argument, which dates from the eighteenth-century European Enlightenment, is the claim that human beings possess inalienable 'natural' rights and are therefore entitled to equal treatment (Grayling, 2007). In this context, we can think of the claims for equality in the *Declaration of the Rights of Man and of Citizens*, approved by the National Assembly of France on 26 August 1789, the *Declaration of Independence* of 4 July 1774, and the publication of Tom Paine's *The Rights of Man* (1791–1792) (Paine, 1964). But even in the high noon of the Enlightenment, slaves, workers and women tended to be excluded on gender grounds from those entitled to such natural rights. Nevertheless, however inadequate historically the actual extension of the idea of natural rights, it provided a language, a rhetoric by which the claims for human dignity might be expressed and expanded. This culminates in the United Nations' *Universal Declaration of Human Rights* (United Nations, 2001, p. 136).

If we accept the moral premise that all human beings in some fundamental sense are equal, have equal rights, then the process of stereotyping is something that must run counter to that moral claim. Stereotypes immediately suggest that 'some are more equal than others' and are, as we have noted, used in that way to suggest that some sets of people are just inferior to other, chosen, sets of people. But the 'natural' rights argument is a mirror image of stereotyping itself. Remember that one of the root assumptions in stereotypes is often that the groups are categorized on the grounds of their 'natural' characteristics. A counter view to this is that stereotypes and the attribution of natural rights are essentially social decisions.

The Circularity of a Natural Rights Argument

The moral philosopher Mary Warnock argues, for example, that who is included in the ambit of natural rights must (logically) rest on a decision (Warnock, 1998, pp. 54–56). The problem is, as Warnock points out, claims to natural rights rest on a circular argument. The form of a natural rights argument is as follows: in virtue of being an 'x', then 'a' is entitled to certain rights. For example, in virtue of being human, 'a' has a natural right to 'z'. But this raises some important questions. Firstly, we ask 'What or who counts as an 'x'?' We can substitute for 'x' a person, foetus, mammal, tree, rock, and so on. Secondly, the argument requires us to be able to specify the criteria that an 'x' must satisfy in order to be included. Put more philosophically, 'What are the necessary and sufficient conditions that 'a' must satisfy in order to count as an 'x'?'

Typically, we might want to say that only persons are bearers of rights. Every person has a natural right to privacy (see Chapter 10). But what are the criteria for being a person? Is this simply by being *Homo sapiens*? Or by having interests? Or by being sentient?

> Everyone who tries to come up with factual or scientific criteria for personhood gets into difficulties over what we are to say about infants or those, who, though they once satisfied the criteria, are no longer able to do so,

such as those in a coma, or suffering from dementia. But this is just not a little local difficulty. It is fundamental. For it is essentially for society to *decide* who is a bearer of rights. There is no way of looking at the facts about, say, a demented woman, and deducing whether she is a person. … Deciding who has rights is the very same decision as deciding who is to count as a person. (Warnock, 1998, p. 63)

The decision cannot be read off from facts about the world, so it must involve antecedent criteria and such criteria must involve some evaluation. Thus, in order to make the decision we must invoke moral value. We are back where we started and, in effect, assuming the thing we are trying to prove. And hence the claim that rights are somehow 'natural' seems difficult to sustain; rights must arise from our (collective) decisions to create rights on moral grounds.

THE RELEVANCE OF KANT'S CATEGORICAL IMPERATIVE
The Dignity of Persons: Treating People as Ends

Kant's moral philosophy provides the relevant principles here. His account provides an underpinning for the talk about rights. Kant's second formulation of the categorical imperative (see Box 9.1) sets out the principle of the fundamental respect due to each person, that everyone ought to be treated as 'an end rather than a means'. This, Kant claims, we can derive from Reason rather than Nature. What he means by this is that we can know the moral law without making reference to experience except in so far as experience is necessary in understanding the terms. This is what he means by morality being 'pure practical reason'; it is derived from Reason alone, but instructs us about our behaviour in the world. If Kant is right, this would mean that he could avoid the type of criticism represented by Warnock's circularity argument about rights. In addition, Kant's claim is that there is 'moral knowledge', which is known independently of experience precisely because it is a priori, unconditioned and universal. An analogy here would be to think of the basic principles of morality as having something like the status we might attribute to mathematical knowledge.

In Chapter 7 we saw how Kant's categorical imperative could be used as a formal (logical) test for morality. Our subjective maxims require that they be willed as universal laws (akin to the universality of the laws of natural science), laws applicable, without exception, to all rational beings (Sullivan, 1997, p. 65). For example, this conception of universality underpinned the morality of truth-telling. Maxims that attempted to prescribe lying as a universal law would simply destroy the very concept of communication. The very notion of the media as vehicles of human communication would be rendered null. If lying was deemed morally acceptable on any occasion, we could never trust what we were being told. Lying simply could not become a universal practice. Lying is parasitic on the concept of truth-telling. Human communication itself is predicated on truth-telling.

On the Relationship between the First and Second Formulas

In contrast to the first formula of the categorical imperative – 'Act only on that maxim whereby you can at the same time will that it should become a universal law' – the second introduces a substantive imperative to respect the person in themself as entitled to dignity and respect as a person. Kant's practical imperative is: 'So act so as to treat humanity, whether in thine own person, or in that of any other, in every case always as an end withal, never as a means only' (Kant, 1965, p. 56), or in Sullivan's modern translation, 'So act as to treat humanity, whether in your own person or that of any other, never solely as a means but always as an end' (Sullivan, 1997, p. 29). To treat someone as a means is to treat them simply as an instrument to satisfy my own needs and ends; to treat them as an end in themselves is to treat them as having their own autonomy to shape their lives towards ends that they themselves determine. Before we go on to see what this means in more detail, it is worth observing right away that stereotyping is completely incompatible with Kant's notion that persons ought to be treated as ends rather than means. In other words, in a very fundamental sense, as a person I must be treated with respect and, as we have seen above, stereotypes precisely violate that respect owed to individual persons.

Kant argues that his second formulation is a derivative of the first (see Table 7.1). At the heart of Kant's 'supreme principle of morality' is the idea of reciprocity. This is contained in the notion that for our maxims ('Do not lie') to be moral they must be capable of legislating universally, that is, for all persons irrespective of time or place. In other words, already contained in the notion of a (subjective) maxim being required to be universal law is the idea that rational beings (persons) all have objective, intrinsic worth (Kant, 1965, p. 56). The second formulation means that we must never deny respect to anyone, even ourselves; this includes those who act immorally. Like the first formulation of the categorical imperative, the second has the same requirements of just treatment (Sullivan, 1997, p. 66). Treating people as ends means does not require us necessarily to sympathize or empathize with others but to treat them with respect. Like the first formulation, it is a norm of impartiality which requires us to overcome our subjective preferences. In that sense it is impersonal and disinterested so that our moral judgements are not skewed, biased or partial. We can view this negatively so that in respecting others we must place a limit on our own desires. This aspect of the formula is particularly relevant to why stereotyping is morally wrong and why media practitioners must have a duty not to engage in stereotyping. As we have seen above, stereotyping relies precisely on skewed, biased and partial views. Stereotyping is a symptom of injustice in that it is raised on subjective preferences and biases; it fails to respect personhood by judging individuals through a distorting lens of some devalued characteristic.

The Formula of Respect for the Dignity of Persons

We can understand Kant's argument if we think of the distinction between persons and things. Kant argues that things, whether human-made artefacts or the products of nature, only have value to the extent that *we* might regard them as valuable, have a use for them ('market price'), or have some emotional attachment to them ('affection price'). Things typically have a market price, an exchange value, but that is only the case as long as someone wants them. Rupert Murdoch has remarked that the market is the best means of determining what should go into a newspaper. Newspapers will sell if their readership wants them. In contrast, Kant argues that human beings, unlike commodities, have objective worth and therefore ought to be regarded as an 'end' for everyone. Human beings have worth not because they are wanted or desired by someone, like cameras, fast cars, expensive clothes, but because of 'standards that hold for every human being with reason' (Sullivan, 1997, p. 68).

Kant's argument is that while it is rational, of course, to use artefacts and tools to achieve our ends (if I want to complete this book, I will need to use a computer), we ought not to treat people in the same way. Persons are rational and free agents. Machines, no matter how 'intelligent', are essentially unfree (since they operate according to deterministic rules). They are not therefore accountable for their actions. Being rational and free human beings, they can know what their moral duty is in a way that machines and animals cannot. On this basis, as a journalist, for example, I ought not to treat the subjects of my stories simply as a means to producing a sensational story, boosting the circulation of my newspaper and increasing my own fame or status. This must be absolutely ruled out. I must treat the subjects of my stories with respect. This doesn't, of course, preclude reporting on their moral faults.

Being free and rational, human beings are deserving of a special kind of respect. Now Kant is not saying that if my computer malfunctions I should not use a technician to fix it, or if my son is sick I shouldn't call a doctor. We all, in the course of our everyday lives, use people directly or indirectly – the shopkeeper who sells us our groceries or the engineers running the power station that keeps my computer running. What he argues is that it is morally wrong to use persons solely or purely as a means to an end. From a Kantian point of view this, of course, must apply to the subjects of journalists' stories and documentaries.

The difficult phrase in Kant's formulation, 'So act as to treat humanity, whether in your own person or that of any other, never solely as a means but always as an end', is what do we mean by 'as an end'. What Kant appears to mean is a 'rational autonomous moral agent', and within us resides at least the possibility and potential of being free, autonomous and 'self-legislating subjects'. At the same time in our everyday activities, we might be regarded as someone to be admired, or useful, or likeable, or skilful, and so on. Clearly, we do in our everyday dealings with others use them as means. In the media business, celebrities are 'marketable'; we have minor celebrities, major celebrities or stellar celebrities, who command their various prices, that is, they have 'extrinsic value' (for as long as someone wants to use them!).

Again, there is nothing necessarily wrong with this; we are dependent beings who have to attend to our needs. But the problem is when we *only* regard others from an extrinsic point of view as a means to our ends whatever they may be. For Kant, persons have intrinsic dignity, are intrinsically worthy of respect, and should never be reduced to the status of mere objects or things.

Means, Ends and Stereotyping

Having discussed Kant's formula of respect for the dignity of persons it must be clear that stereotyping must be proscribed by Kant's principle. Stereotyping detracts from the dignity and respect due to persons. The second formula prescribes an unconditional moral duty on everyone to recognize the dignity of every person. This duty must be exercised irrespective of any particular feelings we might have of attraction or aversion. The reductive approach of stereotyping operates at the level of contingent facts about people and their categorization as belonging to some particular group. However, according to Kant, such contingent facts are irrelevant to the duty of respect owed to every person: As Sullivan points out:

> All contingent facts about others as well as any relationships we may have with them are irrelevant both to their inherent value and to the respect we owe to them. Unlike the emotions of affection and dislike, the moral law neither shows preference for nor excludes any particular persons or groups. (Sullivan, 1997, p. 70)

We may, as Kant points out, use people as means in the everyday business of life. I buy a newspaper from the newsagent. But if I treat the newsagent only as a means, then this must be morally wrong. What seems distinctly morally wrong with stereotyping and discrimination is that it is predicated on treating some specific group of individuals solely as means, but not at the same time recognizing them as ends in themselves.

CHAPTER REVIEW

In this chapter we have been engaged in an ethical analysis of stereotyping. Our assumption from a moral point of view is that stereotyping in general and the use of stereotypes in the media are ubiquitous but unjust phenomena. We identified a number of fallacies in the derivation of stereotypes. Firstly, it is wholly fallacious to draw particular conclusions about individual persons from the categorization of groups on the basis of some notional average characteristics. Secondly, we also noted that stereotyping usually involves the commission of the naturalistic fallacy. Evaluative conclusions about the characteristics of groups and individuals are drawn on the basis of an illicit move from some notional factual statements to usually prejudicial, evaluative conclusions.

We then considered moral principles that might be at the core of our sense that stereotyping was simply morally wrong. We rejected the idea of natural rights as logically unsustainable. However, we then argued that a stronger argument can be derived from Kant's second formulation of the categorical imperative: 'So act as to treat humanity, whether in your own person or that of any other, never solely as a means but always as an end'. On Kant's principle, stereotyping is, firstly, at the level of representation, unjust in that it is a partial and biased view of an individual and a group. The skewedness and partiality of stereotypes fail to respect the intrinsic dignity due to every person. Secondly, in that it is partial, it is also unjust. Stereotyping discriminates against persons and colludes in excluding them from access to the broadest possible range of roles and opportunities. The study of the second-class status of women in the film industry exemplified this. Unjust representations may and do have unjust material effects.

FURTHER READING

Alia, V. (2004) *Media Ethics and Social Change*. Edinburgh: Edinburgh University Press. See particularly Chapter 4, 'The ethics of accuracy and inclusion: reflecting and respecting diversity' (pp. 52–67). This chapter argues the case for the connection between the values of accuracy of representation and the value of inclusiveness and respect for diversity. In doing so it presents an important critique of media stereotyping.

Branston, G. and Stafford, R. (2007) *The Media Student's Handbook* (4th edn). London: Routledge (1st edn, 1996). See particularly Chapter 5, 'Questions of representation' (pp. 141–163). This chapter is a good introduction to processes of stereotyping in the media. In particular it considers racial and gender stereotyping and gives examples of changing stereotypes over time.

Gordon, A.D., Kittross, J.M. and Reuss, C. (eds) (1996) *Controversies in Media Ethics*. White Plains, NY: Longman (2nd edn, 1999). See, in particular, Chapter 7, 'The ethics of "correctness" and "inclusiveness": culture, race and gender in the mass media' (pp. 137–162). This chapter debates the issues of whether or not the mass media should make 'special efforts' to deal with concerns about race, gender, culture and ethnicity. This is dealt with in terms of media content and in relation to representation in media industries.

Keeble, R. (2001) *Ethics for Journalists*. London: Routledge. See, in particular, Chapter 6, 'Race/anti-racism matters' (pp. 71–83). This chapter focuses particularly on news media coverage of race and ethnicity.

Sullivan, R.J. (1997) *An Introduction to Kant's Ethics*. Cambridge: Cambridge University Press. See particularly Chapter 4, 'The formula for the respect for the dignity of persons' (pp. 65–83), which provides an accessible account of Kant's thinking on the intrinsic dignity of moral agents and its implications for the morality of social relationships.

HOW TO USE THIS ARTICLE

Go to https://study.sagepub.com/horner to access the following free journal article:

Bissell, K. and Parrott, S. (2013) 'Prejudice: the role of the media in the development of social bias', *Journalism & Communication Monographs*, 15(4): 219–270.

Use this article to explore the role of the media in the production of prejudice. Research on media content shows how the media provide audiences with stereotypical portraits of other people based on attributes such as sex, age, ethnicity, and so on. In their use of stereotypes, the media help to nurture those stereotypes, prejudice and discrimination. This monograph proposes a theoretical model to explain the influence of mediated, individual, social and ideological influences on the development of bias. In addition, an account is given of four experimental studies that examine weight bias in adults and children. The findings of the studies show that the origins of anti-fat attitudes may lie in individual factors, ideology, or cultural norms and media exposure. These studies provide evidential support for the model. The authors conclude that because the development of bias is very individualistic, it is difficult to maintain that any one factor, medium, individual, social or ideological, 'trumps' other factors. Therefore, they propose a model that represents the myriad of factors that have been identified.

10
PRIVACY

In Chapter 4 we discussed John Stuart Mill's (1806–1873) view that the private sphere was inextricably linked to the exercise of individual liberty. According to Mill, the private sphere encompasses three elements. Firstly, it consists of our private thoughts and conscience. Here we have absolute liberty to believe, feel and speculate on whatever we wish. Secondly, we ought to be free to pursue our own tastes, likings and dislikes, and free to frame our plan for our life in accordance with our character and inclinations. We are free to do what we wish as long as we are not harming anyone, even though our conduct may be foolish, perverse and wrong. Thirdly, out of this liberty of each of us, we can also combine with other individuals as long as the same condition is met – that we are not harming anyone (Mill, 1964, p. 75). Mill, in effect, defines an area where we are entitled not to be intruded upon. In this chapter we concentrate on this idea of privacy because the boundary between public and private is a matter of contention. There is an acute tension between the media's investigative function and a perceived entitlement not to be intruded upon.

In the UK, the phone-hacking scandal and the subsequent inquiry by Lord Justice Leveson have appeared to make privacy 'a tipping point' in public debates about media freedoms, the quality of regulation and the extent and role of the law in policing the media. In the Leveson Inquiry, questions about the nature and boundaries of privacy are viewed through the lens of intrusions into the lives of celebrities, public figures and victims of crime. Debates on privacy frequently rest on the inadequacies of regulatory regimes, the inadequacies of media self-regulation and the lack of direct legal protection against violations of privacy (Cram, 1998). However, prior to such concerns must be an understanding of the moral underpinnings upon which such regulation or laws should be built, but, perhaps more significantly, just how we ought to make moral judgements about privacy. As we will see in the next section, the problem with the concept of privacy is that there is by no means any agreement about the value and meaning of privacy or where the boundaries might lie between the private and public spheres. There are a number of competing ways of understanding the concept of privacy and each has different moral implications.

The controversies around privacy, for example, have been cast in the language of rights. On the one side, those whose privacy has been invaded have claimed a right to privacy while the media in general, and the press in particular, claim the right of freedom to investigate and report even when, on occasions, this may breach the law. It is claimed that there is a 'natural' right to privacy antecedent to any particular rights to privacy granted by a particular legal or regulatory system. Much of the critique of media coverage of public figures, celebrities and others has been on grounds that the media consistently violate this natural right to privacy. However, even if we are to accept such natural rights talk about privacy (frequently used by witnesses in the Leveson Inquiry), we need to ask: 'What is the status of such a right?' 'Is it absolute or relative?' We cannot assume that all the values we might want to cherish are compatible with all other values. In this chapter we will aim to understand the tension between media freedom of investigation and expression and privacy.

We will briefly explore the meaning of privacy and consider what it means to invade a person's privacy. For this purpose we will look at a paradigm case of harassment and intrusion – that of the children's author J.K. Rowling. This case illustrates many of the key aspects of current controversies about the press and privacy which were investigated by the Leveson Inquiry. We will analyse key justifications in defence of intrusion into individual privacy. Firstly, there is an argument for the necessary freedom of the media in general and the press in particular. Secondly, we consider the argument that public figures abrogate their right to privacy by virtue of being public figures. Thirdly, there is a more controversial argument that defends the notion that, in addition to public interest being a ground for the invasion of privacy, 'the interests of the public' may also be a legitimate reason for intrusion into individual privacy. Finally, and in spite of such arguments, from a moral point of view, we can ground the protection of privacy in the Kantian imperative (see Table 7.1) to respect the dignity of persons.

10.1 DEFINITIONS
Types of privacy

1. Physical privacy

   Freedom from unwanted physical observation and bodily contact or interaction; restrictions on others' ability to intrude or interfere.

2. Mental privacy

   Freedom from psychological interference or intrusion; restrictions of the ability to access and manipulate the mind.

3. Decisional privacy

Freedom from intrusion and interference in what I choose to do, the decisions I might make and freedom to act on them, and how I choose to live my life; restrictions on others to procedurally interfere with my decisions.

4. Informational privacy

Freedom from interference and intrusion regarding facts about myself; restrictions on information that others may hold about me and to whom information is disclosed.

Sources: Floridi (2013, p. 228) and Adam (2005, p. 152)

DEFINING PRIVACY

Privacy is defined by *The Shorter Oxford English Dictionary* (1972) as 'the state of being withdrawn from the society of others, or from public interest, seclusion', and this does seem to capture what is at the heart of the conflict between a range of public figures and celebrities and the media. It is to claim a right to be withdrawn from the public gaze and to be protected from the intrusions of the media.

Claims to privacy must be distinguished from claims to solitariness. To want to be solitary is to want to absent oneself from the public world. In contrast, privacy expresses a certain need in relationship to a public world. As Grayling points out, we must not confuse privacy and solitude:

> Solitude is the welcome physical absence of others (loneliness – different yet again – is the physical absence of others). Privacy has nothing to do with the presence or absence of others; it is having aspects of one's life, feelings and activities known and reserved only to oneself or the few to whom one chooses to reveal them. (Grayling, 2001, p. 196)

Any unwanted exposure of such aspects would therefore count as an intrusion or an invasion of privacy. Similarly, privacy ought not to be confused with secrecy. Letters or emails are private but not necessarily secret. The private is the sphere over which individuals feel they have, or ought to have, control; where they have the power to invite or exclude without justification. A secret is something that we intentionally hide whereas privacy is something we like to protect. It is no accident that in the definitions given in Box 10.1, there are several different types of privacy. These tend to be expressed negatively in terms of different areas of private life that need to be protected from various kinds of intrusion and interference.

In expressing the need for privacy, individuals are claiming a moral relationship with the public world. It expresses the need to control how we appear to the public world. It appears to be an essential element in maintaining our sense of self-worth by shielding our intimate feelings, relationships and habits from public exposure. 'Infoprivacy' is a term that has been used to describe that sense of there being facts about ourselves, 'personal information', that ought to be non-public

(Boyne, 2004). Access to our private sphere on this account ought to be only by consent. Penetration of this private sphere without consent is a form of moral wrong-doing, whether by the media or any other agency. In opposition to such claims to privacy is the claim that there are grounds on which privacy might justifiably be set aside in the public interest. However, again, as our variety of definitions suggest, there is no necessary essential core to the concept of privacy. There remains considerable scholarly disagreement about how we should characterize privacy (Floridi, 2013; Solove, 2008; Wacks, 2010).

Privacy is a contested concept. The conventional approach has been to try to define some essential quality, some sufficient and necessary conditions, which define the core of privacy and what it is to be private. For Floridi (2013, pp. 228–260), for example, the key to privacy is to reduce questions about privacy to questions about informational privacy. All our different characterizations of privacy may be redescribed in terms of information; all privacy is essentially 'infoprivacy'. Floridi criticizes various attempts to establish a theory of privacy. First is the idea that we can define privacy in terms of utility, that is, privacy is instrumental for us in achieving the ends; this view has much in common with Mill's idea of the private sphere. Secondly, Floridi rejects the idea that we can ground privacy in the idea of ownership in the sense that I own my body, I own information about myself, and so on. Solove, who has contributed especially to debates about the moral and legal aspects of privacy and the internet (Solove, 2004, 2007, 2008), proposes his own theory of privacy which abandons the attempt to identify some essential nature of privacy in favour of defining privacy in terms of a web of interrelated meanings depending on the context of use. Solove (2008) proposes that we might usefully see privacy not as having some essential quality, but in terms of what Wittgenstein calls 'family resemblances'. Our four putative definitions in Box 10.1 have likenesses to one another (for example, in the sense that they entail some form of control by the individual), but are not reducible to some core meaning or unitary concept. Similarly, Solove argues that violations of privacy are various and harmful in different ways.

Consider the following examples: a reporter wearing a disguise gains entry to the private funeral of a person who has died of a drugs overdose; a celebrity is photographed leaving a clinic; the details of a person wrongly suspected of murder are made public; new x-ray devices installed at international airports can 'see' through people's clothing, constituting a 'virtual strip search'; a newspaper hacks into a person's emails; a newspaper hacks into the mobile phone of a murder victim; a magazine markets a list of its subscribers' personal information in spite of having promised not to; a newspaper publishes a list of the members of an extreme organization after obtaining the list from an ex-member. The ethical evaluations of each of these examples of intrusion may be evaluated differently precisely depending on the context. What it means to safeguard privacy may be different in each of these cases.

A Case of Invasion of Privacy

In spite of the disagreement over the meaning, scope and limits of privacy, there is less uncertainty over its importance and the threats to its preservation (Wacks, 2010, p. 50).

Let's consider a typical example of an 'invasion' of privacy: the case of the famous children's author J.K. Rowling. In this example we can see the intersection of a claim to privacy and the counter-claim regarding the maintenance of media freedom. In England there is still no legal right to privacy as such, although elements of legislation protect privacy in specific ways, such as data protection. But a number of high-profile celebrity cases (for example, Kate Moss and Naomi Campbell, Princess Caroline of Monaco and the Canadian singer Loreena McKennitt) have pushed the law in that direction. The case of J.K. Rowling has been particularly significant in the move towards the recognition of privacy as a natural and legal right (see Box 10.2). J.K. Rowling claimed that her child's right to privacy had been violated by an agency photographer taking a photograph in a public street, and this was upheld by the courts (Dyer, 2008). But it might be argued that this was an undue extension of the range of privacy for a number of reasons. Firstly, we might see this as eroding the distinction between the public and private spheres. In effect, the street would become a media-free zone or at least it would become so unless the consent of potential subjects was obtained first. Simply walking down the street would qualify for protection of privacy. Secondly, the UK Human Rights Act did not recognize any such general right to privacy. A right not to be photographed in a public space would, in effect, create a right for most people to the protection of their image. Thirdly, the effect of all this could severely inhibit the activities of the press, tilting the balance to a less open society. Finally, the case illustrates the extent to which 'moral sentiment' or a prior claim to a natural right may be at the root of changing the law. The Murrays appealed to a pre-existing, 'pre-legal' or 'natural' right to privacy (see Box 10.2).

10.2 A JUDGEMENT CALL
J.K. Rowling – a right to privacy?

In 2008, for the first time an English court case established that the publication of an inoffensive photograph of an ordinary activity in the street could amount to an intrusion into privacy. The case concerned the author J.K. Rowling (Mrs Joanne Murray) and her husband, Dr Neil Murray. The Murrays obtained a ban on the publication of a photograph taken in the street of one of their children. They had brought a high court action in their son's name against Express Newspapers and Big Pictures (UK), an agency which had supplied the picture. The complaint was that their son's right to privacy had been infringed. A photographer had taken pictures of their son in the street with a long lens. They sought damages and an injunction banning further publication of the photograph or any other picture taken of him without his consent. The picture agency's defence was that the English courts had refused previously to recognize the right of an individual not to be photographed in a public place, except when special factors such as harassment, distress to a child or disclosure of confidential information were involved. The central point here was that up until this case, routine activity conducted in a public place carried no guarantee of privacy.

From a moral point of view was this an appropriate extension of privacy?

The court action did not end the Murrays' sense of persecution and invasion of their privacy by the press. J.K. Rowling subsequently appeared as a witness at the Leveson Inquiry, launched in November 2011. At the inquiry J.K. Rowling testified to a consistent pattern of harassment by the press. She claimed that she was driven out of her home by constant press surveillance; that a journalist had secretly placed a note inside her daughter's schoolbag; that she had been pursued by the paparazzi a week after giving birth; and that she was afraid that, even in the light of court action, pictures of her children were still on the internet. The scale of the interest of the press in the author and her family is indicated by the fact that she had taken over 50 court actions against the press (Dyer, 2008).

The Leveson Inquiry and Privacy

The conflict between claims to privacy, particularly by public figures and celebrities, and media freedom exploded in the Leveson Inquiry. The first part or 'module' of the inquiry focused on 'the relationship between the press and the public and looks at phone-hacking and other potentially illegal behaviour'. The spark that lit the prairie fire was mounting evidence that the *News of the World*, a paper noted for its long tradition of populism and investigative reporting, had engaged in systematic efforts to invade the privacy of a wide range of individuals from politicians to celebrities to victims of crime. The inquiry was concerned to investigate a range of press wrong-doing, including: electronic surveillance or intrusion; data theft (for example, going through dustbins or stealing diaries); the use of agents provocateur; payments to witnesses or private investigators; phone and email hacking; and a cat-all 'unfair, unethical and underhand' press activities (*Daily Telegraph*, 2011).

Most notably, there were extensive allegations of phone tapping by a private investigator (Glenn Mulcaire, on behalf of journalists at the newspaper). According to Hugh Grant, Paul McMullan, an ex-*News of the World* Features editor, 'boasted' about phone hacking at the paper (*Guardian*, 2011). The numbers of potential victims of phone hacking ran into thousands (Evans, 2012). News International, the owners of the *News of the World*, initially tried to maintain that the phone-tapping incidents were the work of a few rogue reporters. However, through the testimony of witnesses, it soon became clear that not only was there a culture at the *News of the World* which promoted systematic targeting of the private lives of the famous and infamous, but that this went beyond one newspaper. In effect, what was being tested in the Leveson Inquiry was the ethics of the sector generally.

The weight of evidence against the *News of the World* in particular led ultimately to Rupert Murdoch closing the paper in a damage-limitation exercise. The catalyst for the closure was the general public's revulsion at evidence that the mobile phone of the murdered schoolgirl Milly Dowler had been hacked by journalists at the *News of the World*. In 2002, shortly after Milly went missing, voicemail messages on her phone had been deleted. This gave hope to her parents, Bob and Sally Dowler, that Milly was alive. In fact, the voicemails had been deleted by journalists at the paper in order to make space for new messages. Sally

Dowler testified to the Inquiry that: 'It clicked through on to her voicemail so I heard her voice and [said] "she's picked up her voicemail Bob, she's alive"' (quoted in Robinson, 2011). This was a cruel deception. Murdoch subsequently met the Dowlers and News International paid them £2 million in compensation. Bob Dowler said: 'Given the gravity of what became public ... one would sincerely hope that News International and other media organizations would look very carefully at how they procure ... information about stories, because obviously the ramifications are very much greater than just an obvious story in the press' (quoted in Robinson, 2011).

10.3 A JUDGEMENT CALL
Max Mosley versus the *News of the World*

On March 30, 2008 the *News of the World* published an account of a private 'party' held by Max Mosley. At the party Mosley was using the services of a number of prostitutes. All were engaging in the S&M party voluntarily. Unfortunately, one of the women, an experienced professional dominatrix, had been recruited to take compromising photographs of Mosley with a secret video camera. In particular, the *News of the World* wanted to entrap Mosely by showing him giving a Hitler salute. Mosley was a public figure in that he was, at the time, the Head of Formula One motor racing. In addition, Mosley was the son of the deceased British fascist leader, Sir Oswald Mosley, although he had distanced himself from his father's political beliefs. The *News of the World* article alleged that Mosley and his companions were engaged in sado-masochistic activities and, more specifically, that the party was a re-enactment of a Nazi Jewish concentration camp. The article highlighted every suggestion of this that could be extracted from the video recording. Mosley sued the *News of the World* and won the case. The court upheld a view that whatever the nature of the activities, given that all those taking part consented, this was a private matter, and that Mosley's privacy had indeed been breached.

Could there be a public interest defence for the *News of the World*'s intrusion into Mosley's privacy?

Source: Burden (2009, pp. 240–254)

PRIVACY WARS
Conflicting Rights

A right need not be absolute and this is shown by the conflicts which may arise between different rights claims. The central clash in the Leveson Inquiry was between those who want more stringent protections to a right to privacy and those who believe that this may threaten the freedom of the media. A right, according to Boyne (2006), may be prima-facie right. This means that a right may hold as a general principle but may be overridden if good grounds can be established. There is a social consensus that rights to privacy ought to be respected on the basis of the kinds of reasons already suggested. Privacy is 'a condition of human well-being, part of the good life which ethical behaviour seeks to promote or preserve' (Boyne, 2006, p. 4). But rights may conflict. It is when rights appear to conflict that decisions must be made. The Leveson Inquiry is precisely concerned with this problem. The goal of the Inquiry is to make recommendations 'for a more effective policy and regulation that supports the integrity and freedom of the press while encouraging the highest ethical standards' (Leveson Inquiry, 2011). In the J.K. Rowling case (Box 10.2), for example, the reference to the law as it stood did not resolve the issue. Two different interpretations of the law were delivered by the judges. The appeal judge in effect adopted the position that the interest of the public in J.K. Rowling as a celebrity children's writer did not override the right to the protection of the Murray family from press intrusion.

Article 8 of The European Convention on Human Rights (see Box 10.4) notably does not say directly 'everyone has a right to privacy', but that privacy must be 'respected'. Boyne (2006) points out that, in philosophical language, this means that a right to privacy cannot be considered to be an 'absolute' or an 'indefeasible' right. In other words, it is relative to, and contingent upon, rights held by others. For example, it seems reasonable to suggest that the police have a right, in some cases, to override the right to privacy to detect crime of serious nature, such as the threat of terrorist attack. We can say here that the right of public protection supervenes that of the privacy of a suspected terrorist. And the corollary here is that there is a duty placed upon the police precisely to protect the security of the public.

There are two interrelated questions: 'What ought to be the legitimate limits to a right to privacy?' and 'What are its consequences for the ethical behaviour of media professionals?' There is clearly a tension between the preservation of privacy and media freedom in an open society. It has been argued that the Leveson Inquiry, even before it reported, had a 'chilling effect' on press freedom. Although clearly the evidence suggested that journalists at the *News of the World* made systematic attempts to penetrate the privacy of public figures, celebrities and victims of crime, it nevertheless had a strong record in uncovering corruption in various fields of public life. We consider below three arguments that imply legitimate limits to the right to privacy in the interests of an open and democratic society.

10.4 DEFINITION
Article 8 of the European Convention on Human Rights – a right to respect for private and family life

1. Everyone has the right to respect for his private and family life, his home and his correspondence.
2. There shall be no interference by a public authority with the exercise of this right except such as is in accordance with the law and is necessary in a democratic society in the

interests of national security, public safety or the economic well-being of the country, for the prevention of disorder or crime, for the protection of health or morals, or for the protection of the rights and freedoms of others.

European Court of Human Rights (2010, p. 10)

Argument from Freedom of the Media

The strong case for the right of inquiry of a free media in relation to privacy is based on the need to scrutinize the fitness of individuals to hold public office. It is part of the role of the media in an open and democratic society to hold authority to account. The question is 'How far is it legitimate to probe into the private lives of public figures to pursue this purpose?' It is not difficult to see that demonstrating the incompetence, negligence, corruption, inefficiency, and dishonesty of public figures and those holding public office is clearly in the public interest. Thus there are categories of private actions (which are frequently financial!) which demonstrate whether a person is unfit to hold public office. In such cases, there is clearly a legitimate public interest to be served through an 'intrusion' into privacy (Wacks, 2010, p. 88).

For example, a minor member of the royal family was recently exposed as being willing to sell access to members of the royal family in order to promote commercial interests. This exposure was brought about by a process of entrapment. But we may say that this was justified in the public interest. There have been many similar cases of British MPs who were willing to sell their services to promote commercial interests. The misuse of the expenses system by MPs in the House of Commons also provided legitimate grounds for revealing the private details of the MPs' financial claims. The right to infoprivacy was justifiably overridden in the interests of a public right to know what was in the public interest.

However, any evaluation of a public figure's performance must be on the grounds of appropriate criteria, that is, on how well they perform their public tasks. Consider the case of the *News of the World* and Max Mosley, outlined in Box 10.3. It is difficult to imagine how Mosley's sexual proclivities could have had any bearing on his ability to do his job as head of formula one motor racing. Similarly, the public may be interested in the son of an extreme right-wing politician, but there is no real public interest to be served by the kind of entrapment practised by the *News of the World*. The argument for the freedom of the press, and a public right to know, is questionable when it comes to aspects of individuals' private lives, which may only have a tenuous, or indeed no, connection with their ability to be effective in public office. See, for example, Hugh Grant's Myth 8 in Box 10.5. In his testimony to the Leveson Inquiry, Grant argued, 'It seems clear to me, as it does to most judges, that the vast majority of the public interest defences from popular papers for their sex exposés are bogus. The judges recognise that the motive for printing the story was commercial profit, not public interest' (*Guardian*, 2011).

Archard (1998, p. 89) argues that the belief that any form of immorality in one's private life should disqualify someone from public office is simply wrong. The implication that part of the qualification for holding public office is a blameless private life, especially with regard to sexuality, simply does not follow. There is no necessary connection between the fact that I may be unfaithful to my wife and my ability or otherwise to be an effective government minister. A failure of personal sexual morality is no ground for media intrusion. However, if a senior politician has a problem with alcoholism, this may represent a genuine matter of public interest as it may directly affect the politician's judgement in public affairs. And yet the politician has a right of infoprivacy – the medical details about his alcoholism are a personal matter.

Similarly, Archard (1998) suggests that merely being shown to be hypocritical in one's private life does not imply that one is always hypocritical and does not justify intrusion. However, there are forms of hypocrisy which do call into question a politician's fitness for office and which would justify intrusion to disclose it. For example, in 1993 John Major, as leader of the Conservative Party and the then British Prime Minister, launched the so-called 'Back to Basics' campaign at the Party Conference in order to cement his position as leader and improve the Conservatives' poll ratings. The themes of the campaign were distinctly moral, emphasizing issues of moral probity and law and order. In particular, much was made of the immorality of single mothers both for getting pregnant in the first place and then for expecting to obtain social housing. The campaign rebounded badly on Major and the Conservatives as the criminal and immoral activities of a significant number of Conservative politicians were exposed by the media.

Many Tory MPs were revealed as having offered to ask questions and use their influence in Parliament in exchange for money in what became known as the 'cash for questions scandal'. Most notoriously, Neil Hamilton MP was alleged to have accepted cash from the Harrod's boss Mohammed Al-Fayed. This led to the journalist Martin Bell standing for election in Hamilton's constituency on an anti-corruption ticket and defeating him. In addition to a number of financial scandals, there were also sexual scandals. The prominent MP Jonathan Aitken was alleged to have procured prostitutes for Arab businessmen, who paid his hotel bill at the Ritz in Paris. Aitkin robustly denied the allegations, giving a now infamous speech in which, in response to the press stories, he talked of taking up 'the Sword of Truth' and 'the Shield of Justice'. He was subsequently convicted of perjury and sent to prison after losing a court case in which he tried to sue *The Guardian* newspaper for libel. What was not uncovered at the time was that John Major himself had had an adulterous affair with another Conservative MP, Edwina Currie. The campaign was clearly shown to be a piece of hypocrisy in the light of subsequent revelations.

This form of hypocrisy was important as the exposure of private unethical behaviour was at odds with the politicians' public pronouncements. When private morality was made into a public political issue, it seemed reasonable to hold politicians to account. The key decision for the media professional – the judgement call – is whether the journalist can justify the intrusion into this person's privacy on the grounds of a public right to know. This to some extent links to a further argument to set aside privacy in the public interest.

10.5 EXAMPLE: Hugh Grant's 10 common myths about the popular press

Myth 1. That it is only celebrities and politicians who suffer at the hands of the popular papers.

Myth 2. That egregious abuses of privacy only happened at the *News of the World*.

Myth 3. That in attempting to deal with the abuses of some sections of the press you risk throwing the baby out with the bathwater.

Myth 4. That any attempt to regulate the press means we are heading for Zimbabwe.

Myth 5. That current privacy law under the Human Rights Act muzzles the press.

Myth 6. That judges always find against the press.

Myth 7. Privacy can only be a rich man's toy.

Myth 8. That most sex exposés carry a public interest defence.

Myth 9. That people like me want to be in the papers, and need them, and therefore our objections to privacy intrusions are hypocritical.

Myth 10. That the tabloid press hacks are lovable rogues.

Guardian (2011)

Public Figures are Not Entitled to Privacy

This argument proposes that in an open society the media have a right to inquire into the public and private behaviour of people, particularly the powerful, the rich and celebrities, in the public interest. This right 'trumps' any rights to privacy when the public interest is at stake. The principle of free speech in the public interest is a legitimate restraint on the individual's right to privacy. It may be necessary to invade private physical space to obtain information. The use of a telephoto lens or surveillance techniques is justified because public figures are a different category of person from ordinary members of the public. The argument is that public figures, including celebrities, politicians and holders of public office, are in a special category and their natural right to privacy is to some extent abrogated by their social and cultural status (Boyne, 2006; Wacks, 2010, p. 84). This view takes two principal forms. In the first place, public figures, because of their wealth and power, are more fully equipped to resist intrusions of privacy than the ordinary citizen. This is a weak argument on several counts. First, it is a purely instrumental argument rather than a moral one and has nothing to do with rights as such. Secondly, the extent to which the media do in fact garner information about the private behaviour of public figures shows this claim to be false. Public figures may be afforded some protection but they are constantly subjected to media scrutiny, including forms of physical harassment which restrict their ability to live their lives freely.

A stronger argument may be that there is a kind of tacit contract between public figures and the media; celebrities and politicians court publicity and attempt to manage it in their own interests. They should not then complain if things don't go entirely as they wish. This is the risk they take. This view is strongly contested by Hugh Grant (see Myth 9 in Box 10.5):

> In my experience they [i.e. celebrities] seldom want to be in the papers for the sake of it, to promote themselves. In many cases they hate having to be in them at all. The issue only arises when they have something – a film, for example – to promote, when there is a certain pressure to bang the drum a bit in advance of the release. Occasionally this pressure is contractual, but more often it is simply moral. (*Guardian*, 2011)

What Grant means by 'moral' in this context is a duty to try to promote the film, for example, because of the amount of time, human effort and resources that may have been expended by all those involved. He went on to argue that in fact PR generally only made a small contribution to the success or failure of a film .

The argument may then be extended to suggest that it is only fair and just that they give up some element of their privacy in exchange for the media attention they want. However, this notion of some tacit contract is very dubious, or at least, hard to make it stick, it can only be about public performances rather than private behaviours. There is an important distinction to be made between a photo-opportunity that goes wrong and provides the wrong kind of publicity and the right to respect a boundary between public life and private life. For example, when Neil Kinnock was elected leader of the Labour party in October 1987 he provided photojournalists with the opportunity to film him and his wife strolling on Brighton beach (UK). Unfortunately, this ended with Kinnock being swept inelegantly off his feet and ending up briefly in the sea. In addition to the amusement caused, the press interpreted the dousing as prefiguring his defeat at the polls in the following General Election. For those public figures who gain their positions through talent and hard work, it doesn't intuitively seem fair to then expect them to pay an extra price of surrendering a portion of their privacy (see Archard, 1998, pp. 87–88) – another argument made by Hugh Grant in his statement (see Myth 9 in Box 10.5). There can be no question of a 'contract' or 'deal' in cases when people acquire public prominence and celebrity accidentally, for example, by winning the lottery or witnessing a crime.

Debating the Value of Gossip

Conventionally, gossip is regarded as trivial and of little social value. It is the pandering of the media to the voyeuristic interests of the public that gives rise to breaches of privacy. And as we have already observed in this chapter, such intrusions may be harmful and breach the rights of individuals (Cohen-Almagor, 2005, p. 94). However, a contrary view is put by Archard (1998, pp. 90–93). He makes a case for the value of gossip, arguing that the 'interests of public', as well as 'the public interest', are equally grounds for exposing the private lives of public figures. This is, in effect, an argument from prurience. The fact that the public are interested in the details of the lives of the rich and famous constitutes grounds for shifting the boundaries of public and private. He suggests that this interest is natural and even healthy. He wants us to think about journalism as 'print gossip', but it may equally well be 'broadcast gossip' or 'digital gossip'. There are obvious differences in terms of scale, in the fact that it is print (rather than oral), in that the newspaper gossip is usually better researched and subject to legal constraint (laws of slander and defamation), and in that we are the agents of gossip.

The counter-view is that gossip is frequently felt to be distasteful, harmful or vicious (Wacks, 2010, p. 56). As the Leveson Inquiry shows, intrusion into the private lives of public figures frequently involves blackmail, bullying and harassment. Not only is the end pursued not moral, but also the means employed to achieve those ends are frequently immoral. Archard argues, however, that gossip may be functional. Firstly, he draws upon anthropological evidence to suggest that gossip is important in defining a community and consolidating its unity. Secondly, he says that gossip is about the shared values of the community: ' … gossip is a way of testing out or rehearsing those values by exposing conduct that they would seem to proscribe. And finally gossip functions as a deterrent to wrongdoing by its potential to expose wrongdoers to ridicule and public shame' (Archard, 1998, p. 92). The advent of social networking and Twitter gives further support to this particular argument. The great and the good have not been shy in coming forward to 'tweet' to express private views and to talk about their private feelings (the polymath and broadcaster Stephen Fry, for example).

It may be factually true that gossip serves social purposes and sustains the community in various ways. However, such empirical considerations do not of themselves provide a valid argument for the invasion of privacy, as Archard himself acknowledges:

> Rather, gossip provides a forum wherein we affirm our identity as a community, assure ourselves that everyone can behave badly and explore the force of our moral conventions which determine what is and is not bad behaviour. That is not enough to show that the public's interest does warrant invasions of privacy. It shows only that there is a further dimension – one which has been unjustly neglected – to the moral space in which such invasions are evaluated. (Archard, 1998, p. 94)

If we maintain that privacy is a kind of natural right, then this must trump any instrumental social value that might be attributable to gossip.

The problem is that from such general considerations it does not follow that a particular intrusion into a particular person's privacy can be justified. Archard's approach is utilitarian in the sense that the argument for gossip is its contribution to the general pleasure. A typical weakness of utilitarian arguments is that they may be used to justify the overriding of recognized rights and interests. The argument here seems to pit the entertainment and amusement of the many against the hurt and humiliation of the few. In a similar vein, it might be suggested that an occasional public flogging might satisfy the desire among certain sectors of the public for sensational violence and a more robust approach to law and order. That would not make it right, particularly if the 'victim' of the flogging was selected more or less randomly (that is, other and equivalent criminals received different punishments). The contention is that privacy is a *prima-facie right* and, if that is the case, then there would have to be grounds for each specific intrusion to justify overriding that right.

The judgement call for the media professional is 'Are there sufficient grounds to justify intrusion into privacy?' General gestures towards the putative value of gossip simply won't do. Firstly, in trying to resolve the dilemma between intrusion and non-intrusion, we need to consider just where the boundary between the private and the public is. As we have indicated above, this may be a shifting boundary depending on social and cultural factors. It certainly seems to be the case that social networking, for example, has shifted the boundary towards more openness. Secondly, we need to identify what type of privacy we are dealing with and, thirdly, how this might relate to different categories of people (see Box 10.6). Possible categories to consider are ordinary citizens (versus various types of public figure), children, those who are public figures by virtue of occupying some public role (judges), celebrities, politicians, etc.

We may want to treat people differently depending on whether they find themselves in the public spotlight for accidental reasons or whether publicity is something they seek. Grant makes this point strongly in Myth 1 in Box 10.5:

> That it is only celebrities and politicians who suffer at the hands of the popular papers … To an extent, we already know how false this is. There are victims like the Dowlers, like the families of the little girls murdered at Soham, like the families of soldiers killed in Afghanistan, like the victims of the London bombings. They were all identified as capable of making a commercial profit for certain newspapers, and therefore had their privacy invaded. (*Guardian*, 2011)

10.6 A JUDGEMENT CALL
Relative rights to privacy

There is a view held by academics and commentators that in considering media responsibilities in respecting privacy we ought to recognize relative rights to privacy. We ought to make several important distinctions. Firstly, we might distinguish between those who have chosen a career involving self-publicity (politicians, entertainers, models, etc.) and those who have chosen a career that naturally attracts media attention (artists, sports persons, judges, etc.). For the latter category, media attention is not something they will have chosen, but will be an inevitable side-effect of their choice of profession. A second and perhaps a morally more important distinction is between celebrities and public figures who have chosen their way of life and ordinary people who have involuntarily become the centre of media attention because they are a victim of, or witness to, crime, for example. These distinctions may be taken to imply that those who have voluntarily put themselves in the media spotlight have relatively less right to privacy than those who involuntarily find themselves there.

Can we legitimately, from a moral point of view, attribute different degrees of privacy protection to different categories of public figures?

Sources: Kieran, Morrison and Svennevig (2000, pp. 158–159) and Cohen-Almagor (2005, p. 95)

Grounding Privacy as a Moral Value

Privacy does seem to be an integral element to being a person and something that ought to be respected. To derogate from someone's privacy would seem to be a moral harm. According to Immanuel Kant, as we discussed in Chapter 7, we exist in relationship to one another bound by moral law. Mutual respect for privacy is part of a wider duty of respect we owe to others. Kant expressed this in his second formula of the categorical imperative: the formula of respect for the dignity of persons. We must not treat others only as a means to our own ends (getting a story, becoming famous, etc.) but 'always as an end'. What Kant means by persons being 'ends in themselves' is complex. Persons have ends or goals in the sense of striving for moral well-being (virtue) on the one hand, but also in the sense of striving for physical well-being (happiness). He argues that we have duties to promote such ends for others. We might argue that the privacy of the person is intimately bound up with the notion of persons being 'ends in themselves' (see Table 7.1).

At the same time we have a negative duty not to endanger or violate respect for others. There is therefore a categorical requirement for mutual respect among people. This is not optional, although it may be frequently disregarded! Kant argues that we must limit what we do: in the pursuit of our own welfare or benefit we must not humiliate others or fail to acknowledge and be aware that others have an equal dignity to our own person (Sullivan, 1997, pp. 28–45). Privacy is surely bound up intimately with my sense of self and my self-respect. If our privacy is violated, we certainly have a sense of humiliation, of a lack of respect, of a loss of autonomy. Journalistic intrusions into privacy frequently violate this principle of respect for the dignity and autonomy of others. And Kant's principle is universal; it applies to the ordinary person in the street as well as to the celebrity, the politician and the public figure, or even the criminal. Fundamentally, on this account, to intrude on someone's privacy is to treat them as a means only, not an end.

CHAPTER REVIEW

In this chapter we have explored the fundamental dilemma for media practitioners between the competing claims of the right to privacy and the right of the media to free speech. The chapter has argued that the protection of individual privacy is central to being a person. We have also seen that privacy may be abrogated in the public interest by investigative journalism or abrogated in the pursuit of stories that simply interest the public for largely entertainment purposes. In this context, we devoted some attention to the debate over the value of gossip. Calls for tighter regulation of the media have been treated as threats to the continuance of an open society. For these reasons, media industries, and in particular the press, continue to favour self-regulation. Even the critics of the press, such as Hugh Grant, agree that the freedom of the press is an important value to be maintained.

The Leveson Inquiry into the phone-hacking scandal has to some extent revolved around this tension between conflicting values of freedom and respect for privacy. What the Leveson Inquiry has brought to light, particularly through the testimony of 'victims' of intrusion, is the sense of a press being out of control, where the ethical standards expected of journalists have frequently been breached. However, what also emerges is that the there is a lack of symmetry between the competing claims. Firstly, for example, there is a profound asymmetry between, say, the freedom of expression of individuals and the freedom of expression of large multinational media corporations. Secondly, powerful media institutions are in a far better position to exercise freedom of expression than the individual can be in defence of their privacy. The testimony of witnesses at Leveson gives ample proof of this.

A central theme of our discussion is whether or not a right to privacy is a relative or absolute one. In the context of the tension between claims for media freedoms and a right to privacy, a responsible approach might take into account the relative rights of privacy that may be attributed to different categories of public figures. The relevant distinction here is that between those who voluntarily cultivate media attention and those who involuntarily become the centre of media attention. In the first category we can put, for example, politicians and celebrities; in the second category are those who have become the victims of, or witnesses to, crime. This may provide some grounds for recognizing relative rights to privacy which do not compromise the rights of the media. However, in conclusion, we returned to a more absolutist Kantian view of rights and duties. Kant's relevant principle here is that of the respect owed to every autonomous moral agent; it applies to the ordinary person in the street as well as to the celebrity, the politician and the public figure, or even the criminal. Fundamentally, on this account, to intrude into someone's privacy is to treat them as a means only and not as an end. This implies that there ought to be much more rigorous constraints on the media, given the evidence of current practices.

FURTHER READING

Clapham, A. (2007) *Human Rights: A Very Short Introduction*. Oxford: Oxford University Press. See, in particular, Chapter 6, 'Balancing rights – the issue of privacy' (pp. 108–118). This chapter provides an introductory account of the concept of a right to privacy. However, it sets the claim to such a right in the context of other competing rights such as that of freedom of expression.

Cram, I. (1998) 'Beyond Calcutt: the legal and extra-legal protection of privacy interests in England and Wales', in M. Kieran (ed.), *Media Ethics*. London: Routledge. pp. 97–110. A useful account of the history of attempts to regulate and protect individual privacy.

Kieran, M., Morrison, D.E. and Svennevig, M. (2000) 'Privacy, the public and journalism: towards an analytic framework', *Journalism*, 1(2): 145–169. An empirical study which, through focus groups and questionnaires, produced evidence about the range of public attitudes on the rights of the individual, the public good and the regulation of media content.

Morrison, D.E. and Svennevig, M. (2007) 'The defence of public interest and the intrusion of privacy: journalists and the public', *Journalism*, 8(1): 44–65. The authors highlight the unsatisfactory nature of the concept of 'the public interest' and offer an alternative concept, that of 'social importance', as a surer guide to the balance between public interest and privacy.

Solove, D.J. (2008) *Understanding Privacy*. Cambridge, MA: Harvard University Press. This is a substantial contribution to the attempt to clarify many of the conceptual confusions surrounding our understanding of privacy. Solove proposes his own new theory of privacy, which abandons the attempt to identify the essential nature of privacy in favour of defining privacy in terms of a web of interrelated meanings, depending on the context of use.

Wacks, R. (2010) *Privacy: A Very Short Introduction*. Oxford: Oxford University Press. A good overview of the nature and value of privacy. Chapter 4, 'Privacy and free speech', is particular relevant here.

 ## HOW TO USE THIS ARTICLE

Go to https://study.sagepub.com/horner to access the following free journal article:

Cohen-Almagor, R. (2014) 'After Leveson: Recommendations for instituting the Public and Press Council', *The International Journal of Press/Politics*, 19(2): 202–225.

Privacy has been the touchstone issue in the recent crisis in the British media. Use this article to consider what might be a suitable institutional framework (a Public and Press Council) to improve the far from satisfactory situation in Britain (and elsewhere!). Drawing on a range of international material, the article provides a very useful review of relevant codes of practice that may form the basis for the ethical principles that might underpin the new regulatory framework. The author proposes that the new regulator should be empowered with unprecedented authority and greater powers and be able to bring substantial sanctions to bear on breaches of the code. The paper provides useful background on the work of the Leveson Inquiry and the problems arising from the concentration of media ownership in the UK.

PART IV
NEW DIRECTIONS?

11
SECURITY

The emergence of digital media has radically extended the range of Media Ethics. We have already encountered in previous chapters issues around social media. Events associated with the rise of emergent digital media are played out on a global scale and have raised fundamental moral issues about national and international security. The global reach of digital media has enabled the broadcasting (if that is what it is) of sensitive material on an unprecedented scale. The paradigm case here is that of WikiLeaks which we will examine in some detail in this chapter. This case in particular exposes tensions between divergent ethical views of the role of the state in relationship to the media. These to some extent echo the dilemmas we have already encountered in our discussions of freedom of speech and its limits.

The first view, which can be characterized as libertarian or liberal, is that the moral imperative must be always, as far as possible, to minimize the role of the state both in relationship to the liberty of the individual and in relationship to free speech. We encountered this view in the context of John Stuart Mill's famous essay 'On Liberty', discussed in Chapter 4 (see Box 11.1 below). A second view, however, would be that the first priority, the first duty, of the state is to maintain its security and the security of its citizens. In this tradition, certain idealist philosophers, for example, G.W.F. Hegel (1770–1831) and T.H. Green (1836–1882), have taken the state or society to be more fundamental than the individual citizen. In other words, it makes no sense to treat individuals as if they were in some way set apart from social and political relationships. The moral imperative emerging from this way of thinking is always to make the priority the claims of the state rather than the individual. These positions, although arising in the working out of political theory in the nineteenth century, can be seen clearly mirrored in responses to the revelations of WikiLeaks and other putative breaches of state security.

In the light of our discussions in the previous chapter, a further and separate theme which will emerge in this chapter is the extent to which the moral debate about security, which is driven by uses of emergent digital media, presents distinctively new moral problems. Or rather, as Deborah Johnson, a seminal figure in Computer Ethics, argues, 'that we think of the ethical issues surrounding computer and information technology as new species of general, traditional moral issues' (Johnson, 2001, p. 16). This contrasts with claims that emergent media technologies will necessarily generate uniquely new ethical issues. However, this is not to deny that the novel attributes of, say, social media technologies frequently mean that moral issues arise with a new 'twist' because they have created new possibilities for human action. The case of WikiLeaks provides a characteristic 'puzzle case' in that, as I will argue, the very novelty of WikiLeaks means that it is not clear what kind of thing it is we are dealing with and therefore what the appropriate rules or regulations might be that ought to govern its operation. However, its novelty means that we can't settle this question in advance; it's indeterminate. Ultimately, in such cases we need to make a decision in order to know how to deal with it.

11.1 DEFINITION
The liberty principle

'The object of this Essay is to assert one very simple principle, as entitled to govern absolutely the dealings of society with the individual in the way of compulsion and control, whether the means be physical force in the form of legal penalties, or the moral coercion of public opinion. That principle is that the sole end for which mankind are warranted, individually or collectively, in interfering with the liberty of action of any of their number, is self-protection. That the only purpose for which power can be rightfully exercised over any member of a civilised community, against his will, is to prevent harm to others.'

Mill (1964a, pp. 72–73)

WIKILEAKS
Characterizing WikiLeaks

WikiLeaks, according to some, posed major challenges to state and international security and is part of what Schmidt and Cohen (2013, p. 40) have called 'free-information movements'. At the same time, it poses challenges to mainstream news media and to the role of conventional media and professional journalism. It does enable anonymous sources to make information available more easily. In order to do what it did, that is leak sensitive government material, WikiLeaks exploited the then new technical potential of social media. Technically, a wiki is a website that enables its users to create and edit content across a set of inter-linked websites via a web browser. Wikis are operated by wiki software and are now widely used to create community websites, to drive corporate intranets, support knowledge management systems and even for just personal note-taking. One of the most conspicuous uses of this technology has been in the development of Wikipedia. However, unlike Wikipedia, WikiLeaks is not technically a wiki at all, and it has gone through at least four design iterations (Heemsbergen, 2014). Its users are not able to add to it or edit it. In this way, it resembles the operation of more conventional news services. Similarly, like other global media, it is driven by a central personality, Julian Assange, a journalist, software developer and internet activist (see Box 11.2).

11.2 A JUDGEMENT CALL
Does WikiLeaks represent a responsible use of power?

WikiLeaks in some ways resembles more conventional (global) media news services. Firstly, one important similarity is that WikiLeaks is driven by a central, powerful personality, Julian Assange. In this, he bears some comparison to his fellow Australian and media mogul, Rupert Murdoch. Secondly, like Murdoch, Assange is committed to a kind of journalism that feeds on exposure and sensational revelations, especially in relationship to the famous and powerful. Thirdly, Assange is an interesting combination of journalist, software developer and internet activist. However, again, what Murdoch and Assange share is an interest in power. The information disclosures made by WikiLeaks have powerful and lasting impacts. This is why he has been pursued for various alleged crimes by a number of governments. But the key difference between Assange and his fellow media moguls is that Assange distributes his revelations for free, while Murdoch's media empire deals in information as a commodity for profit.

Is WikiLeaks a responsible use of media power and does the fact that it distributes its information freely make a moral difference?

Source: Newey (2011, p. 35)

Assange has been frequently challenged as to whether what he does with WikiLeaks is a morally responsible use of power. He gave his answer to this question to Eric Schmidt, Executive Chairman of Google, and Jared Cohen, Director, Google Ideas, for their book *The New Digital Age* (2013). Schmidt and Cohen's interest is in the future course or next phase of 'free-information movements' and they see such movements as potentially very damaging. Firstly, according to Assange, 'Our human civilization is built upon our complete intellectual record; thus the record should be as large as possible to shape our own time and inform future generations'. Secondly, Assange believes that 'because different actors will always try to destroy or otherwise cover up parts of that shared history out of self-interest, it should be the goal of everyone who seeks and values truth to get as much as possible into the record, to prevent deletions from it, and then to make this record as accessible and searchable as possible for people everywhere'. In contrast (and interestingly given their positions in Google), Schmidt and Cohen believe that the free-information model is a 'dangerous model'. They also believe that bad judgements will be made about what information ought to be released that will lead ultimately to some people being killed. They argue that government systems to control and regulate information are justified, and while they acknowledge that these may be imperfect, nevertheless governments should be deciding what is classified and what is not. So here we have two poles of the moral argument: Assange clearly represents the liberal tradition, while, perhaps surprisingly, Schmidt and Cohen incline to the state control view.

Content

Let's first briefly examine the kinds of information WikiLeaks is disclosing to see what might be at stake here. In the autumn of 2010 there were two waves of releasing material culled from a US database of confidential diplomatic cables. In the first wave of releases there were embarrassing revelations of the private views of diplomats. In the second wave of releases there were documents relating to both private and public strategic installations. These can be broadly classified as relatively mundane, unsurprising disclosures on the one hand, and on the other disclosures that are genuinely 'news' and in the public interest. In the first category of the 'revelations' in 2010, we can include things like: Colonel Gaddafi is an oddball; the Vatican has tried to block an investigation into paedophile priests in Ireland; the revelation that the (ex) French President Nicolas Sarkozy is a short man with a 'Napoleon complex'; the non-fact that Angela Merkel is really a man; and the charge that the Duke of York behaves with 'vulgarian bluster', making indiscreet comments about the British government's defence policy (Newey, 2011, p. 35).

In the second category, there are significant revelations that have been 'speaking truth to power', annoying governments and informing the public. These are the traditional roles of a free media. These disclosures include, for example, the data released through WikiLeaks which increased the estimates of civilian deaths in Iraq since 2003 by some 15,000. An earlier scoop by WikiLeaks was the showing of a US Apache gunship crew in Iraq seeming to treat the killing of terrorist suspects (that in fact included two Reuters reporters) as if it was a video game. A further significant revelation was that of the possible involvement in 1989 of the British Government in the murder of Irish republican lawyer Pat Finucane. This disclosure prompted the British intelligence service, MI5, to make available documents which could form the basis of a public inquiry into the case. Further diplomatic documents revealed that King Abdullah had been urging the US government to attack Iran. Other documents seemed to shed further light on the controversial release of the convicted Lockerbie bomber of Pan Am flight 103, Abdelbaset Ali al-Megrahi, from a Scottish jail. It was disclosed that the Libyan government had threatened revenge if al-Megrahi died in jail. The British envoy had been talking with the Libyan government about his release as a fait accompli before the decision of the Scottish Executive to release him. This seemed to be at odds with the British government's denial that it had neither been influenced by Libya nor in its turn sought to influence the decision to release al-Megrahi. For the relatives of those who had died in the Lockerbie bombing, in particular, this was further evidence that the decision to release al-Megrahi had been made on other grounds than justice or compassion.

Reaction

WikiLeaks' release of such sensitive information was attacked by both national governments and elements of the media establishment. Firstly, the charge was that of irresponsibility, that WikiLeaks had simply 'dumped' 250,000 documents into the public domain with little or no consideration for the consequences or the likely loss of life that might follow, for example in war zones such as Afghanistan (Naughton, 2012, p. 131). Sixty-eight out of 111 stories appearing in US newspapers about the release of embassy cables made these kinds of claims about irresponsibility and potential harm and a further 20 were simply 'ambiguous' (Benkler, 2006). However, these claims were simply untrue as many of the 250,000 documents did not reach the public domain. Similarly, as we will discuss below, much of the material was filtered by WikiLeaks' more mainstream partner organizations. Secondly, as Benkler argues, governments and elements of the mainstream media joined forces to deny that WikiLeaks' release of documents was an act of journalism, but rather that it was akin to an act of terrorism. Secretary of State Hilary Clinton, for example, on 30 November 2010 stated 'Let's be clear, this disclosure is not just an attack on America's foreign interests. It is an attack on the international community – the alliances and partnerships, conversations and negotiations that safeguard global security and advance economic prosperity' (quoted in Naughton, 2012, p. 132). Similarly, Assange was characterized by Vice-President Joe Biden as a 'high-tech terrorist'. According to Naughton (2012, p. 135), the WikiLeaks affair came to be characterized or framed by both government and media not as signalling the emergence of a new form of journalism, but as something akin to the emergence of media terrorism.

11.3 A JUDGEMENT CALL
Whistle-blowing and Bradley Manning

We have already mentioned some similarities between WikiLeaks and other news services (Box 11.2). A further similarity resides in the fact that Assange relies on anonymous sources to provide the material for WikiLeaks. In effect, WikiLeaks provides a drop box into which sensitive material can be uploaded. One of WikiLeaks' major and most controversial sources was Bradley Manning (b. 1987), who subsequently re-designated himself as

(Continued)

(Continued)

Chelsea Elizabeth Manning. Manning was responsible for what is believed to be the release (via WikiLeaks) of the largest ever set of classified documents. However, his identity was discovered and he was subsequently convicted in July 2013 in the USA of violations of the Espionage Act, dishonourably discharged from the army and sentenced to 35 years in jail. The classified material passed to WikiLeaks included videos of airstrikes on Iraq and Afghanistan in 2007 and 2009; 250,000 US diplomatic cables; 500,000 army reports. Manning had been able to get his hands on so much material through his work as an intelligence analyst in an Army Intelligence Unit in Iraq. He used WikiLeaks because his attempts to interest more conventional media (*The Washington Post* and *The New York Times*) had failed. Manning claimed in court that his motive for this obvious betrayal of trust was that he was going 'to help people'. Indeed, some of the material did help to expose violations of human rights. It is also claimed that the leaks exposed government corruption in the Middle East which became a catalyst for the Arab Spring.

Is this kind of whistle-blowing morally justifiable in the public interest?

Source: Chelsea Manning (2014)

It is relatively easy to overestimate the extent to which, from an ethical point of view, emergent media may be different from conventional media. What seems distinctive about WikiLeaks, when it is considered as a medium, is its technological base, the distributed nature of its technology and the fact that its content is free to its users. However, the fact that it doesn't treat its information as a commodity is not particularly special if we consider the extent of the growth of free newspapers or a traditional form of journalism, such as radio broadcasting. A difference between WikiLeaks and more conventional media is that it is not itself creating a story; it is acting as a source, as a database. What it has in common with other news media is its power, as we have seen, to control the flow of information. One of the interesting aspects of the WikiLeaks case is the alliance with *The Guardian* newspaper. For example, in concert with *The Guardian*, the cables were only released in batches, at WikiLeaks behest. *The Guardian*'s defence of this control was that its function was a conventional, professional one of redacting the material to remove the names of individuals who might be in danger because of the disclosure and also to provide the kind of context to the stories which WikiLeaks itself does not do.

John Naughton (2012) argues that this alliance between an emergent and a more conventional medium represents a new 'partnership' model. This model was 'symbiotic', bringing considerable benefits to both 'organizations'. From an ethical point of view, it brought WikiLeaks the established professional skills of journalism: such as sifting, verifying, corroborating, and redacting information that might have endangered life. In other words, certain standards were brought to bear on the material before it entered the public domain. Of course, this cut no ice with the detractors and critics of WikiLeaks. For the collaborating mainstream there were also benefits (Naughton, 2012, p. 129). In bringing the secret material to public attention it showed a continuing commitment to journalism in the public interest, even at some risk to itself. It demonstrated the continuing relevance in the internet age of key journalistic skills of sifting and evaluating controversial evidence. It provided an incentive for mainstream media to consider, for example, developing their own secure electronic drop boxes. Finally, given the highly competitive market, it gave *The Guardian* newspaper 'a slice of some of the biggest journalistic action of the decade' (Naughton, 2012, p. 130).

11.4 A JUDGEMENT CALL
Whistle-blowing and Edward Snowden

Another case that raises similar moral issues to that of WikiLeaks is that of the release of classified documents by Edward Snowden (b. 1983). Snowden was a computer specialist and a former employee of the Central Intelligence Agency (CIA) and had been also a contractor for the National Security Agency (NSA). Snowden was responsible for releasing thousands of classified documents through various news organizations, such as *The Guardian* and *The Washington Post*. The documents that Snowden released were particularly interesting in that they exposed the surveillance work of the security services in a number of countries. These included the surveillance work of the NSA in the USA and similar work, in collaboration, with the security services of the UK, Australia, Canada and New Zealand, together with details of the cooperation of various businesses and European governments. The revelations were the cause of great embarrassment to the governments involved. The exposures began on 5 June 2013. One estimate suggested that Snowden had copied and passed on upwards of 200,000 highly classified documents, only a fraction of which appeared in the media. Nevertheless, this led to a ruthless global pursuit of Snowden by the US government. Snowden now lives in a secret location in Russia. Considerable pressure was also brought to bear on the various newspapers to surrender whatever information they were holding. Snowden has been variously caricatured as a heroic whistle-blower and a traitor. He claims his 'sole motive' for leaking the documents was 'to inform the public as to that which is done in their name and which has been done against them'. Snowden, unlike Chelsea Manning, is self-consciously ideological; he espouses right-wing libertarian beliefs and is anti-government.

Is this kind of whistle-blowing morally justifiable in the public interest?

Source: Edward Snowden (2014)

THE RIGHT TO INFORMATION ARGUMENT

One moral defence of WikiLeaks' and Edward Snowden's activities (see Box 11.4) might be an argument based on human rights. Article 19 of The UN Declaration of Human Rights says that everyone has a right 'to seek, receive and impart information and ideas through any medium and regardless of frontiers' (United Nations, 2001, p. 140). Even if we accept the argument that because our governments have signed up to the Declaration a right has been brought into being, this must be a qualified or *prima-facie* right and not an absolute right. For example, there is a judgement to be made (as we saw in Chapter 10) about the extent to which the value of privacy needs to be respected as well as the value of information: 'The question is whether hum drum diplomatic pillow talk, as well as low skulduggery, is fair game for disclosure' (Newey, 2011, p. 35).

There are a number of reasons why we might want to suggest that this is not simply to be settled by reference to information rights. Firstly, WikiLeaks is putting out information on a global scale and most of that information may not belong to our state but will belong to other national jurisdictions. This may be construed as a violation of others' sovereignty and other countries may not be as eager as we may be to have their dirty linen washed in public. 'Globality' may not be an 'unambiguous good'. Secondly, there are, as we have discussed elsewhere, many sensitive areas of information where it is by no means obvious that publication is necessarily a good. Article 10 of the European Convention on Human Rights (see Box 11.5) specifically qualifies the right to freedom of expression with the interests of national security. The publication of classified documents is on the face of it a breach of the Convention in terms of the duties and responsibilities that come with the right of freedom of expression.

Thirdly, it would be impossible to know what all the consequences of publishing classified and sensitive material might be. In the case of WikiLeaks, the charge has been made that some of the information about military operations in Iraq and Afghanistan may endanger the lives of not only military personnel, but also civilians and aid workers. Fourthly, what the underlying technology of WikiLeaks allows Assange to do is to circumvent the right of the state, in the words of Article 10, to require 'the licensing of broadcasting, television or cinema'. One of the problems, as we have suggested before, is the difficulty of defining quite what it is we are dealing with in the case of WikiLeaks.

11.5 DEFINITION
Article 10 of the European Convention on Human Rights – freedom of expression

1. Everyone has the right to freedom of expression. This right shall include freedom to hold opinions and to receive and impart information and ideas without interference by public authority and regardless of frontiers. This Article shall not prevent States from requiring the licensing of broadcasting, television or cinema enterprises.
2. The exercise of these freedoms, since it carries with it duties and responsibilities, may be subject to such formalities, conditions, restrictions or penalties

as are prescribed by law and are necessary in a democratic society, in the interests of national security, territorial integrity or public safety, for the prevention of disorder or crime, for the protection of health or morals, or for the protection of the reputation or rights of others, for preventing the disclosure of information received in confidence, or for maintaining the authority and impartiality of the judiciary.

European Court of Human Rights (2010, p. 11)

Accountability

This new medium has at least two characteristics that emphasize the question of accountability. In contrast to more conventional media, WikiLeaks illustrates the power associated with the scope of communications and the possibilities of reproducibility. Firstly, the power of the medium is enhanced by the immediacy, the interactivity and its almost permanent availability. What's significant about WikiLeaks and its alliance with *The Guardian* is that the extent of interactivity available to users is highly restricted – unlike Wikipedia. Secondly, power is exercised through reproducibility. Again, WikiLeaks is a paradigm case of technology enabling public reproducibility of massive amounts of information. Assange and his associates have appropriated the intellectual property of others and reproduced it without the permission of the originators. Along with this power we might want to argue comes a commensurate level of responsibility to exercise an even greater duty of care. This, of course, is not a new moral issue in any sense. However, the enabling power of the technology raises it in a heightened way. The normal processes of accountability that we would naturally expect of a conventional news organization are circumvented, whereas more established media are subject to forms of state and industry regulation this is not the case for WikiLeaks. This may explain why Assange has been pursued in the courts on a charge (of sexual assault) that is unrelated to the activities of WikiLeaks. His supporters and conspiracy theorists see the legal action brought by two women in Sweden as an indirect form of attempted censorship. This has led to a form of 'cyberwar' as Assange's supporters have attempted to hack into, and paralyse, online organizations such as Amazon and PayPal who have withdrawn their services from WikiLeaks.

THE PUBLIC INTEREST ARGUMENT: WHISTLE-BLOWING

Defenders of WikiLeaks maintain that its actions have been in the public interest in the sense that what has been exposed has been the various nefarious activities of governments. Similarly, in the case of Edward Snowden, it is claimed that what has been exposed has been the extent to which the security forces are out of control, maintaining, for example, surveillance on masses of innocent citizens and the heads of state of friendly countries. These may be described as classic cases of whistle-blowing.

Sisela Bok (2003) has defined a whistle-blower as a person who makes 'revelations meant to call attention to negligence, abuses or dangers that threaten the public interest'. Bok notes that whistle-blowers usually operate from within organizations. This is true of both Chelsea Manning and Edward Snowden. In addition, we can also see whistle-blowing as a conscious form of dissent. This is also certainly in the case of Edward Snowden. Another characteristic of whistle-blowing is that it is an act of last resort, when all other options have been explored. However, this is a more contentious argument for both Manning and Snowden.

There have been many notable cases were individuals have leaked government information in the public interest. One of the most celebrated cases in Great Britain was in 1984 when a senior civil servant in the Ministry of Defence, Clive Ponting, leaked secret information about the sinking of the battleship, the *General Belgrano*, during the Falklands War. Ponting passed information, which directly contradicted the government's account of how and why the battleship was sunk, to the Labour MP Tam Dalyell. The documents revealed that the *General Belgrano* had been outside the exclusion zone imposed by the British Navy and had been steaming away from the Royal Navy taskforce when it was attacked. This removed the government's justification for its sinking, which resulted in the deaths of hundreds of Argentinean sailors. Ponting was charged under the Official Secrets Act (1911) and tried by a jury. His defence was that of the public interest and that of the protection of parliamentary privilege, given that the information went directly to a Member of Parliament. Ponting expected to be found guilty and imprisoned, but the jury accepted the public interest argument in spite of the fact that the judge's summing up clearly indicated that Ponting was in breach of the Act. Ponting went on to write a number of important books about the 'culture of secrecy' in the British government and contributed to a growing movement for reform of the official secrets legislation in favour of more open government (Ponting, 1985, 1990).

Other celebrated examples of whistle-blowing include Daniel Ellsberg's release of the so-called 'Pentagon Papers' in 1971. Ellsberg worked at the Rand Corporation and had security clearance, which enabled him to have access to classified documents about US government decision making during the Vietnam War. Ellsberg made copies of the documents, amounting to some 7,000 pages. Increasingly disaffected by the conduct and course of the war, he eventually allowed them to be published. After many legal battles, the Pentagon Papers made it into the public domain and contributed in no small part to public disenchantment with the war and the campaign to bring it to an end. What the papers demonstrated was that President Johnson and his executive had lied to the public and to Congress about the prospects for victory and the likely levels of casualties through a continuation of the war. Like Ponting, Ellsberg faced trial, but there was also a covert operation to discredit him and prejudice the outcome of the trial. But again, like Ponting, Ellsberg eventually won the court battle. The covert operations against him were organized and executed by the same group who were responsible for the bugging of the Democratic Headquarters in the Watergate complex: Gordon Liddy and the so-called 'White House Plumbers'. According to Newey, there is a qualitative difference between WikiLeaks and actions such as those of Ponting and Ellsberg. We can see these as local and specific actions with a clear moral purpose. In these cases, we have individuals in government employment who have jeopardized their careers and faced possible imprisonment. Newey (2011, p. 35) suggests that WikiLeaks institutionalizes whistle-blowing so that it is no longer an act of individual conscience and that 'information is not an unambiguous good. It depends on how it is presented, for what purpose, and at what expense. You can have too much of it'.

WIKILEAKS: A PUZZLE CASE

As was pointed out earlier, the underlying technology of WikiLeaks allows Assange more easily to circumvent the right of the state to regulate publication. Article 10 of the European Convention on Human Rights, acknowledges the right of the state to require 'the licensing of broadcasting, television or cinema' (European Court of Human Rights, 2010). There is a clear clash between the right to know and the right to regulate. One of the problems, as we have suggested, is therefore the difficulty of defining quite what it is we are dealing with. What is important is to be able to determine what the appropriate rules might be. WikiLeaks is a paradigm example of a 'puzzle case' (see Box 11.6). When we talk about WikiLeaks, are we talking about a news organization or some other kind of information service, or a database or the means of expression for its creator? This is just not clear. This indeterminateness lies at the heart of moral disagreements about WikiLeaks, its activities and their moral evaluation. Certainly, the US government views the activities of Assange (and Snowden) as treason. But it is important also to consider what the relevant conventions and regulations ought to be to cover WikiLeaks and similar emergent media. The importance of novelty here is that we cannot answer this question *in advance* precisely because it is a new thing. In order to decide on appropriate, specific regulatory or moral frameworks we have to *decide* what it is. Given the current rate of advance in media technologies, the future is likely to be about having to make such decisions. This takes us beyond 'new ways of breaking old laws'. We have to know what the relevant rules are (and new ones may need inventing) in order to be able to identify wrongdoing.

11.6 A JUDGEMENT CALL
Dealing with 'puzzle cases' arising from emergent technologies

Our moral concepts and language have evolved historically to meet the situations and predicaments that human beings have encountered. Present meanings are constructed by actual present correct usage. However, emergent technologies may create

(Continued)

(Continued)

predicaments where it is unclear how we ought to apply existing moral concepts, rules and standards.

(a) A puzzle case can be either an imaginary or actual case that gives rise to the need to make a decision about the meaning of words.

(b) There is no antecedent correct answer; we cannot know what it means in advance. There is no previously existing correct linguistic usage. The problem in a puzzle case is that by its very nature it is indeterminate.

(c) Thus puzzle cases constitute 'decision issues'. In reaching a decision there may be good or bad reasons for making a decision one way or another. And in that sense there may be correct or incorrect decisions.

Consider applying this pattern of inquiry to, say, Twitter. Does Twitter create new areas of moral uncertainty? Are new rules required for its (formal or informal) governance?

Source: Flew (1994, pp. 454–459)

The decision we might take about the meaning of WikiLeaks has important consequences. WikiLeaks does not obtain the documents it makes public in a direct manner. Files are uploaded anonymously to a Wiki from which they can be subsequently downloaded for anonymous release. In addition, like more conventional journalists, it protects its sources. However, if information is obtained illegally, it is the person who obtains the information who is legally responsible if the law is broken. If material is passed to a news organization which publishes this, then the publisher is protected by the First Amendment. If this is the case with WikiLeaks, then Assange must be protected by the First Amendment. The issue is then a genuine 'decision issue': 'What are the reasons that we might use to argue that WikiLeaks is a news organization?' Again, the answer is not pre-given. For example, WikiLeaks does not operate conventionally in the sense that it distributes information to the public using wiki software. It doesn't have the variety of content of more conventional news services. Thus, in order to make moral sense of emergent, novel media technologies we must go through this kind of decision procedure.

CHAPTER REVIEW

In this chapter we have pursued two themes. Firstly, we discussed the tension between two views of security at the level of the state. The liberal ethic suggests that the moral imperative must always be to minimize the role of the state, especially in relationship to the freedom of the media. This may be presented both in terms of utility, that is that the best state of affairs is always the one where individuals and the media have the greatest freedom of speech and publication or in the language of rights. An alternative view suggests that security precedes freedom and that the first priority of the state must be the security of the state and of its citizens. We saw this tension played out in the controversies over the dissemination of classified information by WikiLeaks and its collaborating newspapers and in the case of Edward Snowden. At its most extreme, one camp saw the free publication of classified material as an act of 'media terrorism'. However, the liberal camp saw the actions of Chelsea Manning and Edward Snowden as heroic acts of whistle-blowing.

The second theme of the chapter was concerned with the problem of whether emergent media technologies create new moral dilemmas or whether they create new species of generic moral problems. The cases we have considered seem to suggest that digital media show every sign of presenting familiar moral dilemmas (for example, the morality of whistle-blowing) but in new forms. WikiLeaks displays evidence of continuity with other and more conventional media forms while at the same time it has elements of discontinuity and novelty. Its moral status is not pre-given but must be the result of a decision. But again, this is not to suggest that we need a new 'digital ethics' since some of the moral arguments relevant to WikiLeaks arise in the case of more conventional media. Ultimately, what are required are cogent reasons for deciding how to characterize WikiLeaks and what may or may not be morally (or legally) appropriate. We can take WikiLeaks as a paradigm case of what happens when we are confronted with genuine novelty and the means by which we might dissolve indeterminacy to achieve a clearer moral view.

FURTHER READING

Alia, V. (2004) *Media Ethics and Social Change*. Edinburgh: Edinburgh University Press. See, in particular, Chapter 10, 'Changing technologies: prospects and problems' (pp. 147–159). Alia, in this chapter, takes a fairly radical approach to the potential social and political impacts of transformations in media technologies. She reviews ethical questions around media ownership, control, censorship and public trust.

Hamelink, C.J. (2000) *The Ethics of Cyberspace*. London: Sage. See particularly Chapter 4, 'Equal entitlement in cyberspace' (pp. 79–106). In this chapter Hamelink takes an egalitarian rights-based approach to access to content in cyberspace. He focuses on 'the digital divide', the importance of access and global governance.

Johnson, D.G. (2001) *Computer Ethics* (3rd edn). Upper Saddle River, NJ: Pearson/Prentice-Hall. This book is a foundational discussion of the nature and purpose of Computer Ethics. Johnson argues against others that in many cases ordinary moral principles can be extended to situations created by the information and communications technologies. Computing creates new species of generic moral problems.

Naughton, J. (2012) *What You Really Need to Know about the Internet: From Gutenberg to Zuckerberg*. London: Quercus. This is a popularizing account but a good mix of history, analysis and useful case studies. See, for example, 'Case Study 3: WikiLeaks and the powers that be' (pp. 123–135).

Schmidt, E. and Cohen, J. (2013) *The New Digital Age: Reshaping the Future of People, Nations and Business*. London: John Murray. See particularly Chapter 2, 'The future of identity, citizenship and reporting' (pp. 32–81), for a discussion of the current and possible future impact of the digital revolution on media, media industries and media ethics.

Tavani, H.T. (2011) *Ethics and Technology: Controversies, Questions, and Strategies for Ethical Computing*. Hoboken, NJ: John Wiley & Sons. See especially sections on 'Are cyberethics issues unique ethical issues?' (pp. 9–14) and 'Whistle-Blowing' (pp. 115–119). In the first of these sections Tavani considers the extent to which new cybertechnologies give rise to uniquely new moral issues or whether we are confronted by traditional moral problems but simply in new forms and contexts. This discussion is applicable to the impact of new media technologies on conventional media ethics. In the second extract Tavani briefly discusses the moral status of whistleblowing.

HOW TO USE THIS ARTICLE

Go to https://study.sagepub.com/horner to access the following free journal article:

Heemsbergen, Luke J. (2014) 'Designing hues of transparency and democracy after WikiLeaks: vigilance to vigilantes and back again', *New Media & Society* [Online], 24 February, http://nms.sagepub.com/content/early/2014/02/21/146 1444814524323 (accessed: 23 April 2014).

Use this article to explore in more depth the relationship between WikiLeaks and democracy. The article reflects on the origins and history of WikiLeaks, tracing iterations of WikiLeaks between 2006 and 2011. It seeks to match the evolving design iterations of WikiLeaks with corresponding paradigms of digital democracy advanced by Lincoln Dahlberg, an expert on media politics at the University of Queensland. The author aims to explain how different political positions may be created in new media apparatus through the design process.

12
DIGITAL ETHICS

In the previous chapter, in looking at the impact of WikiLeaks, we considered whether or not emergent media technology raised new species of generic moral problems or whether it gave rise to uniquely new moral problems. In this chapter we take that discussion further. It may be that the transformative power and global scope of digital technologies require us to rethink the foundations of Media Ethics. The computer ethicist Charles Ess (2009), for example, suggests that the impacts of the current wave of innovative media technologies are so profound that we require nothing less than a correspondingly new Digital Media Ethics. The transformation of existing media (film, television, newspapers, etc.), together with the emergence of new forms of media (social media, Twitter, and so on), pose new moral issues and create new types of wrong-doing. In order to address this, we will explore the relationship between work that has already been done in the areas of Computer Ethics and its relevance to the development of Media Ethics.

We know from our previous experience of 'technological revolutions' in media technologies that technologies reconfigure media industries, institutions and audiences (see Box 12.1). One view might be that technologies are in themselves ethically neutral. But media technologies create new possibilities for human action and in that way may give rise to new moral problems and dilemmas that might not have been encountered before. New technological possibilities are not always morally beneficial and may come with human and environmental costs. It is right, therefore, that the developments in digital media technologies should be subject to moral evaluation and scrutiny (Johnson, 2001, p. 5). It is in this context that conventional moral frameworks may need to be radically revised. The aim of this chapter is to investigate various responses to this situation. In this chapter, the term 'emergent media' is used to indicate generic innovation in media technologies, platforms and services because of the accelerating rate of media innovations; new media very quickly now become old media. We will analyse a range of interpretations drawn from Information Ethics, Computer Ethics and Digital Media Ethics.

12.1 A JUDGEMENT CALL
The implications of the
digital transformation of the music industry

Pete Townshend, the legendary rock guitarist, in his John Peel Lecture of 1 November 2011, took a strong line on the technological revolution that the music industry is undergoing (Townshend, 2011). He felt that new forms of distributing music threatened both the rewards that creative musicians might earn from their work and the ability of new artists to develop creatively and be heard:

> Radio is not like internet radio, or torrent sites. Radio pays musicians a fee when music is heard. Radio does not take the position that the public has a right to decide after hearing music played whether to pay for it or not. Radio stations pay and the public pay directly or indirectly in order to listen and make the judgement.

Townshend believes we are in transition from one model of the music industry to another, determined by new media technologies. Conventional industry supported artists financially, creatively, in editorial guidance, manufacturing, publishing, marketing, distribution and payment of royalties. In contrast, the iTune's publishing model only supports artists in the distribution of their work and the payment of royalties, which according to Townshend, is bad for creative work. In addition, the ease of music piracy deprives the creative artist of her/his *just* rewards – a moral question! At the heart of Townshend's lecture was the central enabling role of information and communications technologies in transforming the music landscape.

Does Townshend have a moral case against the new directions in the music industry?

Source: Townshend (2011)

12.2 DEFINITIONS
Computer Ethics, Information Ethics and Digital Media Ethics

Computer Ethics has been defined by James Moor (1985, p. 266) in this way:

> On my view, computer ethics is the analysis of the nature and social impact of computer technology and the corresponding formulation and justification of policies for the ethical use of such policies.

Similarly Deborah Johnson (1985, p. 1) in a further seminal definition writes that Computer Ethics is:

> ... a concern for the way in which computers pose new ethical questions or, more accurately, pose new versions of standard moral problems and moral dilemmas, exacerbating the old problems, and forcing us to apply ordinary moral norms in unchartered realms.

Luciano Floridi (2010, p. 103) conceives Information Ethics, by analogy, as a type of environmental ethics and so it is concerned with 'the ecological management and wellbeing of the infosphere'.

Charles Ess (2009, p. 8) defines the focus of Digital Media Ethics, at least initially, as 'the distinctive features of digital media – what sets them apart from earlier media – that makes them ethically challenging and interesting'.

EMERGENT MEDIA
New Possibilities for Action

Technologies in general, whether digital or analogue, 'instrument human action' in other words we use technologies to go beyond our natural physical capacities and thereby extend the nature, scope and range of human actions. Media technologies are no different in this respect. Emergent media technologies create new possibilities for human action. Making moral choices is about rejecting some possibilities for action on moral grounds. Physical events that occur when an individual acts in a computerized environment are different from those that occur in an environment with no computers. In discussing the relationship between digital and analogue photography in Chapter 8, we saw both continuities and discontinuities in photographic practices and their possible moral implications. Ethical approaches to digital media technologies concern what we should or shouldn't do; what possibilities through technologies we ought or ought not to realize. When we are confronted with genuinely novel situations, generated by emergent technologies, new possibilities for choice and action may outstrip existing legal, regulatory and moral rules. A number of applied ethical approaches have been developed in response. However, there is by no means a consensus view of the field.

COMPUTER ETHICS
A Framework for Identifying Moral Issues

Moor argues that there are three significant characteristics of computing technologies that generate social and ethical impacts: (1) 'logical malleability' (the computer as a 'universal tool'); (2) the creation of 'policy vacuums' (the lack of relevant pre-existing rules, although this is not always the case); and (3) 'conceptual muddles', concerning how best to characterize the new situations created by digital technologies. While this framework was first conceived in the 1980s to define the problems of computing technologies, arguably this approach is now equally applicable to the impact of emergent digital technologies on media institutions and practices.

What Moor means by 'logical malleability' is that most technologies have very specific functions. A computer, depending on its software, can perform a range of diverse tasks – as a video game, a spreadsheet, a word processor, a communications device, an image editor, an interface ... even as a robot! The logical malleability of computing ('the universal tool') leads to 'new possibilities for human action'. Contrast analogue televisions, for example, which were only capable of receiving terrestrial television signals, with the wide range of functions now performed by a standard digital television and the wide scope given to new forms of subscription services. In fact there has been much speculation about the eventual convergence of the television with computers. Another example we have already encountered is the transformation of the processes of photojournalism through digital technologies. New moral questions arise in relationship to the ease with which digital images can be manipulated. A particular aspect of this is the extent to which photography through mobile phones and the possibilities afforded by software such as Photoshop have democratized the creation of images (De Saulles and Horner, 2011).

Moor argues that the logical malleability of digital technologies is likely to create 'policy vacuums'. Digitally-based media technologies can create situations for which our conventional moral compasses may not be equipped. Conventional moral guidelines, legal rules, commercial rules, policies are no longer readily applicable. For example, there could have been no concept of 'hacking' before there were not only computers, but also networked computers. The puzzle when the first hackings began to take place was what kind of an action was hacking from a moral point of view? Hacking came to be defined as the accessing of a computer system or network without authorization from the owner (Tavani, 2011, p. 179). Early legal attempts to deal with hacking tried to treat it as a form of trespass, but hacking involved no observable, tangible, physical intervention. If the hacker had done no harm, was there anything wrong here? And could a distinction be made between benign hacking, malicious hacking and justified hacking as a form of civil disobedience?

12.3 A JUDGEMENT CALL
A policy vacuum in copying computer software

With the advent of the personal computer in the 1980s some users found that they could relatively easily copy proprietary software such as word-processing software, spreadsheets and video games. In the absence of any particular laws or rules covering such actions, users did not necessarily consider they were engaging in wrong-doing; once purchased, there were no rules governing the subsequent use and distribution of the software packages. In other words, there was a *policy vacuum*. Software was not protected by either copyright or patent law.

This situation led to what Moor calls a *conceptual muddle*. Existing rules related to physical theft, that is, of a machine itself or of a hard disk. The muddle was about how we understand software. Was software to be understood as essentially an idea (not protected by IP law) or was it to be understood as a form of writing protected by copyright law or as a set of machine instructions protected patents? The answer could not (logically) be known in advance. Hence appropriate moral principles and argument needed to be applied in order to make a decision and develop policy for the regulation and protection of software (if that was appropriate!).

In the absence of a clear policy or legal framework would it be morally appropriate for users to continue to copy software and would it be appropriate at the same time for creators and producers to assume a 'natural right' to control and/or profit from what they created?

Sources: Tavani (2011, p. 13) and Moor (1985)

Hacking also illustrates Moor's third significant characteristic – that of 'the conceptual muddle'. This occurs when we try to use our existing concepts and rules to cover cases where they will not work. We are confronted with new entities such as websites, videogames, social media etc. There is a policy vacuum because there may be a conceptual muddle about what things actually are and what they mean. Once the concepts have been defined, then the policies, rules and conventions to inform practice can be devised. To dispel the muddle and formulate sound policies we then need to clarify what, for example, hacking is. However, this clarification is largely a matter of deciding to define things in certain ways. For example, you cannot make rules about the duplication of computer software until there is a general understanding about what 'software' is. There is a policy vacuum on these issues because there is a conceptual muddle about what things are and what they mean. Is it like physical property? Is it like intellectual property? Is software an idea or a set of machine instructions? Should copying software be treated as theft? Once the concepts have been defined, then the policies, rules and conventions to inform practice can be devised. My point is that there is not necessarily a right answer. The answers are not given in advance. It's about deciding what it is and then prescribing appropriate rules!

For Moor, it is the job of Computer Ethics to help us to identify the policy vacuums and clarify the conceptual muddles when they arise. Moor's account provides a widely accepted rationale for Computer Ethics. We might similarly argue that Digital Media Ethics is in the same business and that Moor's analysis can be transposed to the impact of digital media technologies on the more conventional media landscape. Conceptual muddles constitute what may also be called 'puzzle cases' (see Box 11.6).

An Alternative View

However, Moor's approach is not without its critics. Another seminal figure in the development of Computer Ethics, Deborah Johnson (2001, p. 7), argues that while Moor provides insight into aspects of Computer Ethics, this is not without its limitations. Johnson proposes a new, alternative account and characterizes this as 'a socio-technical computer ethics'. Johnson observes that Moor's standard account is widely accepted and has provided a rationale for the field. The identification of the need to fill the vacuums provides a case for philosophical analysis and also normative analysis – to examine, critique, debate and propose policies. However, although this has led to a rich body of work over a couple of decades, Computer Ethics is still evolving.

Johnson makes three fundamental criticisms. Firstly, Moor's account is not exclusively an account of ethical issues in relationship to computers and information technology. His account is true of any radically new technology in that most new technologies are likely to create policy vacuums. As I have already suggested, it is relatively easy to see how Moor's idea might be applied in trying to understand the impact digital media technologies.

Secondly, Moor tends to emphasize novelty. The focus tends to be on the early phases of the lifecycle of technologies. Attention is skewed towards innovation and the introduction of new products to users and the public. This neglects the pre- and post-adoption phases of emergent technologies. Computing and information technologies are no longer new. New applications are introduced, but already on the basis of well-founded concepts in computer science and technology.

Finally, the standard account is embedded in a 'social impact' framework. Social and historical contexts tend to be 'black boxed', that is left out of account and not investigated. The fundamental model is one in which the technology impacts on society and history, but there is little to suggest how the technologies themselves may be shaped by social, economic and cultural forces. For example, the formation of WikiLeaks springs out of a particular ideology and political activism. Moor's underlying model seems to be that computer professionals produce for clients who then choose and use. The emphasis is then on the social effects (impacts) caused by technology: computers causes social change.

What's wrong with this framework? It makes a difference in that it leaves out social shaping by human beings and their interests and values. It neglects the research that has been done in the field of Social Studies of Science and Technology, which demonstrates how technologies are socially constructed and do not just emerge from purely technical imperatives (Bijker, Hughes and Pinch, 2001). Johnson claims that our moral experience, our moral ideas and our practice are shaped and shaping. On Moor's reading, agency and power seem to be attributed to computers, whereas the narratives should be staged around what people do –for example, how media professionals appropriate and use the technologies they have at their disposal.

Johnson suggests some general principles for an alternative framework which is founded on the idea that digital technologies are designed and shaped. This is Johnson's understanding of a socio-technical Computer Ethics. Firstly, technologies and societies co-create each other over time. And, of course, values are fundamentally implicated in that process of shaping. The media technologies that we get don't just drop from the sky, but are shaped by the interests of powerful groups. Historically, the shift from pre-digital printing technologies to the computerized printing of newspapers in the UK was precisely driven by the needs and interests of newspaper owners. The owners wanted to break the power of the print unions over the production process. The design and introduction of computerized printing and the shift of the production process from its traditional home in Fleet Street to new sites of production in Wapping were a carefully worked out strategy to wrest control from the print unions.

Secondly, Johnson argues that the unit of analysis should be socio-technical systems rather than simply technological entities. In other words, we begin with combinations of artefacts and humans. Moor's emphasis on the logical malleability of computing technology is misleading in this sense. The malleability must be malleability in response to human needs, wants, interests and goals. It's not just a matter of coding, but of complex interactions between people, institutions and circumstances as well.

Thirdly, technology is not purely neutral but is often shaped by the interests of particular powerful groups. Again, the example of the newspaper printing industry is instructive here. The design of the computerized presses was influenced by the desire of management to shift power from the print workers on the shopfloor. This involved partly deskilling the existing print shop workers to break the power of the unions. This also involved giving journalists direct access to the production process.

According to Johnson, these considerations take Computer Ethics (and for us, Digital Media Ethics) out of the grip of a 'social impact' framework. This provides a better answer to the question 'Why Computer Ethics?' or 'Why Digital Media Ethics?' The socio-technical approach shows that the role of digital technologies in society is a subset of Technology Ethics more generally. However, we now appreciate that that technology is not something 'exogenous' to society, which is impacting somehow from outside, but is 'endogenous' to society, and is closely bound up with social processes and human values. Technology does, more generally, play a role in constituting human lives. But then why isn't Computer Ethics (or Digital Media Ethics) just ethics? The defence here is that they help to focus on the technology component of ethics, and specifically the role of the computer and IT in moral practice, norms and issues. Technologies instrument human actions but they are still human actions.

12.4 A JUDGEMENT CALL
Twitter Trolls and new forms of wrong-doing

A pair of Twitter Trolls have been jailed as a result of sending anonymous and threatening tweets. The pair threatened to kill and rape a feminist for campaigning to have the face of Jane Austen on the £10 note. Isabella Sorley, 23, was described as a binge-drinking college graduate. Her collaborator, John Nimmo, 25, was a jobless recluse living on benefits. They bombarded

(Continued)

(Continued)

journalist Caroline Criado-Perez with vile messages threatening her with attacks 'worse than rape'.

The threatening tweets began in July 2013 after the Bank of England revealed that Jane Austen, the author of the *Pride and Prejudice,* would replace Charles Darwin as the face of the £10 note. The announcement was greeted as a 'brilliant day for women' by Caroline Criado-Perez. She had led a high-profile campaign on social media to ensure a female face would remain on the banknotes. This arose after the Bank of England removed the nineteenth-century social reformer Elizabeth Fry from the £5 note in favour of Winston Churchill. Criado-Perez then began receiving a stream of abuse from 86 different Twitter accounts. Sorley and Nimmo had opened many different accounts with false identities in order to launch the attack.

Does the use of Twitter rather than any other medium make a moral difference in this case?

Source: Camber (2014)

Old Wine – New Bottles?

Part of Johnson's argument is that traditional accounts of Computer Ethics tend to be innovation-centric, concentrating on novelty and discontinuity rather than continuity. We now consider to what extent the role of digital technologies creates uniquely new moral problems, or rather, as Johnson argues, new species of generic moral problems. If Johnson is right, then generally our established moral frameworks remain relevant. (We will discuss below the ethical theories of Luciano Floridi, who advocates a more radical turn in Information Ethics particularly and Ethical Theory more generally.)

Hamelink (2000, p. 35) argues that 'the speed of digital communication does not create new forms of immorality, but makes it possible to commit immoral acts so fast one hardly notices' and 'old moral issues … acquire a new dimension in a digital context' (Hamelink, 2000, p. 34). Specific properties of information and communication technologies, such as speed, scope, ease of manipulation and the capacity of users to retain anonymity, may heighten existing moral problems. Importantly, these properties may significantly reduce the chances of getting caught. For example, the distribution of child pornography may benefit from such properties as distributors are able to mask their identities. At the same time, this may give rise to dilemmas for Internet Service Providers (ISPs). The extent to which they may collaborate with law enforcement agencies may be in conflict with their duties to respect their clients' privacy. Recent policy debates have centred on the question of just who ought to be morally and legally responsible and to what extent.

What Hamelink seems to mean by old moral issues acquiring new dimensions is the creation of 'moral distance'. Committing deceptions via the internet may be somehow easier because the victim of the deception is at some remove. The idea is that it is easier to inflict harm if the consequences are less immediately present. We may be prepared to say or do things at a distance via some medium which we would not say or do 'face to face'. This may be empirically true, but indicates a failure of moral imagination. It is also not clear whether this is necessarily a phenomenon only of emergent media technologies. The example of so-called Twitter Trolls is relevant here (see Box 12.4). The protection of anonymity through the use of false Twitter identities seems to empower malign individuals to verbally attack others on Twitter in the most outrageous (and frequently illegal) way. Johnson argues that computer-ethical issues generally involve familiar moral concepts (such as duty, harm and so forth). However, the instrumentation of human action through computer and information technology may enhance or constrain human actions in morally significant ways. Certainly this seems to be the case for the Twitter Trolls!

DIGITAL MEDIA ETHICS
Morally Relevant Features of Emergent Digital Media

Charles Ess, in *Digital Media Ethics* (2009), sets out to define both what's new about current emergent digital media and the implications for moral behaviour and ethical theory. The focus of the book is on 'the distinctive features of digital media – what sets them apart from earlier media – that makes them ethically challenging and interesting' (Ess, 2009, p. 8).

Firstly, Ess argues, is that the media are digital. What's important about that is the extent to which different types of media share the same technological platform and enable a greater scope for convergence. The contrast here is with the distinctiveness and relative degrees of separation of analogue media. Digital media much more easily combine image, text and music, for example, and this creates new ethical challenges. With more established media technologies and institutions there are codes, regimes and processes in place to regulate and control content. For example, there are rules governing permissions about when and where it may be appropriate to take photographs. In contrast, the ability of individuals to post photographs, for example, on Facebook, making images public in a new way, joins up issues around copyright in publication and consent in photography.

Secondly, borrowing a phrase from James Moor, Ess believes that a distinctive feature of the 'new' digital media is that the information they capture, record and transmit is 'greased'. This means that these media can deliver up their content both instantaneously and potentially globally. For Ess this has important implications for privacy. The ever greater potential for data storage, processing and retrieval poses new threats to the protection of personal and private information. In addition, the copying of material in analogue form was always possible – in the 1970s and 1980s particularly, there was extensive private copying of music on tape cassette. What is distinctive about digital media is the ease of copying, reproduction and distribution.

The third distinctive feature highlighted by Ess is the way that digital communications technology is characterized by its global reach, enabling the emergence of the new media forms with which we are now familiar. These include email, social networking sites (Facebook, MySpace), video and photographic distribution sites (Flickr, YouTube, etc.), personal blogs, Twitter sites and wikis (Wikipedia, WikiLeaks). The scope, speed and scale of these web-based media might be described as a democratization of the media landscape. The technology allows individuals to transcend their familiar geographical, cultural and linguistic communities to engage in 'cross-cultural encounters online' (Ess, 2009, p. 15). It can be argued that such developments have extended the possibilities of abuse and exploitation.

This opening-up, of course, extends the scope for offence to be given to those who may not share our beliefs and values. Ess argues that the new media technologies make us 'cosmopolitans' – citizens of the world. This in turn enlarges the scope for a clash of ethical and cultural values. He cites the case of the Mohammad Cartoon controversy (Ess, 2009, p. 16). The cartoons were published in 2006 in a relatively small circulation Danish newspaper, *Jyllander-Posten*. In pre-internet days these cartoons may have just sunk without trace. However, they very quickly appeared online and became the focal point for a widespread and violent reaction. The result was many deaths and much destruction of property. As we have already seen in Chapter 4, the questions of freedom and expression, offensiveness and censorship, are not new moral issues. What is new here, Ess argues, is 'how a globally distributed digital media thus amplifies the consequences of our communicative acts far beyond the boundaries familiar to us with traditional media' (Ess, 2009, p. 16). This 'amplification of consequences' may require us to reconsider our accepted ideas about moral responsibility. The amplification of the impact of our actions through digital media is going to have a commensurately greater impact, which means that we have, as media practitioners and as ordinary citizens, a commensurately greater 'duty of care'.

Fourthly, the interactive property of digital media technologies is again a distinctive feature. This has meant that digital texts, and here Ess uses a phrase first used by Phil Mullins (1996), tend to be characterized by 'fluidity'. More conventional media have traditionally been dominated by a model of distribution which tends toward 'top-down' and 'one-to-many'. The advent of the internet and the Web means readers, viewers and listeners are increasingly encourage to 'talk back' by emailing or blogging in response to a newspaper story or a TV or radio broadcast. The BBC, for example, has invested heavily in not only translating its analogue broadcasting services into digital form, but also in developing interactive web-based services.

More radically, Wikipedia is an example of what we might traditionally have thought of as an encyclopaedia. However, Wikipedia is new in that it is an encyclopaedia constructed, expanded and modified by its users with a minimum of editorial intervention. Wikipedia has been frequently criticized on the grounds that its very fluidity will make it inherently unreliable – a potentially moral issue.

However, the evidence appears to be that its democratic and self-regulating nature renders it increasingly reliable as an information source.

A RADICAL ALTERNATIVE: INFORMATION ETHICS
The Information Revolution

The features of digital technologies highlighted by Ess have also led Luciano Floridi (2013) to suggest that this amounts to nothing more or less than a revolution, which is fundamentally altering the way in which human beings see themselves and their relationships both to the natural and the artificial environment. For Floridi, the shift from the analogue to the digital is of 'ontological' significance, that is, it constitutes a new and fundamental shift in our understanding of 'being' itself. Being is, at bottom, information, and because of this revolution in information and communication technologies we increasingly live in what Floridi calls the 'infosphere'. We are information-processing beings – the human mind can be understood in 'computational' terms: the mind is to the brain as software is to hardware. People are 'inforgs', that is intrinsically informational beings, but digital computers are information handlers *in their own right*. To be is to be information. People are not ' … standalone entities, but rather interconnected informational organisms or *inforgs*, sharing with biological agents [*sic*] and engineered artefacts a global environment ultimately made of information, the infosphere' (Floridi, 2010, p. 9). All objects in the universe are 'data structures'. The world is constituted by 'informational objects' interacting with each other. This metaphysical vision underpins Floridi's radical ethical theory: the information turn in ethics. It rests, as we will see, on the fundamental claim that information has intrinsic value. If we accept Floridi's 'information turn' in ethical theory, then Media Ethics will be absorbed by the new Information Ethics (Floridi, 2013).

A Non-standard Approach to Ethical Theory

Floridi has developed what he describes as a 'non-standard' approach to ethical theory in relation to information and communication technologies in particular, and to ethics in general (Floridi, 1999, 2008, 2010, 2013). His approach is modelled on environmental ethics. Floridi starts from the question 'What is the best strategy to construct an information society which is ethically sound?' His general answer is to found a moral system on the idea that we should treat the world and human beings as now fundamentally informational entities constituting a new environment: 'the infosphere' (Floridi, 2010, p.111). This conception of the infosphere embraces all informational entities, practices and situations. It includes media practices, organizations and processes. Meeting the global challenges generated by the revolution in information and communication technologies must be on the basis of respect for information, its conservation and valorization. This approach is founded on the premise that specific characteristics of digital communications and media technologies – in particular their pervasive and global nature – demand a fundamentally new approach to moral theory.

Floridi (2008, p.47, original emphasis) defines this radical version of Information Ethics as 'an *ontocentric, patient-oriented, ecological* macro-ethics'. He also characterizes it as 'non-standard ethical theory' (Floridi, 1999, p.49). We might better understand this by thinking, as Floridi does, of Information Ethics as analogous to Environmental Ethics. Environmental (ecological) Ethics tends to assume that there is an intrinsic value or worthiness to all forms of life. Included in this is any biological entity or ecosystem. In this view, suffering is intrinsically negative or, more strongly, morally wrong. The point here is that environmentalism is not human-centred, not anthropomorphic, but attributes moral value much more widely than the interests of human beings. What follows from this is that Environmental Ethics and, by analogy, Information Ethics, are both 'patient centred', that is primarily concerned with the 'victims' or receivers of actions, but those 'victims' are not limited to human beings only. For example, environmentalists have traditionally been concerned with the preservation and conservation of species threatened by extinction or ecosystems threatened with destruction. Thus a moral agent's concern ought to be with the nature and well-being of any 'patient': 'the "receiver" of the action is placed at the core of ethical discourse' (Floridi, 2008, p. 47). This constitutes what Floridi calls the 'ontocentric' nature of Information Ethics. In contrast, standard ethical theories tend to focus on agents or actions rather than on the 'patient' (receiver or victim) of an action. But Floridi goes beyond this environmental approach by replacing any form of life as intrinsically of moral worth with the claim that any form of being has at least some minimal if overrideable moral worth. His argument goes something like this: (i) all information has value; (ii) everything is information; (iii) therefore *all beings* may be attributed with at least some moral worth.

Our moral concerns, then, must be with the flourishing of all entities. This amounts to an 'Information Turn' in ethical theory generally. What detracts from such flourishing? For Floridi, this is encompassed by the concept of entropy, the general tendency for any ordered system to run to disorder. However, Floridi is at pains to point out that his use of the concept of 'entropy' is not strictly in the sense in which physicists might use it. In his usage, entropy means any sort of corruption, destruction, depletion or pollution of the infosphere and, more specifically, of 'information objects'. These would include anything from a stone to a tree to a human being to a news report. In this sense, Information Ethics is both impartial and universal. From a media perspective, then, our moral concern would embrace equally the whole universe of media entities. From an Information Ethics point of view, it would be morally wrong to bring about a reduction in the quantity, content, quality or value of any media entity.

He formulates four basic laws of Information Ethics which indicate what it means to be a responsible and caring agent in the infosphere (see Box 12.5). On the basis of these laws or principles, it may be readily seen that the duty of any moral agent must be to contribute to the flourishing of the infosphere. If an agent acts in such a way to negatively affect the whole infosphere (not only an informational object) this may be judged as an instance of evil because it increases the level of entropy. Praise or blame may therefore be attributed on the extent to which a person's decisions (although it may be some other type of moral agent, such as a computer) enhance or detract from the infosphere. We must take into account the ethical claims that being an information entity entails and the impact on the wider infosphere. In other words, informational entities cannot be treated in isolation from their relationship to the infosphere.

The extent of moral praiseworthiness or blameworthiness is dependent on the extent to which individual principles are satisfied or not satisfied. An action or a process is commendable, for example, if it satisfies the conjunction of the so-called null law with at least one of the other laws. An action is in effect morally neutral if it only satisfies the null law since the level of entropy in the infosphere is unchanged. Floridi writes that:

a) An action is *unconditionally* commendable only if it never generates any entropy in the course of its implementation; and
b) The best moral action is the action that succeeds in satisfying all four laws at the same time. (Floridi, 2008, p. 59)

12.5 DEFINITION
The laws of Information Ethics

1. Entropy ought not be caused in the infosphere (null law);
2. Entropy ought to be prevented in the infosphere;
3. Entropy ought to be removed from the infosphere;
4. The flourishing of informational entities as well as of the whole infosphere ought to be promoted by preserving, cultivating and enriching their properties.

Floridi (2008, pp. 58–59)

However, it is unlikely that most of our actions will satisfy such strict criteria as indicated in the conditions (a) and (b). More likely, in performing an action we may generate some entropy as well as create some positive moral value, that is we are in a position to claim that the infosphere is in a better state after the event. We might compare this to a utilitarian approach to evaluating moral actions by weighing the costs and the benefits of any action in terms of their consequences. Also like utilitarianism, evaluation is based on the extent to which the total welfare is increased or, in Floridi's language, the total extent of entropy is reduced as far as we can judge.

A problem with the Floridian framework is that it may be difficult to translate it into our everyday understanding of moral situations. The plot deepens because Floridi specifically warns us not to confuse Information Ethics with an ethics of the BBC news. But this would be to mistake the Level of Abstraction (LoA) at which his theory operates. To understand this is perhaps to understand the heart of the theory:

By defending the intrinsic moral worth of informational objects, IE [Information Ethics] does not refer to the moral value of any other piece of well-formed and meaningful data such as an email, the Britannica or Newton's Principia. What IE suggests is that we adopt an informational LoA to approach the analysis of being in terms of a minimal common ontology, whereby human beings as well as animals, plants, artefacts, and so forth are interpreted as informational entities. (Floridi, 2008, p. 60)

We begin with the idea of informational objects as the 'lowest common denominator', but more human-centred values may then be invoked at other appropriate levels of abstraction. In the next section we briefly consider how Floridi deals with a particular moral issue to illustrate just how the use of Information Ethics may explicate our moral experience. Floridi's claim, of course, would be that his approach gives us better moral insight.

Privacy Revisited

In our previous discussion of privacy we saw that as a moral category it is a somewhat slippery customer. It is not easily accommodated in standard ethical theory, partly because it is essentially 'a property of a class of entities as patients, not of actions' (Floridi, 2013, p. 258). From a moral point of view, privacy appeared not to be a unitary concept; we talk of physical privacy, mental privacy, information privacy, decisional privacy. Justifying claims include those of ownership, of natural rights, of the instrumental importance of the maintenance of the private sphere, the distinction between the private and the public sphere, and justifications of privacy are made on a range of different grounds. For example, it is claimed that we own personal information about ourselves and therefore we have a right to its concealment or disclosure. This is frequently asserted by celebrities who wish to profit from the selective release of information about themselves. This form of privacy is said to be violated when such personal information is acquired without permission – such as in the notorious cases of phone hacking investigated by Lord Leveson. Other claims include those for the instrumental value of privacy for the pursuit of our interests (political, religious, sexual, and so on) and the conduct of our intimate personal relationships with friends and family.

The moral focus has been conventionally on the violation of privacy and the fact that to the persons concerned it may bring shame, embarrassment and distress. But Floridi suggests that the value of privacy may be more clearly understood when in fact the information acquired is innocuous, as in case (a) in Box 12.6. Floridi argues that even this minimal intrusion is still morally wrong. In order to understand this, we have to refer to the fundamental insight that a person is an 'informational entity'. The wrongness of the action lies not in the consequences of the action but in 'a lack of care and respect for the individual as an informational entity' (Floridi, 2013, p. 259).

12.6 A JUDGEMENT CALL
Reading another's diary

Consider the following two cases.

a) Suppose I read a friend's diary without their permission. I find that the diary contains only the most generous accounts of our meetings, dinners, travels, and concert goings. It could be argued here, particularly from a consequentialist position, that no harm has been done. There are no embarrassing revelations; no suggestion that in fact he had not enjoyed these events and had resented the time they had taken up.

b) Kate McCann had kept a diary after her daughter, 3-year-old Madeleine, had disappeared from a holiday apartment in 2007 in Portugal. The diary was seized by the Portuguese police as part of their inquiry into the child's disappearance. In her evidence to the Leveson Inquiry, Kate McCann testified that in September 2008 the *News of the World* published the diary under the headline: 'Kate's Diary: In Her Own Words'. The publication was without her consent. It is not known how the *News of the World* obtained the diary from the Portuguese police: 'The publication of this material with a picture on the front page suggesting she had provided this herself left her feeling mentally raped...'

Compare the extent to which both these cases may or may not constitute violations of privacy and on what grounds?

Source: Evans (2011)

As we may now appreciate, the point of view here is that of a person as 'a packet of information'. In the scenario outlined above, my friend is the patient, the receiver, of my actions and in accessing his personal information I have violated a moral right. The moral right rests on the basis that a person is constituted by information. The unauthorized access is an intrusion into and then an alienation of my information. In that sense, case (a) and case (b) in this analysis are symmetrical. Floridi writes:

> Privacy is nothing less than the defence of personal integrity of a packet of information, the individual, and the invasion of the individual's informational privacy, the unauthorized access, dispersion and misuse of her information is an infringement of her me-hood and a disruption of the information environment. The violation is not a violation of ownership, of personal rights, of instrumental values, or of consequentialist rules, but a violation of the nature of the informational self. (Floridi, 2013, p. 260)

CHAPTER REVIEW

In this chapter we have been considering the extent to which the nature of Media Ethics may need to be revised in the light of emergent digital media technologies. We seem to be confronted by two distinct ideas. Firstly, that we have been here before and that even though the current digital technologies appear to be revolutionary, we nevertheless remain confronted with traditional generic moral problems albeit in new forms. Secondly, that in fact we are confronted with a new moral landscape thrown up by these revolutionary technological changes. To explore these issues we looked at the relationship between Media Ethics, Computer Ethics, Digital Media Ethics and Information Ethics. It is evident that there is no immediate consensus.

We looked at two related but distinct approaches to Computer Ethics. James Moor (1985) provides a framework in which we might understand the generation of new moral problems. He develops the notion that we can understand the impacts of emergent media technologies by considering the policy vacuums and conceptual muddles which they give rise to. Deborah Johnson (2001), however, suggests that this approach places too much emphasis on the impact of technology rather than on the ways in which technologies may be shaped to human ends. WikiLeaks may be a useful example of an ideologically and morally driven technology. Charles Ess, by contrast, stresses those features of digital technologies which seem to give rise to new moral dilemmas. He argues for a new Digital Media Ethics. Finally, we considered the work of Luciano Floridi, which involves a radical 'informational turn' in moral theory. On this account, we should look to a radical reappraisal of Media Ethics in the light of Floridi's Information Ethics.

FURTHER READING

Ess, C. (2009) *Digital Media Ethics*. Cambridge: Polity Press. This is a helpful, comprehensive textbook on key moral issues generated by digital media.

Floridi, L. (2008) ' Information ethics: its nature and scope', in J. Van Den Hoven and J. Weckert (eds), *Information Technology and Moral Philosophy*. Cambridge: Cambridge University Press. pp.40–65. A good succinct overview of Floridi's ethical theory.

Floridi, L. (2010) *Information: A Very Short Introduction*. Oxford: Oxford University Press. This is a relatively accessible account of Floridi's approach to information in general and Information Ethics in particular.

Floridi, L. (2013) *The Ethics of Information*. Oxford: Oxford University Press. A comprehensive and detailed account of Information Ethics, its general principles and its relationship to other ethical theory. Contains useful examples embodying the theory.

Hamelink, C.J. (2000) *The Ethics of Cyberspace*. London: Sage. See particularly Chapter 4, 'Equal entitlement in cyberspace' (pp. 79–106). In this chapter Hamelink takes an egalitarian rights-based approach to access to content in cyberspace. He focuses on 'the digital divide', the importance of access, and global governance.

Johnson, D.G. (2008) *Computer Ethics* (4th edn). London: Prentice Hall. A seminal account of Computer Ethics which stresses the extent to which human values and interest shape our information and communications technologies as much as we are shaped by them.

Moor, J.H. (1985) 'What is Computer Ethics'?, *Metaphilosophy*, 16(4): 266–275. A key paper in the development of Computer Ethics. It presents a valuable framework for understanding how new moral issues may be generated by developments in information and communications technologies.

Rogerson, S. (2002) 'Computers and society', in R.E. Spier (ed.), *Science and Technology Ethics*. London: Routledge. pp. 159 – 179. A brief but helpful overview of Computer Ethics from a professional perspective.

HOW TO USE THIS ARTICLE

Go to https://study.sagepub.com/horner to access the following free journal article:

Dijck, J. Van and Poell, T. (2014) 'Making public television social? Public service broadcasting and the challenges of social media', *Television and New Media* [Online], 21 March. http://tvn.sagepub.com/content/early/2014/03/20/152747 76414527136 (accessed: 25 March 2014).

Use this article to take a closer look at the relationship between emergent social media and television broadcasting. The paper argues that platforms such as Twitter, Facebook and YouTube affect the social practice of television and its cultural form, disrupting broadcasters' conventional production and distribution logistics. In particular, the article studies how the rise of social media has affected European public service broadcasting. This is explored at a number of levels: the level of institutions, professional practice and content. The ethical question addressed through this study is the extent to which the values of public sector broadcasting may be maintained as public television engages with social media their ability to relate to new young audiences. The article considers the argument that public service broadcasting (PSB) should translate into public service media (PSM), extending public service values beyond radio and television to embrace the full spectrum of the internet.

13

WRONG-DOING

In this book we have been trying to understand what ought to constitute the ethical commitments of media practitioners through a variety of principles, arguments and cases. We can readily enumerate the kinds of actions that, from a moral point of view, may be called vicious: the wilful commission of untruths, lies, bribery, scurrility, obscenity, invasions of privacy, triviality, distortion, exaggeration, bias, a deliberate commitment to poor production values, and so on. Intuitively at least, we can picture the kinds of virtuous actions, in no particular order, which in a democratic society media practitioners ought to be committed to: honesty, truth, balance, respect for audiences, accuracy, fairness, respect for the subjects of media coverage, the promotion of high production values, and so on (Belsey, 1998, p. 10). In this chapter we show that to do the right thing is always the rational course of action.

Our theme, then, in this final chapter is to try to understand the nature of wrong-doing as something irrational. Most media practitioners are aware of the laws, regulations and codes of practice which govern their professions. Nevertheless, the evidence is that wrong-doing is widespread and media scandals are nothing new. Kant, as we have seen in Chapter 7, gives us some insight into the moral drama involved in the tension between our inclinations (desires) and our moral knowledge of what we ought to do ('practical reason'). To begin this excursion into what is called 'moral psychology' we disentangle various meanings of reason. If we are to show that to act morally is to act reasonably, and that to act wrongly is to act unreasonably, then we have to know what may count as appropriate reasons in making moral judgements. This returns us to our discussion of the elements of moral judgement in Chapter 1 (see Table 13.1). We distinguish 'reasons as motives' from 'reasons as grounds' and 'reasons as causes'. A further dimension to wrong-doing is the attribution of praise and blame. We discuss the conditions under which it is appropriate to attribute blame for the actions we have taken or failed to take. We highlight four conditions: the violation of norms, causal responsibility, foreseeability and freedom to act. This approach is applied to the controversy surrounding the role of the paparazzi in the death of Diana Princess of Wales. Finally, we examine some sources of wrong-doing, including weakness of will, shamelessness and ignorance.

Table 13.1 Summary: elements of moral judgement

Element	Description
Facts	In order to arrive at a reasonable judgement we need to know as far as we can the 'facts of the case'.
Relevant ethical principles	To determine how we ought to act, or what policy should be adopted, we need to consider what relevant universal rules or principles bear on the situation and what are their relative weights; for example, does justice or fairness have priority over others such as benevolence?
Argument	In coming to a judgement we need, if called upon, to show we have reasonable grounds for believing what we do believe to be the right judgement.
Moral imagination	We need to consider the relevant interests of all those involved or affected; this may not just be a question of imagining myself in someone else's place, but also of imagining what it is like to be them.

Adapted from Hare (1963, pp. 86–111)

REASON AND REASONS
Having Good Reasons and Being Persuaded

Doing the wrong thing is choosing to do the wrong thing. It is important in this context to grasp the distinction between *coming to believe something* because the arguments and the evidence are sound and simply *being persuaded of something*. The advertising industry, for example, is in the business of persuasion and not of reasoning. It endeavours to persuade us to buy products in many different ways but usually these ways involve, at some level, an appeal to our emotions, our desires (conscious or unconscious), our interests, our preferences, and so on. The language of advertising is well understood as a language of persuasion rather than reasoning.

However, advertising codes of conduct proscribe the use of outright lies in promoting products. Thus we may be persuaded to buy a product on the strength of an advertisement's appeal to our motives and aspirations. This is quite different from choosing a product on the basis of a reasoned judgement on the evidence of the superiority of its performance over other similar products. Advertisements are rarely about a reasoned assessment as a basis for rational justification for the purchase of a product. They deploy the arts of persuasion rather than deception. Critiques of advertising are frequently misplaced for that reason – that is, we just do know the rules of the advertising game!

The relevance of this to moral action is that I may be persuaded to choose to do the morally wrong thing. I know what the right action is, but I may be persuaded by my colleagues or the general culture in a newsroom or by the demands of my editor, or my desire for promotion. In the case of the *News of the World*, for example, one of the claims that recurs in the Leveson Inquiry was that there was a culture in which intrusion into the privacy of celebrities, public figures and those inadvertently finding themselves in the public gaze, was perfectly acceptable. Phone hacking, along with other known tricks of the journalist's trade, was deemed not only acceptable but also necessary. This, it is claimed, was very persuasive in encouraging journalists to go along with what was not only morally wrong, but also frequently illegal.

Motives, Grounds and Causes

It is also important to distinguish reasoning as a psychological process from reasoning as a process of rational justification. We can examine from a psychological point of view the psychology of making a decision, but rather like our distinction between description and evaluation, a psychological account of how a decision is made is not a form of justification, rational or otherwise. Seeking rational justification involves an appeal to an independent standard, as we discussed in Chapter 1. The difficulty is that we frequently use the word 'reason' in several different senses (Flew, 1975, pp. 57–66). We use the word as meaning: (i) a motive to do something; (ii) a ground or evidence for belief or action; and (iii) a causal explanation (see Table 13.2).

Table 13.2   Summary: types of reasons

Type	Illustration
(i) Reason in the sense of a motive for holding some belief or judgement to be true.	The tabloid press may have strong commercial motives for opposing tighter regulation to protect individual privacy from intrusion. However, such motives do not constitute 'reason as grounds' for establishing whether such legislation might be morally right or not.
(ii) Reason in the sense of having grounds or evidence for the truth of some belief or judgement.	Evidence of widespread phone hacking and intrusion into the private lives of public figures, however, would constitute grounds (evidence) for tightening press regulation.
(iii) Reason in the sense of a physical cause of an event.	The cause of death of the Princess of Wales was the injuries sustained in the car crash in the tunnel. This kind of reason gives us a physical explanation.

Subject/Motive Shift

It is important to mark these three different ways in which we might use the word 'reason'. It frequently is the case in presenting an argument that there is an illegitimate shift or slide from one meaning to another. The philosopher Antony Flew refers to this as 'the Subject/Motive Shift'. For example, we may begin in a discussion defending the truth or falsity of a proposition by giving the reasons (grounds or evidence) for its truth or falsity and then slip into the altogether different issue of the motives for some person, group or institution accepting or rejecting the proposition. In other words we move from a genuine discussion of evidence to one of a discussion of motives. In addition questions of motives for acting or evidence for believing something to be true are again very different from questions of what caused something to happen (Flew, 1975, p.58).

For example, we might in this context consider the closure of the *News of the World* by Rupert Murdoch in the light of the phone-hacking scandals. Clearly there was considerable evidence from the Leveson Inquiry that some journalists had been guilty of breaches of the law and of various forms of moral wrong-doing. Did this constitute sufficient evidence for the closure of the newspaper? There was plenty of evidence to suggest that many of the employees had not been involved in the phone hacking over a long period (Burden, 2009). But the reasons for its closure were 'reasons as motives' rather than 'reasons as evidence'. The paper had a strong record of investigative journalism and the exposure of corrupt practices by politicians, minor royals and sports personalities. There was evidence, therefore, that if the specific corrupt practices had been addressed, the paper could have continued. In closing the paper Rupert Murdoch was motivated by the desire to limit the damage done by prolonged revelations of the paper's wrong-doing. An important motivational element was the promotion of News Corporation as a competent body to take a controlling interest in Sky Television, for which government approval would be required. Such approval was partly dependent on Mr Murdoch demonstrating the competence of his organization to manage a media institution. We might conclude that what was important in the closure of the *News of the World* were various motivational factors (reasons as motives) rather than necessarily good evidential grounds. Even up to its closure, the paper had remained one of Britain's best-selling tabloids.

We can make a useful distinction between individual corruption and corporate corruption (Dupré, 2013, pp. 137–138). Virtuous persons are those predominantly disposed to do the morally right action appropriate to the situation in which they find themselves. Acting professionally, that is, according to the moral code of your profession, is part of what it means to be virtuous. However, as we know, individuals may be corrupted; they may choose or be induced to act it immoral ways, for example, to tell lies for financial gain or bribe policemen to obtain confidential information. These are corrupt practices. Equally, we might also talk of institutional corruption. What we might mean here is that an institution or organization behaves in such a way as to undermine its primary purpose. In the case of the press, we could say this is evident when the culture of the organization undermines its processes and prevents it from achieving its purpose. In the case of the *News of the World*, it was alleged at the Leveson Inquiry that a culture had developed in which malpractice (phone hacking) was not only tolerated but encouraged. The price to be paid, as we have seen above, is that the corrupt practices undermined the investigative purpose of the paper, ultimately leading to its closure. The *News of the World* was the victim of the wider financial interest of Murdoch's media empire.

Motives and Ethical Codes

Professional ethical codes often seem to have little influence on those concerned with, for example, significant breaches of privacy. Professional codes of practice, in general, and in the media in particular, are frequently criticized for their apparent ineffectiveness. A number of explanations are usually advanced for this. For example, there may be a lack of understanding by the membership of professional bodies and technical societies and a consequent lack of endorsement of the codes. Other problems include the lack of any method to enforce ethical codes and often out-of-date and cumbersome mechanisms for revision. Importantly, codes are too general to provide sufficient direction in specific cases, especially given that important moral dilemmas arise from conflicting values and courses of action. This has led to the view that in many respects ethical codes of practice are pointless, unnecessary and a form of professional window-dressing. A stronger criticism made by the medical ethicist Robert Baker of even medical codes is that they are not merely an irrelevance but in fact are positively undesirable 'because they are useful only to persons who, lacking decent character, wish to pretend they had one' (Baker, quoted in Buchanan and Henderson, 2009, p. 96).

In defence of professional ethical codes, it might be said that codes are useful on a number of counts. They remind us that professional behaviour transcends technical concerns and competencies. They provide a framework for thinking (systematically) about moral dilemmas. In addition, codes may 'mediate externalities', that is, they embed within themselves the impact of laws, rules and policies drawn from the surrounding social and legal culture. Professional ethical codes may provide a resource in negotiating positions which may challenge community or individual values. Finally, the expectation regarding what codes and regulations can achieve may be just too high.

However, an important reason for rejecting the criticisms of ethical codes is that it misses the point. Such criticism is based again on the subject/motive confusion. In the criticisms discussed above, the fundamental assumption is that codes of practice are motivational and on that basis fail because the majority of the membership are not moved by them or are not immediately familiar with them. This motivational theory of codes of practice is simply false. What counts about a code of practice is the moral reasons (grounds) it supplies for certain kinds of actions in the situations that professionals are likely to encounter. And as we have already argued, such reasons say something about the individuals or institutions to whom they apply, that is something about the reasons for them to act in one way or another, whether or not they recognize that, and whether or not, if they do recognize it, they also act on it as they should (Foot, 2001, p. 18).

Codes of practice that function as guides are not primarily intended to motivate. If I am a member of the National Union of Journalists, then I am *committing* to the NUJ's code of practice. If I subsequently commit acts which are at odds with the code, then either I haven't understood what it says, or in my contrarian behaviour I am just not accepting them. Thus if we want to praise or blame media professionals as being moral or immoral, being just or unjust, for example, then what we mean is that they recognize and try to act on certain kinds of reasons (grounds) as reasons for action. But further critics of codes of practice miss the point because primarily doing morally good actions is not just following a set of rules. As we have seen before when discussing Kant (see Chapter 7), moral or immoral actions are performed according to a subjective maxim we might have (for example, phone hacking is permissible in order to expose political corruption). Acting according to that maxim does not mean we are necessarily and explicitly repeating it to ourselves under our breath. It is, for example, something we might make explicit if called to account subsequently for our actions. We can act according to a rule (maxim) without necessarily 'following' a rule.

Kant argued, for example, that a morally good action is an action done *for the sake of duty*. Performing an action simply because it conforms to a moral code, an external law, is on this account not really being done for the sake of duty. I go through the motions, but what counts is my intention whether or not I act with a pure will. Thus to act for the sake of duty is to act according to a self-imposed law which may or may not conform to an external rule or law (as we noted in the Introduction, acting legally and acting morally are not necessarily the same thing). In extreme circumstances, we may be able to perform a morally good action only if we defy the law of our community. (Think, for example, of those bloggers in oppressive regimes who try to present the truth to the world under the threat of imprisonment or worse.) This is what Kant means when he argues that when we act according to a maxim we become 'universal legislators', which is why his test, the categorical imperative, is about whether or not the subjective maxim could also become a universal rule, that is, an objective principle (see Chapter 7). We are at once both subjects and legislators and this gives human beings their special and peculiar status among all creatures.

BLAMEWORTHINESS

However, we may be mistaken about our duties just as we may be mistaken about facts. We may act on maxims or laws which are wrong, that is, that do not conform to Kant's categorical imperative test: 'Where there is the possibility of universally valid (objective) principles, there is also the possibility of error' (Körner, 1966, p. 149). If I am in error, should I be blamed? In this section we will briefly consider the idea of blameworthiness. What, then, are the relevant conditions for attributing blame? To be blameworthy is to be morally responsible for our wrong-doing. We need to understand when it is reasonable to hold media practitioners to account for their judgements and their actions. What are the conditions under which it is morally right to attribute blame?

13.1 A JUDGEMENT CALL
The paparazzi and the death of Princess Diana

A major question arising from the death of Princess Diana on 31 August 1997 was to what extent the pursuit by the paparazzi contributed to the tragedy in the tunnel? If the photographers and journalists had not been in pursuit, would Diana have died? In this case, we have a set of individual decisions by each of the photographers involved. The motives (the interests) of the paparazzi were purely in 'the money shot': the princess with Dodi Al Fayed. The paparazzi were in hot pursuit through the tunnel when the crash occurred. Much of the media coverage of the crash implicated this pursuit in the crash and the subsequent death of Diana. A consequence was a period of vilification of the activities of the paparazzi in the case of Diana, but also more generally. The French judicial investigation concluded, however, that the cause of the crash was the loss of control of the car by Al Fayed's driver. Henri Paul had three times the permitted level of alcohol in his blood. It was likely, therefore, that the immediate reason (cause) of the crash was loss of control by a drunk driver. Subsequent inquests in London in 2004 and 2007 attributed the crash to Henri Paul, but also implicated the paparazzi. The UK's Ministry of Justice stated, however, that the Crown Prosecution Service could not prosecute the paparazzi because they were not British nationals. This was the case even though the victim was British.

Should the photojournalists be blamed for what happened? What would you have done in their place?

Source: BBC News (2008)

We can stipulate at least four conditions for attributing moral blame to persons or institutions. These include: (i) the violation of some moral rule or norm; (ii) a real causal contribution to the event for which they are being held responsible; (iii) the outcome of the judgement or action at the time could have been foreseen; and (iv) freedom of action – they were not acting under constraint. We will consider each of these criteria with the role of the paparazzi in the death of the Princess of Wales in mind (see Box 13.1).

Violating Norms

To be blameworthy is to have done something which is morally wrong by some standard. As we have already discussed, moral norms or obligations may or may not be embedded in legislation or in the specific rules of an organization. In this book, we have been primarily concerned with moral norms rather than legal or organizational ones. In the case of the paparazzi, even though the British courts could not prosecute, we would still want to say that they were blameworthy. They were blameworthy in the sense that the individual and mass pursuit of the Princess Diana ultimately contributed to her death. In other words, we clearly have the violation of a moral norm that it is our duty, all things considered, not to cause harm. This is the case taking either a utilitarian or a Kantian moral account.

Causal Contribution to Consequences

A second condition is that for a person or an institution to be held blameworthy they must have made a causal contribution to the consequences for which they are being held responsible. A number of important considerations should be borne in mind when considering the relationship between causes and effects here. Firstly, a failure to act may make a positive contribution to bringing about some event. We say, for example, in the case of Jonathan Ross and Russell Brand controversy that failures in the editorial procedures at the BBC contributed to the subsequent moral outrage at the broadcast of the programme (see Chapter 2). Secondly, a simple causal contribution is usually not by itself a sufficient condition for some event to take place. In other words, events are usually the outcome of many contributory causes. But in order to establish blameworthiness we must be able to say that the action was a *necessary* contributory factor. In the case of Diana's death, we have at least two principal contributing causes: firstly that Henri Paul had been drinking alcohol before taking the wheel and, secondly, the car was then pursued by the paparazzi. The pursuit contributed to Henri Paul driving faster and more dangerously than under normal circumstances, leading to the accident. It is also the case that we could not say that any one of the pursuing paparazzi was responsible, but the aggregate of their individual decisions was a contributory cause of the accident. Hence they were morally blameworthy if not legally so.

Foreseeability

The third criterion relevant to blameworthiness is that a person or an institution is culpable if they were in a position to predict the likely consequences of their actions. The relevant consequences are the morally adverse consequences of the action, usually expressed as some form of harm. (This, of course, is an essential factor in any consequentialist account of moral rightness or wrongness.) What would be unreasonable would be to attribute blame when the person, for example, could not have been in a position to foresee the consequences of their actions. (We deal with the relationship of ignorance to wrong-doing below.) But it is also reasonable to expect moral agents to do as much as is reasonably possible, all things considered, to try to understand the likely outcomes of their actions. Again, if we consider the case of the death of Princess Diana, the detrimental effects of alcohol on a driver's performance are well known scientifically. Equally, a mass car chase on normal urban roads is likely to increase the risk of a crash. Our knowledge of the future course of events is severely limited and fallible, but this doesn't preclude the possibility of a reasonable risk assessment of the likely outcomes of our actions. Of course, as we will discuss below, such rational approaches to our decision making are often easily overwritten by other and more pressing motives and interests. We may, for example, be more motivated to gain professional recognition (laudable in itself) than to consider the moral consequences of our actions.

Freedom to Choose and Act

A final criterion goes to the very core of moral responsibility. We must, in a fundamental sense, be free to choose in order to be held responsible for our actions. In other words, we must not be acting under the pressure of some overwhelming compulsion. I may choose to be the toast of the paparazzi fraternity by gaining a telling but intrusive shot of a public figure rather than respect that person's right to privacy. But I must be free to make that choice in order to be subsequently blamed for doing the morally wrong thing. Now there may be degrees of coercion and to the extent that I may be under pressure to perform in one way or another may be a mitigating circumstance when considering responsibility. It is clear, for example, that the pressures of 'industrial journalism', to use Belsey's phrase (1998, p. 11), may override our individual moral sense. The prevailing culture of the *News of the World*, for example, was such that journalists were constrained to do things which they knew to be morally and legally wrong. But in a deep sense they were always free to refuse to act wrongly, even if the price might have been losing their job. Many, if not most journalists, manage to negotiate successfully the pressures to deliver stories at any cost and act in a morally responsible manner. Again, in the case of the death of the Princess of Wales those members of the paparazzi who were in pursuit of her car had freely chosen to do what they were doing and were, therefore, culpable in her death.

SOME SOURCES OF WRONG-DOING

Moral judgement must rest on reasons to act rightly or wrongly. Reasons for moral action apply whether I choose to recognize them or not. As an investigative journalist, I ought to promise my sources that I will keep their identities secret. Making such a promise then constitutes a strong moral reason for not revealing my sources. I know that making such a promise entails that I ought not to disclose their identities. If I choose subsequently not to recognize the compelling nature of such a promise, this does not, all things considered, relieve me of the duty to keep my promise. The duty remains whether I choose to recognize it or not. I may recognize the duty but still break the promise. As the moral philosopher Philippa Foot points out, 'One who is the subject of a true moral judgement does not always do what he says he should do, since he may not recognise its truth, and may not act on it even if he does' (Foot, 2001, p. 18). A shadow falls between moral judgement and action. Understanding this involves understanding some key aspects of what we can call 'moral psychology'. So we now consider three explanations of the failure to carry through moral judgements, or what we know to be right into action. These include weakness of will, shamelessness and ignorance.

13.2 A JUDGEMENT CALL
Facebook and 'beheading clips'

Facebook is allowing videos showing people being decapitated to be posted and shared on its site once again. Facebook originally pulled decapitation videos after the Family Online Safety Institute complained that it had 'crossed the line'. In May 2013 Facebook introduced a temporary ban on the showing of clips of beheadings. The social network had introduced the ban following complaints that the clips could cause long-term psychological damage. Dr Arthur Cassidy, a former psychologist who runs a branch of the Yellow Ribbon Programme in Northern Ireland, a suicide prevention charity, claimed that 'It only takes seconds of exposure to such graphic material to leave a permanent trace – particularly in a young person's mind. The more graphic and colourful the material is, the more psychologically destructive it becomes.' Facebook permits anyone aged 13 and above to be a member. The US firm confirmed that it now believes its users should be free to watch and condemn such videos. However, it said that it was considering adding warnings. In its terms and conditions Facebook now states that it will remove photos or videos that 'glorify violence' in addition to other banned material, which includes, for example, a woman's 'fully exposed breast'.

Is this a case of weakness of will on Facebook's part or is it a morally defensible action?

Source: Kelion (2013)

Weakness of Will

Weakness of will is sometimes also described as moral 'incontinence' or a lack of self-restraint; a tendency to yield to temptation although one knows better than to yield. Part of our moral experience is the drama of moral decision making as our desires, inclinations and preferences come into conflict with what we know we ought to do. Hence, the 'continent' person is someone who consistently acts morally and may justly be described as virtuous. If, as an investigative journalist, for example, I am careful to protect my sources, then I may be described, and indeed praised, as 'continent'.

13.3 DEFINITION
Incontinence or weakness of the will

Aristotle makes a distinction between *akrates* and *enkrates*: the former is the term for a morally weak person and the latter means a person who can resist temptation.

Akrasia [Greek for weakness] means incontinence or weakness of the will.

Source: Flew (1979)

According to the philosopher Donald Davidson (1969), there are conventionally three elements in defining an 'incontinent' action. An agent (a person or an institution) acts incontinently if, and only if: (a) the agent intentionally performs an action x; (b) the agent holds the belief that there is an alternative course of action, y, open to them; and (c) the judgement of the agent is that, all things considered, it is better to do y than x (Davidson, 1969, p. 93). However, the problem is that there is a plausible alternative account to the effect that we might generally act intentionally in order to achieve some kind of good. So that in so far as I intentionally ignore the moral value of respect for privacy in pursuit of a good story, then I must, on this view, really think that getting a good story is better than respecting someone's privacy. Hence it is difficult to see where the question of weakness of will enters the picture. In other words, why would I do something when I actually believed that another course of action was better altogether? If I am prepared to break the NUJ's Code of Practice, then mustn't I really think that acting in my own interest, and in that of my employer, trumps any moral considerations?

What we ought to say, however, is that what is going on here is that although the weak-willed person recognizes the moral reason for doing the right thing, they just act irrationally. As David Wiggins points out:

> Almost anyone not under the influence of theory [*sic*] will say that, when a person is weak-willed, he intentionally chooses that which he knows or believes to be the worst course of action when he could choose the better course; and that, in acting in this way, the weak-willed man acts not for *no* reason at all – that would be strange and atypical – but irrationally. (Wiggins, 1998, p. 239)

I am culpable because although I can recognize compelling moral reasons for a certain action I do not carry it through. I act badly in relation to my own judgement. I ought not to join a pack of photographers and journalists verbally abusing and spitting at Sienna Miller while pursuing her down the street. But I do! The weak-willed, incontinent person knows that in choosing the morally wrong action they are acting badly and may feel regret or shame. But what are we to make of those who are shameless in their wrong-doing?

Shamelessness

In behaving shamelessly I am aware of doing the morally wrong thing but evince no shame in doing it. As Philippa Foot (2001, p. 19) points out, we must be aware that shamelessness can coexist with the use of moral language without this necessarily being insincere. On the one hand, we have the raft of revelations of wrong-doing by the *News of the World* journalists, but on the other hand this coexists with the press industry's claims to free speech in the public interest. In November 2011 David Sherborne (the barrister representing 51 of the press victims) at the Leveson Inquiry laid out an indictment of the tabloid's behaviour:

> Illegally accessing people's private voicemails, bribing employees into divulging personal information, blagging sensitive details through

deception and trickery, blackmailing vulnerable or opportunistic individuals into breaking confidences about well-known people, the blatant intrusion into the grief of victims of crime, the vilification of ordinary members of the public unwittingly caught up in such events, the hounding of various well-known people, their families and friends, purely because this sells newspapers, and finally, the bullying of those, who in seeking to question these practices, are therefore merely exercising the same freedom of speech behind much of this behaviour is sought to be shielded or excused by the press. (Hill, 2011)

Here we have as set of vicious practices but at the same time a shameless defence of a self-regulated press by the industry in general. Also, there is the shamelessness of disregarding morality altogether. We ought never to underestimate the extent to which individuals or organizations, particularly in the entertainment sector, may be shameless in their vices (see Box 13.4).

13.4 A JUDGEMENT CALL
Reality TV and shamelessness

The press release for a UK reality TV show, *Geordie Shore*, celebrates the fact that 'Our favourite Tyneside residents spent the first series fighting, shagging and drinking'. Other reality shows, for example E4's *Desperate Scousewives* ('a desperate title, as there are no wives'), Channel 5's recent *Tamara Ecclestone: Billion $$ Girl*, similarly reveal their subjects in a less than flattering light. Consider media critic Alison Graham's view of a whole menu of such 'reality TV'. Graham argues that under the banner of entertainment participants in this type of show are subjected to various forms of humiliation, often through public exposure of their insecurities. At the same time, the general message of the programmes (including others, such as *Made in Chelsea*, *Celebrity Big Brother* and *The Only Way is Essex*) is the promotion of 'the eavesdropping on lives dedicated to the pursuit of leering, grubby hedonism'. The press release issued by *Geordie Shore* demonstrates a shameless indifference to moral values, even to the point of celebrating its own negative reviews – Lorraine Kelly writing in *The Sun* (!) said that it had no redeeming features whatsoever.

How far do you agree with Alison Graham's assessment of reality TV shows?

Source: Graham (2011, p. 51)

Ignorance

We may do the wrong thing because of ignorance; I may fail, out of ignorance, to recognize certain practical reasons (grounds) for acting. Ignorance of moral reasons for acting in the right way may excuse or mitigate our wrong-doing. Aristotle makes several important points about ignorance in *Nichomachean Ethics* (Achrill, 1987, pp. 151–152). Firstly, he distinguishes between knowledge of what may be morally or legally required from ignorance of material facts. For example, if I am the editor of a national newspaper, I ought to know what the Press Complaints Council code says about intrusive photography. Aristotle argues that we are just required to know relevant moral norms or laws. This must be particularly the case when we claim to be acting in a professional capacity.

Secondly, Aristotle thought that ignorance of material facts is not necessarily an excuse for wrong-doing: 'Acting by reason *of* ignorance seems also to be different from acting *in* ignorance' (Achrill, 1987, p. 389). Agents are culpable for what they might do in ignorance if they are responsible for that ignorance by, say, getting themselves drunk or failing to find out the relevant facts of the situation. We need, therefore, to ask whether or not a person or organization is to some extent responsible for their ignorance? Aristotle's analysis discusses failures to act out of ignorance (sins of omission rather than commission), but this is very relevant to the phone-hacking scandal. There was a failure of management to act to stop the misdeeds and it does seem that a failure to prevent wrong-doing must be culpable. James Murdoch's defence to the House of Commons Select Committee inquiring into the *News of the World* was essentially a defence based on an ignorance of what was happening and consequently failing to act. He claims that he was simply unaware of vital emails which suggested that phone hacking at the newspaper was not the work of one rogue reporter but, in fact, was much more widespread. Under these circumstances, we could argue that ignorance is equally no defence; he was responsible for his own ignorance of what was happening. He certainly had the power, as head of News International, to find out or instruct others to find out.

Thirdly, Aristotle also recognizes the complexities of situations in which we might find ourselves and the unwitting ignorance that might arise as a consequence. As we have already discussed earlier in the book, some approaches to ethics require us to know the consequences of our actions in some detail and for varying lengths of time in the future. However, our knowledge of the future course of events is extremely fragile and it is common to find that things just turn out differently from what was intended. There are inbuilt limits to our knowledge and it would be unreasonable to apportion blame on the basis for something which is, in principle, unforeseeable.

CONCLUSION: THE REAL AND THE IDEAL

The idea of ethical media practice, then, represents an ideal of virtuous conduct by media institutions and media practitioners. However, as we have seen, there is much evidence to suggest that institutions and practitioners frequently fail to live up to the highest standards of professional practice. Much print and broadcast journalism is biased, highly selective, intrusive, playing to the prurient interests of its audience, crudely populist, untrustworthy, and so on. Cynics may claim that on these grounds virtuous media practice is simply a pipedream – a self-justifying story the media tell themselves in order to maintain their social and political privileges, to justify their supposed 'contract' with society. In other words, there is more myth than reality to the idea of ethical media practice.

We can make several responses to such claims. Firstly, there is often confusion by both popular and professional critics between the logical aspects of 'all' and 'some'. It doesn't follow that because *some* media professionals may be indifferent to the claims of morality that *all* media professionals are necessarily amoral or immoral, just as it doesn't follow that because some swans are white that necessarily all swans are white. Secondly, if the media are as untrustworthy and debased as some critics and media theorists suggest, it is hard to imagine why audiences continue to want to consume the products of those media industries. To suggest that everyone everywhere is simply a dupe of the system is deeply patronising. Thirdly, it is logically intrinsic to the concept of an ideal that it is a condition we aspire to but may not reach. If we always and everywhere fulfilled our ideals, the ideal would cease to be an ideal and would simply become reality. There is a meaningful and intrinsic contrast between the real and the ideal, but this does not devalue the ideal. Our moral ideals set the standards to which we as professionals and human beings ought continuously to aspire.

FURTHER READING

Coleman, R. (2010) 'Moral development and journalism', in C. Myers (ed.), *Journalism Ethics: A Philosophical Approach*. Oxford: Oxford University Press. pp. 25–33. This article looks at how people develop into ethical beings and particularly at ethical development in the professions. It uses Kohlberg's moral development theory as its basic psychological framework.

Sanders, K. (2006) *Ethics and Journalism*. London: Sage. See, in particular, Chapter 14, 'The good journalist' (pp. 160–170), for a discussion of professionalism, the qualities of a good journalist and contemporary challenges.

Skovsgaard, M. (2014) 'A tabloid mind? Professional values and organisational pressures', *Media, Culture and Society*, 20(10): 1–19. This article is an interesting empirical study of the values of tabloid journalists contrasted with other kinds of journalists.

Zelizer, B. (2012) 'How to make meaning of hand-wringing after scandal', *Media, Culture and Society*, 34(5): 625–630. A useful commentary on the current spate of media wrong-doing and their origins and implications. The argument of the piece is that the 'hand-wringing' over scandals must be made to be something more than a 'rhetorical pressure valve'.

HOW TO USE THIS ARTICLE

Go to https://study.sagepub.com/horner to access the following free journal article:

Pihl-Thingvad, S. (2014) 'Professional ideals and daily practice in journalism', *Journalism* [Online], 5 February: 1–20. http://jou.sagepub.com/content/early/2 014/02/04/1464884913517658 (accessed: 18 February 2014).

Use this article to study in greater depth the 'discrepancies' between the ideals of professional practice and everyday working practices in the media. The author begins from the assumption that professional ideals are essential for the journalistic profession. This article is an empirical examination of the discrepancies in the case of the generation of news by Danish journalists. The discrepancies considered include actual practice and ideals, such as the ability to provide reliable and objective information, to provide a product of high quality, and to have autonomy in the work, for example. In addition, it investigates the reaction of the journalists to these discrepancies in the context of their organizational commitments. The author concludes that discrepancies have a negative impact on commitment.

REFERENCES

Achrill, J.L. (ed.) (1987) *A New Aristotle Reader.* Oxford: Oxford University Press.

Adam, A. (2005) *Gender, Ethics and Information Technology.* London: Palgrave Macmillan.

Albertazzi, D. and Cobley, P. (eds) (2010) *The Media: An Introduction* (3rd edn). London: Pearson Education (1st edn, 1998).

Alia, V. (2004) *Media Ethics and Social Change.* Edinburgh: Edinburgh University Press.

Almond, B. (1997) 'Rights', in P. Singer (ed.), *A Companion to Ethics.* Oxford: Blackwell.

Archard, D. (1998) 'Privacy, the public interest and a prurient public', in M. Kieran (ed.), *Media Ethics.* London: Routledge. pp. 82–96.

Aristotle (1960) *The Politics of Aristotle,* translated with Notes by Sir Earnest Barker. Oxford: At the Clarendon Press.

Asai, R. (2011) 'Social media as a tool for social change', in A. Bissett (ed.), *Proceedings of the Twelfth International Conference: The Social Impact of Social Computing, ETHICOMP 2011, Sheffield Hallam University, Sheffield UK, 14–16 September 2011.* Sheffield: Sheffield Hallam University, pp. 44–50.

Austin, J.L. (1970) *Philosophical Papers.* Oxford: Oxford University Press.

Ayer, A.J. (1967) *Language Truth and Logic* (2nd edn). London: Gollancz (1st edn, 1936).

Baggini, J. and Fosl, P.S. (2007) *The Ethics Toolkit: A Compendium of Ethical Concepts and Methods.* Oxford: Blackwell.

BBC2 (2007) *The Conspiracy Files: 9/11.* Broadcast 18 February.

BBC News (2008) 'Princess Diana unlawfully killed'. Monday 7 April. http://news.bbc.co.uk/1/hi/uk/7328754.stm (accessed: 9 August 2012).

BBC News (2012) 'Leveson Inquiry: Michael Gove warns Leveson on liberty'. 29 May. www.bbc.co.uk/news/uk-18245965 (accessed: 8 August 2012).

Beauchamp, T.L. (2001) *Philosophical Ethics: An Introduction to Moral Philosophy* (3rd edn). Boston, MA: McGraw-Hill.

Bell, M. (1998) 'The journalism of attachment', in M. Kieran (ed.), *Media Ethics.* London: Routledge. pp. 15–22.

Belsey, A. (1998) 'Journalism and ethics: can they co-exist?', in M. Kieran (ed.), *Media Ethics.* London: Routledge. pp. 1–14.

Benkler, Y. (2006) *The Wealth of Networks: How Social Production Transforms Markets and Freedom.* New Haven, CT: Yale University Press.

Bentham, J. (1969) *An Introduction to the Principles of Morals and Legislation,* in D.D. Raphael (ed.), *British Moralists: 1650–1800. Volume II: Hume–Bentham.* Oxford: Clarendon Press. pp. 313–346 (1st edn, 1789).

Berlin, I. (1998) 'Two concepts of liberty', in I. Berlin, *The Proper Study of Mankind*. New York: Farrar, Strauss and Giroux. pp. 191–243.

Bijker, W.E., Hughes, T.P. and Pinch, T. (eds) (2001) *The Social Construction of Technological Systems: New Directions in the Sociology and History of Technology*. Cambridge, MA: The MIT Press.

Bissell, K. and Parrott, S. (2013) 'Prejudice: the role of the media in the development of social bias', *Journalism & Communication Monographs*, 15(4): 219–270.

Blaagard, B.B. (2013) 'Shifting boundaries: objectivity, citizen journalism and tomorrow's journalists', *Journalism* [Online], 3 February, http://jou.sagepub.com/content/early/201 3/01/15/1464884912469081 (accessed: 13 February 2013).

Black, B. (2012) *An A-Z of Critical Thinking*. London: Continuum.

Blackburn, S. (2001) *Being Good: A Short Introduction to Ethics*. Oxford: Oxford University Press.

Blackburn, S. (2006) *Dictionary of Philosophy* (2nd edn). Oxford: Oxford University Press (1st edn, 1994).

Bok, S. (1980) *Lying: Moral Choice in Public and Private Life*. New York, Vintage Books.

Bok, S. (2003) 'The morality of whistle-blowing', in M.D. Ermann and M.S. Shauf (eds), *Computers, Ethics and Society*. New York: Oxford University Press. pp. 42–47.

Boyne, C. (2004) 'Private lives and public interests', unpublished lecture, University of Brighton, December.

Boyne, C. (2006) 'War reporting – some thoughts', unpublished lecture, University of Brighton, December.

Boyne, C. (2008a) 'New media, access and equity', unpublished paper, University of Brighton, November.

Boyne, C. (2008b) 'Obligations of communication professionals: truth-telling as a *prima facie* moral duty', unpublished paper, University of Brighton, December.

Branston, G. and Stafford, R. (2007) *The Media Student's Handbook* (4th edn). London: Routledge (1st edn, 1996).

Brock, G. (2012) 'The Leveson Inquiry: there's a bargain to be struck over media freedom and regulation', *Journalism*, 13(4): 1–10.

Brooker, P. (1999) *Cultural Theory: A Glossary*. London: Arnold.

Brown, A. (2014) 'Perhaps it doesn't matter if the *Daily Mirror*'s weeping child is a lie', *The Guardian* [Online], 16 April, www.theguardian.com/commentisfree/andrewbrown/2014/ apr/16/daily-mirror-weeping-child-lie-food-banks (accessed: 17 April 2014).

Buchanan, E.A. and Henderson, K.A. (2009) *Case Studies in Library and Information Science*. Jefferson, NC: McFarland.

Burden, Peter (2009) *News of the World? Fake Sheiks and Royal Trappings*. London: Eye Books.

Burns, J. (2013) 'Students win LSE apology over T-shirt ban', *BBC News Education and Family* [Online], 20 December 2013, www.bbc.co.uk/news/education-25463263 (accessed: 21 December 2013).

Butcher, S.H. (1898) *Aristotle's Theory of Poetry and Fine Art* (2nd edn). London: Macmillan (1st edn, 1885).

Camber, R. (2014) 'Twitter trolls who made rape and death threats to Jane Austen banknote campaigner plead GUILTY to sending "menacing" messages', *Mail* [Online], 7 January, 3.15 pm. www.dailymail.co.uk/news/article-2535270/Twitter-trolls-rape-death-threats-Caroline-Criado-Perez-plead-GUILTY.html#ixzz2q0ZVKM2s (accessed: 10 January 2014).

Clapham, A. (2007) *Human Rights: A Very Short Introduction*. Oxford: Oxford University Press.

Cohen, S. (2002) *Folk Devils and Moral Panics: The Creation of the Mods and Rockers* (3rd edn). London: Routledge (1st edn, 1972).

Cohen-Almagor, R. (2005) *Speech, Media and Ethics*. London: Palgrave Macmillan.

Cohen-Almagor, R. (2014) 'After Leveson: recommendations for instituting the Public and Press Council', *The International Journal of Press/Politics*, 19(2): 202–225.

Coleman, R. (2010) 'Moral development and journalism', in C. Myers (ed.), *Journalism Ethics: A Philosophical Approach*. Oxford: Oxford University Press. pp. 25–33.

Collins, T. (2010) 'Not the Army I know', *Radio Times*, 20–26 November: 9.

Cornell, D. (ed.) (2000) *Feminism and Pornography*. Oxford: Oxford University Press.

Cram, I. (1998) 'Beyond Calcutt: the legal and extra-legal protection of privacy interests in England and Wales', in M. Kieran (ed.), *Media Ethics*. London: Routledge. pp. 97–110.

Cumberbach, G. (2010) 'Effects', in Daniele Albertazzi and Paul Cobley (eds), *The Media: An Introduction* (3rd edn). London: Pearson Education. pp. 354–368 (1st edn, 1998).

Daily Telegraph (2011) 'Leveson Inquiry: first day as it happened', *The Daily Telegraph*, 14 November. www.telegraph.co.uk/news/uknews/leveson-inquiry/8890596/Leveson-Inquiry-first-day-as-it-happened-November-14.htm (accessed: 15 November, 2011).

David, M., Rohloff, A., Petley, J. and Hughes, J. (2011) 'The idea of moral panic: ten dimensions of dispute', *Crime, Media Culture*, 7(3): 215–228.

Davidson, D. (1969) 'How is weakness of the will possible?', in J. Feinberg (ed.), *Moral Concepts*. London: Oxford University Press. pp. 93–113.

Davies, N. (2009) *Flat Earth News*. London: Vintage.

De Saulles, M. and Horner, D.S. (2011) 'The portable panopticon: morality and mobile technologies', *Information and Communication & Ethics in Society*, 9(3): 206–216.

Dear, J. (2014) 'A country where the truth can kill', *British Journalism Review*, 25(1): 50–55.

Death of Osama bin Laden (2012) Wikipedia. http://en.wikipedia.org/wiki/Death_of_Osama_bin_Laden#Release_of_photographs (accessed: 9 April 2012).

Dijck, J. van and Poell, T. (2014) 'Making public television social? Public service broadcasting and the challenges of social media', *Television and New Media* [Online], 21 March. http://tvn.sagepub.com/content/early/2014/03/20/15274776414527136 (accessed: 25 March 2014).

Dupré, B. (2013) *50 Ethics Ideas You Really Need to Know*. London: Quercus.

Dworkin, A. (2000) 'Against the male flood: censorship, pornography, and equality', in D. Cornell (ed.), *Feminism and Pornography*. Oxford: Oxford University Press. pp.19–38.

Dyer, C. (2008) 'J.K. Rowling wins ban on photos of her son', *The Guardian*, Thursday 8 May.

Ellis, A. (1998) 'Censorship and the media', in M. Kieran (ed.), *Media Ethics*. London: Routledge. pp. 165–177.

Ess, C. (2009) *Digital Media Ethics*. Cambridge: Polity Press.

European Court of Human Rights (2010) *European Convention on Human Rights*. Strasbourg: European Court of Human Rights.

Evans, M. (2011) 'Leveson Inquiry: Kate McCann felt "mentally raped" after NOTW published private diary'. *The Telegraph* [Online], 17 November 2011. www.telegraph.co.uk/news/uknews/Leveson-inquiry/889338/Leveson-Inquiry (accessed: 17 November 2011).

Evans, M. (2012) 'Rooney and Burrell among dozens of new hacking claims', *Daily Telegraph*, Saturday 21 April.

Feinberg, J. (ed.) (1969) *Moral Concepts*. London: Oxford University Press.

Financial Post (1993) 'Turn of century poses a computer problem', Saturday 23rd May, p. 37.

Fishman, J.M. (2003) 'News norms and emotions: pictures of pain and metaphors of distress', in L. Gross, J.S. Katz and J. Ruby (eds), *Image Ethics in the Digital Age*. Minneapolis, MN: University of Minnesota. pp. 53–69.

Flew, A. (1975) *Thinking about Thinking*. Glasgow: Fontana.

Flew, A. (1976) *Sociology, Equality and Education*. London: Macmillan.

Flew, A. (ed.) (1979) *A Dictionary of Philosophy*. London: Pan Books.

Flew, A. (1985) *Thinking about Social Thinking*. Oxford: Basil Blackwell.

Flew, A. (1994) *An Introduction to Western Philosophy: Ideas and Argument from Plato to Popper*. London: Thames & Hudson.

Floridi, L. (1999) 'Information ethics: On the philosophical foundation of computer ethics', *Ethics and Information Technology*, 1(1): 37–56.

Floridi, L. (2008) 'Information ethics: its nature and scope', in J. Van Den Hoven and J. Weckert (eds), *Information Technology and Moral Philosophy*. Cambridge: Cambridge University Press. pp. 40–65.

Floridi, L. (2010) *Information: A Very Short Introduction*. Oxford: Oxford University Press.

Floridi, L. (2013) *The Ethics of Information*. Oxford: Oxford University Press.

Foot, P. (2001) *Natural Goodness*. Oxford: Oxford University Press.

Foster, P. (2010) 'Lockdown for dissident's wife as Beijing condemns Oslo "farce"', *The Daily Telegraph*, Saturday 11 December, p. 20.

Frost, C. (2000) *Media Ethics and Self-regulation*. Harlow, Essex: Pearson Education.

Gaber, I. (2012) 'Rupert and the "three card trope" – what you see ain't necessarily what you get', *Media, Culture and Society*, 34(5): 637–646.

Gibbon, E. (1930) *The History of the Decline and Fall of the Roman Empire*, in J.B. Bury (ed.), Seven Volumes. London: Methuen, (1st edn. 1783).

Global Grind (2014) 'Well look at that: new study shows Rap music and violence are not linked' [Online], 7 January. http://globalgrind.com/2014/01/08/study-rap-music-violence-not-linked-details/ (accessed: 14 April 2014).

Gordon, A.D., Kittross, J.M. and Reuss, C. (eds) (1996) *Controversies in Media Ethics*. White Plains, NY: Longman (2nd edn, 1999).

Graham, A. (2011) 'Beauty and the beastly', *Radio Times*, 31 December–6 January, p. 51.

Graham, G. (1998) 'Sex and violence in fact and fiction', in M. Kieran (ed.), *Media Ethics*. London: Routledge. pp. 152–164.

Grayling, A.C. (1997) *The Future of Moral Values*. London: Phoenix.

Grayling, A.C. (2001) *The Meaning of Things: Applying Philosophy to Life*. London: Weidenfeld & Nicolson.

Grayling, A.C. (2003) *What is Good? The Search for the Best Way to Live*. London: Weidenfeld & Nicolson.

Grayling, A.C. (2007) *Towards the Light: The Story of the Struggles for Liberty and Rights that Made the Modern West*. London: Bloomsbury.

Grayling, A.C. (2010) *Ideas that Matter: A Personal Guide for the 21st Century*. London: Phoenix.

Gross, L., Katz, J.S. and Ruby, J. (eds) (1988) *Image Ethics: The Moral Rights of Subjects in Photographs, Film, and Television*. Oxford: Oxford University Press

Gross, L., Katz, J.S. and Ruby, J. (eds.) (2003) *Image Ethics in the Digital Age*. Minneapolis, MN: University of Minnesota Press.

Guardian (2011) 'Hugh Grant's witness statement to the Leveson Inquiry [full text]', 23 November. www.guardian.co.uk/media/2011/nov/23/hugh-grant-leveson-inquiry-statement (accessed: 25 November 2011).

Hamelink, C.J. (2000) *The Ethics of Cyberspace*. London: Sage.

Harcup, T. (2007) *The Ethical Journalist*. London: Sage.

Hare, R.M. (1963) *Freedom and Reason*. Oxford: Clarendon Press.

Hasinoff, A.A. (2013) 'Sexting as media production: rethinking social media and sexuality', *New Media and Society*, 15(4): 449–465.

Heemsbergen, Luke J. (2014) 'Designing hues of transparency and democracy after WikiLeaks: vigilance to vigilantes and back again', *New Media & Society* [Online], 24 February, http://nms.sagepub.com/content/early/2014/02/21/1461444814524323 (accessed: 23 April 2014).

Helmore, E. (2013) 'The naked truth: Hollywood treats its women as second class citizens', *The Observer*, 1 December, p. 36.

Herodetus (2013) *The Histories*. Translated by Tom Holland. London: Penguin Hardback Classics.

Hill, A. (2011) 'Leveson Inquiry: indictment of a 'tawdry' press', *Guardian*, www.guardian.ac.uk/commentisfree/2011/nov/16/leveson-inquiry-twdry-press (accessed 17 November 2011)

Honderich, T. (ed.) (1995) *The Oxford Companion to Philosophy*. Oxford: Oxford University Press.

Independent on Sunday (2011) 'A peaceful protest', *The Independent on Sunday*, 27 March, p. 1.

Johnson, D.G. (1985) *Computer Ethics*. Englewood Cliffs, NJ: Prentice-Hall.

Johnson, D.G. (2001) *Computer Ethics* (3rd edn). Upper Saddle River, NJ: Pearson Prentice-Hall (1st edn, 1985).

Johnson, D.G. (2008) *Computer Ethics* (4th edn). London: Prentice-Hall (1st edn, 1985).

Kant, I. (1923) 'On a supposed right to tell lies from benevolent motives', in *Kant's Critique of Practical Reason and Other Works on the Theory of Ethics*. Trans. T.K. Abbott. London: Longmans, Green & Co. pp. 361–365. (1st German edn, 1797).

Kant, I. (1965) *Fundamental Principles of the Metaphysic of Ethics* (10th edn). Trans. T.K. Abbott. London: Longmans (1st German edn, 1785).

Kant, I. (1989) *The Moral Law: Groundwork of the Metaphysic of Morals*. Trans. H.J. Paton. London: Routledge (1st German edn, 1785).

Kapidzic, S. and Herring, S.C. (2014) 'Race, gender and self-representation in teen profile photographs', *New Media Society* [Online], 27 January. http://nms.sagepub.com/content/early/2014/01/24/1461444813520301 (accessed: 26 January 2014).

Keeble, R. (1998) 'The myth of Saddam Hussein: new militarism and the propaganda function of the human interest story', in M. Kieran (ed.), *Media Ethics*. London: Routledge. pp. 66–81.

Keeble, R. (2001) *Ethics for Journalists*. London: Routledge.

Keen, A. (2007) *The Cult of the Amateur: How Today's Internet is Killing Our Culture and Assaulting Our Economy*. London: Nicholas Brearley Publishing.

Kelion, L. (2013) 'Facebook lets beheading clips return to social network', *BBC News Technology* [Online], 31 October, www.bbc.co.uk/news/technology-24608499 (accessed: 24 April 2014).

Kieran, M. (ed.) (1998a) *Media Ethics*. London: Routledge.

Kieran, M. (1998b) 'Objectivity, impartiality and good journalism', in M. Kieran (ed.), *Media Ethics*. London: Routledge. pp. 23–36.

Kieran, M., Morrison, D.E. and Svennevig, M. (2000) 'Privacy, the public and journalism: towards an analytic framework', *Journalism*, 1(2): 145–169.

Körner, S. (1966) *Kant*. Harmondsworth: Penguin.

Lægaard, S. (2007) 'The Cartoon Controversy: offence, identity, oppression'? *Political Studies*, 55: 481–498.

Laachir, K. (2010) 'Social class sexualities', in D. Albertazzi and P. Cobley (eds), *The Media: An Introduction* (3rd edn). London: Pearson Education. pp. 427–443 (1st edn, 1998).

Langford, D. (ed.) (2000) *Internet Ethics*. London: Macmillan.

Law, S. (2007) *The Great Philosophers: The Lives and Ideas of History's Greatest Thinkers*. London: Quercus.

Leveson Inquiry (2011) 'About the Inquiry', www.levesoninquiry.org.uk/about/ (accessed: 15 November 2011).

Lunceford, B. (2011) 'The new pornographers: legal and ethical considerations of Sexting', in B.E. Drushel and K. German (eds), *The Ethics of Emerging Media: Information, Social Norms and New Media Technology*. New York: Continuum. pp. 99–118.

MacKinnon, C.A. and Dworkin, A. (eds) (1997) *In Harm's Way: The Pornography Civil Rights Hearings*. Cambridge, MA: Harvard University Press.

Mackie, J.L. (1990) *Ethics: Inventing Right and Wrong*. London: Penguin.

Macintyre, B. (2010) 'My role in the Lady Chatterley court case: interview with Bernadine Wall', *The Times Saturday Review*, Saturday 16 October, p .4.

Macrury, I. (2010) 'Advertising', in D. Albertazzi and P. Cobley (eds), *The Media: An Introduction* (3rd edn). Harlow, Essex: Pearson Education. pp. 258–275 (1st edn, 1998).

Mail Foreign Service (2010) 'Chinese screens blacked out as jailed dissident is awarded the Nobel Prize against the country's wishes', *Daily Mail* [Online]. www.dailymail.co.uk/news/article-1337510/Chinese-screens-blacked-Liu-Xiaobo-awarded-Nobel-Peace-Prize.html#ixzz17inXaP4m (accessed: 10 December 2010).

Maltby, S. (2014) 'Broadcasting graphic war violence: the moral face of Channel 4', *Journalism*, 15(3): 289–306.

Manning, C. (2014) Wikipedia, available at en.wikipedia.org/wiki/Chelsea_Manning (accessed 24th March, 2014).

Martin, N. (2008) 'BBC system that carried Ross to the gutter', *The Daily Telegraph*, Saturday 22 November, p. 4.

Marx, K. and Engels, F. (1976) 'Manifesto of the Communist Party', in K. Marx and F. Engels, *Collected Works, Volume 6: Marx and Engels, 1845–1848*. London: Lawrence and Wishart. pp. 477–519 (1st edn, 1848).

Merrill, J.C. (1996) 'Overview: foundations for media ethics', in A.D. Gordon, J.M. Kittross and C. Reuss (eds), *Controversies in Media Ethics*. White Plains, NY: Longman. pp. 1–28.

Midgley, M. (1991) *Can't We Make Moral Judgements?* Bristol: The Bristol Press.

Midgley, M. (2001) *Wickedness*. London: Routledge.

Mill, J.S. (1940) *Autobiography*. London: Oxford University Press (1st edn, 1873).

Mill, J.S. (1964a) 'On Liberty', in A.D. Lindsay (ed.), *John Stuart Mill, Utilitarianism, Liberty and Representative Government*. London: Dent. pp. 61–170 (1st edn, 1859).

Mill, J.S. (1964b) 'Utilitarianism', in A.D. Lindsay (ed.), *John Stuart Mill, Utilitarianism, Liberty and Representative Government*. London: Dent. pp. 1–60 (1st edn, 1861).

Moor, J.H. (1985) 'What is computer ethics'? *Metaphilosophy*, 16(4): 266–275.

Moor, J.H. (2008) 'Why we need better ethics for emerging technologies', in J. Van Den Hoven and J. Weckert (eds), *Information Technology and Moral Philosophy*. Cambridge: Cambridge University Press. pp. 26–39.

Moore, G.E. (1993) *Principia Ethica*. Cambridge: Cambridge University Press (1st edn, 1903).

Morrison, D.E. and Svennevig, M. (2007) 'The defence of public interest and the intrusion of privacy: journalists and the public', *Journalism*, 8(1): 44–65.

Mulgan, T. (2011) *Ethics for a Broken World: Imagining Philosophy after Catastrophe*. Durham, UK: Acumen.

Mullins, P. (1996) 'Sacred text in the sea of texts: the Bible in North American electronic culture', in C. Ess (ed), *Philosophical Perspectives on Computer Mediated Communication*. Albany, NY: SUNY Press. pp. 271–302.

Myerson, G. (2001) *Mill's On liberty: A Beginner's Guide*. London: Hodder & Stoughton.

Naughton, J. (2012) *What You Really Need to Know about the Internet: From Gutenberg to Zuckerberg*. London: Quercus.

Newey, G. (2011) 'Diary', *London Review of Books*, 33(1), 6 January, p. 35.

Norman, B. (2010) 'My movies', *Radio Times*, 20–26 November, p. 47.

Norman, R. (1991) *The Moral Philosophers: An Introduction to Ethics*. Oxford: Clarendon Press.

Nowell-Smith, P.H. (1965) *Ethics*. Harmondsworth: Penguin (1st edn, 1954).

O'Neill, O. (2002) *A Question of Trust: The BBC Reith Lectures 2002*. Cambridge: Cambridge University Press.

Orwell, G. (1949) *1984*. London: Secker and Warberg (1st edn.).

Osgerby, B. (2010) 'Youth', in D. Albertazzi and P. Cobley (eds), *The Media: An Introduction* (3rd edn). London: Pearson Education. pp. 471–484 (1st edn, 1998).

Paine, T. (1964) *The Rights of Man*. London: Dent (1st edn, 1791–1792).

Paton, H.J. (1971) *The Categorical Imperative: A Study in Kant's Moral Philosophy*. Philadelphia, PA: University of Philadelphia Press (1st edn, 1947).

Petheram, M. (2002) *J.S. Mill: A Beginner's Guide*. London: Hodder & Stoughton.

Pigden, C. (2011) 'Hume on Is and Ought', *Philosophy Now*, 83(March/April): 18–20.

Pihl-Thingvad, S. (2014) 'Professional ideals and daily practice in journalism', *Journalism* [Online], 5 February: 1–20. http://jou.sagepub.com/content/early/2014/02/04/1464884913517658 (accessed: 18 February 2014).

Plaisance, P.L. (2009) *Media Ethics: Key Principles for Responsible Practice*. London: Sage.

Plamenatz, J. (1949) *The English Utilitarians*. Oxford: Basil Blackwell.

Plamenatz, J. (1993) *Man and Society: Political and Social Theories from Machiavelli to Marx. Volume II. From Montesquieu to the Early Socialists*. London: Longman.

Ponting, C. (1985) *The Right to Know: The Inside Story of the Belgrano Affair*. London: Sphere.

Ponting, C. (1990) *Secrecy in Britain*. Oxford: Basil Blackwell.

Press Complaints Commission (2012) *Editors' Code of Practice*. www.pcc.org.uk/assets/696/Code_of_Practice_2012_A4.pdf (accessed: 6 August 2012).

Raphael, D.D. (1989) *Moral Philosophy*. Oxford: Oxford University Press.

Robinson, J. (2010) 'It is time Sky pulled its weight, says BBC chief', *The Guardian*, Saturday 28 August, p. 15.

Robinson, J. (2011) 'Leveson Inquiry: phone hacking "made Dowlers think Milly was alive"', *The Guardian* [Online], Monday 22 November. www.guardian.co.uk/

media/2011/nov/21/leveson-inquiry-phone-hacking-dowlers (accessed: 25 November 2011).

Rogerson, Simon (2002) 'Computers and society', in R.E. Spier (ed.), *Science and Technology Ethics*. London: Routledge. pp. 159–179.

Rolph, C.H. (ed.) (1961) *The Trial of Lady Chatterley Trial: Regina v. Penguin Books Limited*. Harmondsworth: Penguin.

Rorty, R. (1989) *Contingency, Irony and Solidarity*. Cambridge: Cambridge University Press.

Ross, C. (2010) 'Sexualities', in D. Albertazzi and P. Cobley (eds), *The Media: An Introduction* (3rd edn). London: Pearson Education. pp. 397–409 (1st edn, 1998).

Runciman, D. (2009) 'Like boiling a frog' [Book review: *The Wikipedia Revolution* by Andrew Lib.], *London Review of Books*, 28 May: 14–16.

Rusbridger, A. (1998) 'Privacy rights and a free press', *The Guardian*, 7 February, pp. 12–13.

Ryan, A. (1974) *J.S. Mill*. London: Routledge and Kegan Paul.

Sabbagh, D. (2009) 'James Murdoch blames 'state-sponsored' journalism of BBC for choking choice', *The Times*, Saturday 29 August, p. 13.

Sandbrook, D. (2010) 'This "filthy" book set us free – then fettered us forever', *The Daily Telegraph*, Saturday 16 October , p. 23.

Sandel, M. J. (2009) *Justice: What's the Right Thing to Do?* London: Allen Lane.

Sanders, K. (2006) *Ethics and Journalism*. London: Sage.

Schmidt, E. and Cohen, J. (2013) *The New Digital Age: Reshaping the Future of People, Nations and Business*. London: John Murray.

Schwartz, D. (2003) 'Professional oversight: policing the credibility of photojournalism', in L. Gross, J.S. Katz and J. Ruby (eds), *Image Ethics in the Digital Age*. Minneapolis, MN: University of Minnesota. pp. 27–51.

Scruton, R. (1982) *A Dictionary of Political Thought*. London: Pan.

Sheehan, S. (2001) *Wittgenstein: A Beginner's Guide*. London: Hodder & Stoughton.

Shin, W. (2014) 'Being a truth-teller who serves only the citizens: a case study of *Newstapa*', *Journalism* [Online], 24 March. http://jou.sagepub.com/content/early/2014/03/18/1464 884914525565 (accessed: 25 March 2014).

Skorupski, J. (2006) *Why Read Mill Today?* London: Routledge.

Skovsgaard, M. (2014) 'A tabloid mind? Professional values and organisational pressures', *Media, Culture and Society*, 20(10): 1–19.

Edward Snowden (2014) Wikipedia, en.wikipedia.org/wiki/Edward_Snowden. (Accessed 24th March 2014)

Solove, D.J. (2004) *The Digital Person: Technology and Privacy in the Information Age*. New York: New York University Press.

Solove, D.J. (2007) *The Future of Reputation: Gossip, Rumor and Privacy on the Internet*. New Haven, CT: Yale University Press.

Solove, D.J. (2008) *Understanding Privacy*. Cambridge, MA: Harvard University Press.

Stebbing, L. (1939) *Thinking to Some Purpose*. Harmondsworth, Middlesex: Penguin.

Strangroom, J. (2010) *Would You Eat Your Cat?* London: New Holland.

Sullivan, R.J. (1997) *An Introduction to Kant's Ethics*. Cambridge: Cambridge University Press.

Swami, P. (2010) 'An empty chair and China's lost souls', *The Daily Telegraph*, Saturday 11 December, p. 20.

Tavani, H.T. (2011) *Ethics and Technology: Controversies, Questions, and Strategies for Ethical Computing*. Hoboken, NJ: John Wiley & Sons.

Thompson, D. (2008) *Counterknowledge: How We Surrendered to Conspiracy Theories, Quack Medicine, Bogus Science and Fake History*. London: Atlantic Books.

Thompson, M. (1999) *Ethical Theory*. Abingdon: Hodder & Stoughton.

Thompson, M. (2000) *Ethics*. London: Hodder & Stoughton.

Townshend, P. (2011) 'Pete Townshend's John Peel Lecture in full', *The Guardian* [Online], Tuesday 1 November. www.guardian.co.uk/media/2011/nov/01/pete-townshend-joh-peel-lecture (accessed: 1 November 2011).

Tropeano, E. (2006) 'Does rap or rock music provoke violent behaviour?', *Journal of Undergraduate Psychological Research*, 1: 31–34.

United Nations (2001) 'Appendix: United Nations' Universal Declaration of Human Rights', in S. Blackburn, *Being Good: A Short Introduction to Ethics*. Oxford: Oxford University Press. pp. 136–143.

Van Den Hoven, J. (2000) 'The internet and varieties of moral wrong doing', in D. Langford (ed.), *Internet Ethics*. London: Macmillan. pp. 127–157.

Vardy, P. and Grosch, P. (1999) *The Puzzle of Ethics*. London: Fount.

Wacks, R. (2010) *Privacy: A Very Short Introduction*. Oxford: Oxford University Press.

Walker, J. (ed.) (2000) *Halliwell's Film and Video Guide 2001* (16th edn). London: Harper/Collins.

Walker, R. (1998) *Kant*. London: Phoenix.

Warburton, N. (1998) 'Ethical photojournalism and the electronic darkroom', in M. Kieran (ed.), *Media Ethics*. London: Routledge. pp. 123–134.

Warnock, G.J. (1971) *The Object of Morality*. London: Methuen.

Warnock, M. (1960) *Ethics since 1900*. London: Oxford University Press.

Warnock, M. (1998) *An Intelligent Person's Guide to Ethics*. London: Gerald Duckworth.

Wheeler, T. (2002) *Phototruth or Photofiction? Ethics and Media Imagery in the Digital Age*. Mahwah, NJ: Laurence Erlbaum Associates.

Wiggins, D. (1998) *Needs, Values, Truth* (3rd edn). Oxford: Oxford University Press (1st edn, 1986).

Wiggins, D. (2006) *Ethics: Twelve Lectures on the Philosophy of Morality*. Cambridge, MA: Harvard University Press.

Williams, B. (2008) *Morality*. Cambridge: Cambridge University Press.

Williams, R. (1979) *Communications* (3rd edn). Harmondsworth: Penguin (1st edn, 1962).

Wright, G.H. von (1963) *The Varieties of Goodness*. London: Routledge & Kegan Paul.

Zelizer, B. (2012) 'How to make meaning of hand-wringing after scandal', *Media, Culture and Society*, 34(5): 625–630.

INDEX

Printed in Great Britain
by Amazon

26970689R00152